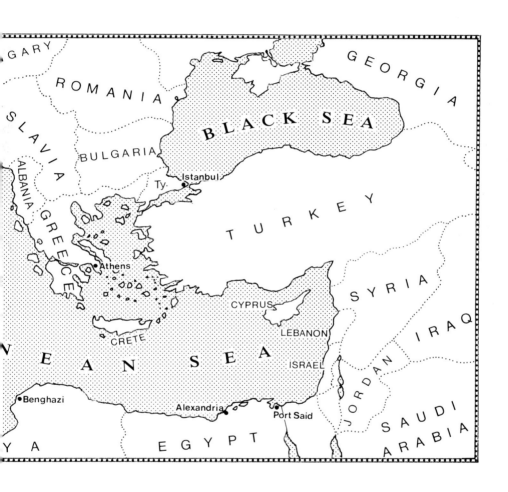

Map 1   THE MEDITERRANEAN

THE BRITISH
IN THE
MEDITERRANEAN

THE BRITISH
IN THE
MEDITERRANEAN

Peter Dietz

BRASSEY'S
LONDON • WASHINGTON

First English edition 1994

UK editorial offices: Brassey's, 33 John Street, London WC1N 2AT
UK orders: Marston Book Services, PO Box 87, Oxford OX2 ODT

North American orders: Macmillan Publishing Company,
201 West 103rd Street, Indianapolis, IN 46290

Distributed in North America to booksellers and wholesalers by the
Macmillan Publishing Company, NY 10022

Peter Dietz has asserted his moral right to be
identified as author of this work

Library of Congress Cataloging in Publication Data
available

British Library Cataloging in Publication Data
A catalogue record for this book is
available from the British Library

0 08 037716 5 Hardcover

Typeset by M Rules
Printed in Great Britain by BPC Wheatons Ltd

Contents

For My Grandson Peter Marsh,
May He Enjoy The Mediterranean
In Peace.

Acknowledgements

I would like to thank the Chief Librarians, archivists and staff of the following institutions for their unfailing courtesy, kindness and attention to my requests for books and information: The Ministry of Defence Central Library, Whitehall; The Prince Consort's Library, Aldershot; The London Library; The Gibraltar Garrison Library; The Malta Library; The Cornwall County Library Service, especially its branches in Penwith; The Penzance Library, Morrab Gardens, Penzance.

The following publishers have kindly given permission for me to quote from the material shown, for which they hold the copyright: Harper Collins for material from *The Mediterranean in the Age of Philip II* by Fernand Braudel; Thomas Cook Group Ltd. for information contained in *The Mediterranean Ferry Guide*; Martin Secker and Warburg for permission to use material from *Thomas Cook* by Piers Brendon; The Princeton University Press for permission to quote from *The Struggle for the Mediterranean* by Raymond de Belot, translated by James A Field Jr.; Faber and Faber for permission to quote from *Bitter Lemons* by Lawrence Durrell; Weidenfeld and Nicolson for permission to quote from *SUEZ*, by Keith Kyle; T Dalton Ltd. and Helen Long to quote from her *Change Into Uniform*.

I am indebted to many individuals throughout the Mediterranean for their help and interest in my project. Particularly I would like to thank Cecil Gomez for his hospitality and assistance 'on the Rock' and in southern Spain. As always, my wife Vivien has been my chief support, critic and technical assistant and without her constant encouragement this book would not have been completed.

List of Illustrations

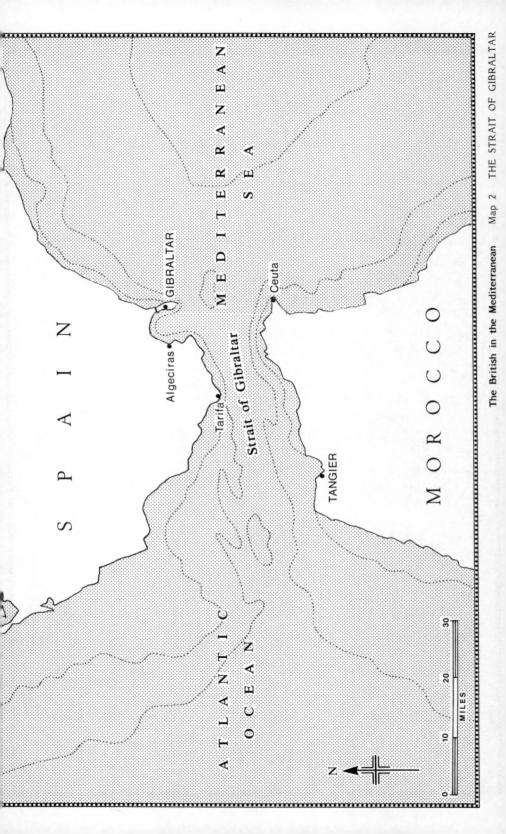

The British in the Mediterranean   Map 2   THE STRAIT OF GIBRALTAR

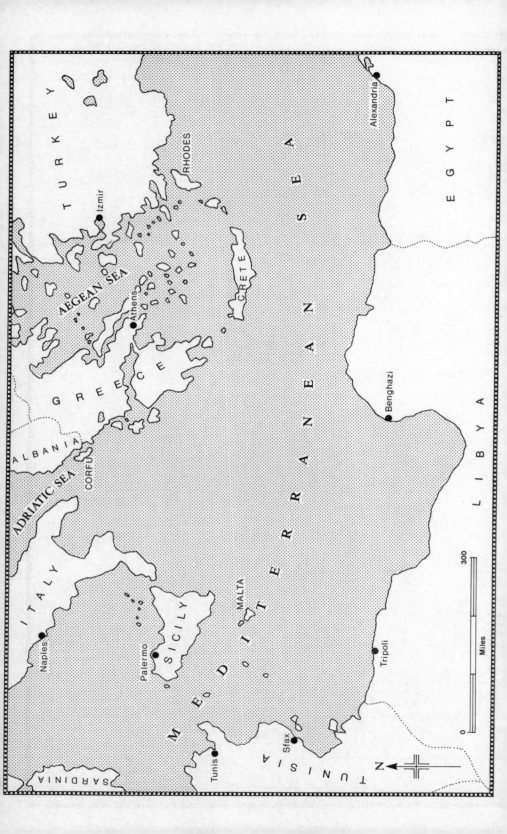

MEDITERRANEAN SEA

CYPRUS

NICOSIA

Famagusta

DHEKELIA S.B.A.

Larnaca (Lárnax)

Limassol

AKROTIRI S.B.A.

Paphos

N

| S.B.A. | U.K. SOVEREIGN BASE AREA |
| ● ● ● | GREEN LINE |

0   20   40
MILES

The British in the Mediterranean   Map 4 - CYPRUS

Introduction

For centuries the Mediterranean – the Middle Sea – has been a battle-field and a playground, with the British deeply involved in both aspects. In this book I have tried to give today's travellers an easily-digested account of the endemic power struggles of the region as well as a record of the exploits and experiences of some of their often intrepid forebears which, I hope, will provide a wider dimension to their appreciation and enjoyment of the United Kingdom's long association with the Mediterranean.

Although the English involvement can be traced back to the Crusades and even earlier, I have mainly concerned myself with the military and naval bases, in some cases small colonies, whose establishment and development since the 17th Century has given us a more permanent relationship with the region and its inhabitants. The first of these settlements was Tangier which was occupied in 1662. Although the port and town were abandoned only 20 years later, this experience of setting up a base in the Mediterranean area – both its successes and its disasters – provided a useful model for future interventions elsewhere.

The British presence in the Mediterranean spread from west to east over a period of almost 250 years, from the Strait of Gibraltar, for long the only entrance from the oceans of the wider world, to the shores of Egypt, Palestine and the island of Cyprus in the east. The expansion and development followed chronologically. Gibraltar was captured in

1704 and the occupation of Minorca followed soon afterwards in 1708. The central Mediterranean bases, exemplified most clearly and most permanently by the Maltese islands, were occupied from the beginning of the 19th Century, largely as a result of the wars with Napoleonic France. The acquisition of the eastern bases, Cyprus, Egypt and the Canal Zone Base, and the Mandate of Palestine date from the 1880s to the period immediately after the First World War.

Popular British tourism, which commenced on a large scale only with the arrival of cheap charter flights, cruises and package holidays after the Second World War has moved in roughly the same direction, from the beaches of Spain in the west through the central resorts and islands towards the more distant, exotic and expensive eastern Mediterranean holiday resorts.

The main focus of interest will be on the more permanent areas of diplomatic and military activity, which in some locations, notably Gibraltar and Cyprus, is still manifested in a British uniformed presence. Places like Tangier, Minorca and Corfu which were occupied for a short period either during or under threat of war, can only be briefly discussed. Even more, the rôle of the British in the countries bordering the Mediterranean is beyond the scope of this book. Suffice it to say that British armies have won some of their most illustrious honours in Spain, Italy, Turkey, the Crimea and North Africa.

I have tried to provide a comprehensive view of British activity in the Mediterranean and an explanation of how that involvement came about as well as some assessment of the impact of the area on the literary and social consciousness of some of the British transients and more permanent settlers. Of course, many British men and women have settled in Mediterranean countries; Byron lived in Venice; D.H. Lawrence, if only for a tragically short time, in the Italian islands; Robert Graves, longer and more fruitfully on Majorca; whilst Lawrence Durrell lived most of his later life in the south of France and his brother Gerald in Corfu. Even James Joyce and his steamy heroine Molly Bloom have their place in the pantheon and how could one leave out the author of *Ulysses* in a book about the Mediterranean? In truth, there does seem to be a continuity of artistic endeavour and consciousness in the work of these authors which it is perhaps not too fanciful to attribute to their proximity to the Middle Sea.

Finally, I have tried, without producing yet another guide book, to

Introduction

give some information about the still existing features of interest in the areas referred to in this book. The Mediterranean has been a popular attraction for the British from the time of the 'Grand Tour' which, despite the comparatively small numbers involved, produced an impact on some areas out of all proportion to its size. The Grand Tour could in fact, be said to have prepared the base for the modern mass tourist industry. The Englishman Abroad has always presented a controversial figure and the modern British hooligans seen in some of the more notorious Mediterranean resorts can, not unfairly, be represented as the descendants of the young bucks who, in the name of enlightenment and painless education, drank, gambled, whored and bullied their way around the classical and less classical attractions in the south of Europe during the 18th and 19th Centuries. *Plus ça change*! Most resort areas in Europe and perhaps all over the world, have their Magaluf and their Monte Carlo as well as their Ephesus and their Epidaurus. The opening up of the sites and attractions in the Mediterranean, for better and for worse, owes much to the British and the appreciation of the discerning visitor is likely to be enhanced by a wider understanding of the history and politics of those places of special British interest.

CHAPTER I

The British Arrive in the Mediterranean

Hakluyt dates the first entry of the English into the Mediterranean as 1511. No doubt he was referring to entry on a significant scale because he also notes that English ships were recorded in the port of Genoa in 1412 and ships from Bristol were carrying pilgrims to the Holy Land in 1446 and 1456/57. He also reports with some pride that a small group of English vessels was able to fight off a Sicilian galley squadron near the island of Pantelleria in 1586. It is likely that the English ships were up to no more good than the Sicilians. At a time when piracy and Corsair raids were increasingly common in the Mediterranean and the Atlantic, and the defeat of Philip II's 'Invincible' Armada at the hands of the English was only two years into the future, incidents of this kind would have been both sought and provoked.

In 1586, too, the English ship *Hercules* brought back 20 Turkish prisoners to Constantinople having 'liberated' them from the Spanish in the West Indies. The Captain and his crew were well rewarded for their humanity and they sailed home from Turkey to England with a rich cargo of exotic spices, oil and silks. England, like France and Venice too, though less successfully, tried to stay neutral in the religious wars of the 16th Century in the Mediterranean. Fortunately, unlike France and Venice, she could not be accused of working against the interests of her co-religionists but merely of pursuing trade and commerce in the few places open to her in the face of the bitter enmity of the Catholic Mediterranean.

The progress of the English in the Mediterranean was slow at first, partly because no base was then available to them; but eventually trade began to increase so that in 1581 the Levant Company was set up by Royal Charter, followed by the Venice Company in 1583. From its first year the Levant Company never made less than 300 per cent profit. Although trade was improving and English ships were now welcomed in many Mediterranean ports from which they had previously been excluded, dangers still existed, especially from the Corsairs operating from their North African bases.

The threat from pirates and the continuing hostility of Spain led, in the early 17th Century, to the setting up of the first convoy system which appeared to be effective and was the envy of the other maritime nations. The severe battles in the Atlantic between the Spanish and Portuguese on one side and the Dutch and English on the other, joined by privateers from almost every other country in northern Europe, made the Mediterranean a much safer and more profitable area for trade. Another factor favouring the Mediterranean was that after the great sea battle of Lepanto in 1571, the Turkish Sultan failed to re-establish control of the western half of the Middle Sea and the North African Emirates took advantage of this to throw off their allegiance to the Sublime Port (Constantinople) and began to emerge as independent states. Eventually the rise of the whole of Barbary against the Turks, in theory at least, opened up the North African coast to Christian trade.

After the series of Anglo-Dutch Wars which dominated maritime affairs in the 17th Century the Dutch were left so exhausted that England achieved complete naval superiority on all the oceans of the world. At last she was able to take advantage, in the Mediterranean as much as elsewhere, of her victory over the Spanish Armada in 1588. But between the First and Second Dutch wars, 1660 saw the Restoration of Charles II to the English throne. Charles was as bad a ruler as the rest of his dynasty but his reign had a consequence of great importance to the English and to the history and development of their armed forces.

In 1661 he married Catherine of Braganza and as part of her dowry she brought with her not only the Island of Bombay but also a small Portuguese settlement at the Atlantic end of the Strait of Gibraltar. King Charles and his government may well have been more interested in the large cash payment which also accompanied Catherine but the acquisition of Tangier, short-lived and unprofitable though it was, provides a logical starting point for the study of the English penetration of the Mediterranean and the establishment of settlements and bases there, some of which endure to this day.

The Gift of Tangier

In 1656 Admiral Blake, the hero of the Anglo-Dutch naval wars, and Lord Sandwich, a supporter of the Commonwealth under Cromwell, were given joint command of a fleet sent into the Mediterranean to harass Spain in pursuance of Cromwell's expansionist policies. After the death of Cromwell, Sandwich and General Monck accepted appointments as 'Generals at Sea', and together they brought the new King Charles II home from exile after the Restoration. Samuel Pepys was with Sandwich on the journey and no doubt his subsequent successful career at the Navy Board owed much to Sandwich's patronage. But it is also clear that Pepys made a favourable impression on Charles and his brother the Duke of York and both recognised the qualities which made him an inspired and dedicated administrator of the navy. Sandwich went on to become Ambassador to Spain, a post he does not seem to have enjoyed, and then in 1669 he became President for the Council for Foreign Plantations. He only resumed his naval command at the outbreak of the Third Dutch War in 1672 and died bravely in the opening battle at Sole Bay. It was through Sandwich and his own growing reputation for industry and incorruptibility that Pepys became involved with the prototype British Mediterranean Base at Tangier.

Although Blake had ensured British domination of the western Mediterranean at least temporarily even before the occupation of Tangier, it was still difficult to deal with the Corsair fleets operating along the Barbary coast under the protection of the North African Emirates. The 'uncivilised behaviour' of the petty – and sometimes more important – chieftains along the whole of the coast was a constant irritant and hindrance to trade which was not finally removed until well into the 19th Century when France began to occupy the territories which were later to become Tunisia, Algeria and Morocco. During the reigns of Charles II and James II many European adventurers joined the Corsairs, taking the skills required to handle the square-rigged northern ships into the Moorish service. Many of the renegades became very rich and acquired great prestige amongst their Moorish comrades. The Moorish galleys had been discredited in the Mediterranean by the end of the 16th Century, especially after the battle of Lepanto, even though that was almost entirely a galley affair. By the middle of the next century Corsair square-riggers were able to venture further afield cruising to Newfoundland, the Cornish coast and even to the mouth of the Thames. For a short season a Corsair crew even established itself on Lundy Island without being disturbed. Hence, the acquisition of Tangier , in Queen Catherine's dowry was hailed as a great safeguard for English shipping and trade.

The Moors however continued to apply unrelenting pressure on the settlement throughout the Portuguese and British occupations. In this respect Tangier was in the same position as Tripoli under the reluctant rule of the Knights of St. John a hundred years earlier. With a permanently hostile hinterland and the constant requirement for succour and provisioning by sea, the small colony was exorbitantly expensive to maintain. It is perhaps surprising, given the fairly obvious disadvantages that accompanied it, that Charles, and presumably his advisers, accepted Tangier as a worthwhile gain since he was considered to be an extremely eligible bachelor whose hand had been sought for several European Princesses. The ready cash element of the dowry was probably important but there is evidence that Catherine's reputation for exceptional grace and beauty had some influence on the 'Merry Monarch'.

In any event England, and by now we should perhaps say Britain, entered into her new responsibilities with optimism. Sandwich had cruised off Tangier with Blake's squadron during the Commonwealth and would have heard Blake's opinion of the strategic importance of the place and been impressed by the famous admiral's views. Sandwich was sent at all speed by Charles to take over Tangier from the Portuguese and forestall any attempt by the Spanish to seize the new possession before Lord Peterborough, the designated governor, and his garrison could arrive. Even as Sandwich arrived the town was under severe attack by the Moors who, like the Spanish, were hoping to take possession before the new authorities could take effective control. With great presence of mind and determination Sandwich landed soldiers and sailors from his own ship to assist the Portuguese in the defence of Tangier. The British action sent a signal to the Moors that Britain was prepared to stay and fight for her first Mediterranean possession. The settlement was finally handed over to the British at the end of January 1662.

Tangier remained solely in the hands of the military until June 1668 when it was incorporated as a Municipality. Meanwhile Samuel Pepys had been appointed to the Privy Council's Committee for Tangier, presided over by the Duke of York. The importance which Charles assigned to Tangier is emphasised by the appointment of his brother to be head of the Committee. In the same way the appointment of Pepys, already a member of the Naval Board, acknowledged the important role the Navy would have in supporting and safeguarding the new colony. Pepys considered his own appointment as a great honour, and one likely to be very profitable to him. Merchants and contractors dealing with the colony pressed *douceurs* on him so that Tangier, in his own words, became one of the finest flowers in his garden. When he succeeded the incompetent Povey as Treasurer of the Tangier Board in 1665 even brighter prospects opened up, although he had agreed to hand over half the proceeds of his office to his predecessor – no doubt an early but widely accepted form of pension arrangement. Pepys was continually troubled by bad and sometimes non-existent account-keeping in Tangier. He says that when the contract for building the Great Mole at Tangier was finally signed and sealed, the Board, like he himself, were uneasy since few of them understood the contract. At a meeting of the Tangier Committee on 9 May 1667 Pepys complained of the bad accounting, but without effect.

Another cause of friction between the military and the merchants of Tangier was the seeming incompatibility between the requirements of a military base on the one hand, and on the other, commercial interests of the British civilians who had arrived to open up trade with the interior and with the Mediterranean as a whole. The merchants had of course been encouraged in their business ambitions by the King and the Tangier Committee who hoped that the colony would become at least self-sufficient, and in time a substantial revenue-earner for the crown. When Pepys met John Bland, an important merchant and Tangier's first Mayor, after the colony's incorporation as a Municipality, he was told in no uncertain terms that 'things were out of order in Tangier and likely to be whilst the soldier governs all'.

However the military problems of Tangier were never ending and, apart from a few short periods of uneasy truce, the long, defended perimeter of the colony was under more or less continuous attack. Sandwich landed about 300 troops to help in the initial defence of Tangier against the Moorish attacks of 1661 and 1662 and these were replaced by a permanent garrison of 100 horse and 1,000 foot which provided the nucleus for the 1st Tangier Regiment. Lord Peterborough, the first governor, raised the original regiment and the troop of horse and each new governor was, in turn, appointed to command the Tangier Regiments. But the garrison was never sufficient to man the defences adequately and any sortie like the Earl of Teviot's cavalry ride of 1664 was always likely to end in a similarly disastrous massacre. Teviot was the second governor of Tangier, succeeding Peterborough after the latter had been in office for only a few months. Pepys regarded him as a 'cunning fellow' but the inhabitants thought highly of him. He met his death gallantly riding at the head of his troops when they were attacked by a well-arranged ambush outside the walls of the town.

When Charles sold Dunkirk to the French for £200,000, the remnants of the three British regiments stationed there were brought to Tangier. Teviot had commanded the regiments as Governor of Dunkirk from 1660–1662 and continued to command them as the new Governor of Tangier. The transferred regiments, being of Irish origin and almost all Catholics, immediately became the subject of controversy. Teviot, who became Lord Rutherford in 1663, was also a Catholic and Pepys, in his diary, recorded that after the arrival of the Irish regiments almost all the officers were Catholic. Complaints of obvious and excessive Catholicism in the garrison mounted during the 1670s, long before the deliberately pro-Catholic policies of James II were put into effect after his succession in 1685. Tangier was caught up in the ramifications of the Popish Plot and the fear, in overwhelmingly Protestant England, of a Catholic army based in Tangier bedevilled Charles's reign and prevented the build-up of an adequate garrison in the embryo colony.

However, for Charles the necessity to maintain some kind of garrison in Tangier allowed him to increase the small regular army that was reluctantly sanctioned by a suspicious Parliament. The Regiment of Foot raised by Peterborough especially for Tangier was the first regiment after the Guards to be placed on the permanent establishment. After a particularly bitter and nearly successful siege in 1680, fickle public opinion in England called for reinforcements to be sent to the settlement, and the King's Battalion, 600-strong, joined the garrison under Colonel Charles Trelawny. The new battalion became the 2nd Tangier Regiment in 1682 and later the 4th or King's Own (Royal Lancaster) Regiment. By the time of the evacuation the Light Horse had increased to four troops and when they arrived in England two more troops were added; together they became the Royal Regiment of Dragoons.

By 1680 the civil population of Tangier was about 600; the two regiments comprising the garrison numbered 1400 and there were about 300 prisoners-of-war, who were kept fully employed in building fortifications and the great New Mole, which was intended to provide a safe harbour in place of the existing exposed anchorage. Work on the Mole and the town defences went on throughout the occupation but as the attacks of the Moors proved to be unrelenting the costs mounted. Doubts about retaining the settlement increased in England. In addition, Tangier had not shown itself to be a very satisfactory base from which to counter the Corsairs who continued to use harbours and anchorages within a few days sail of the town. Indeed, some of the Tangier merchants were alleged by the garrison to be selling arms and munitions to the Corsairs who then supplied them to the Moors besieging the colony.

It was impossible to get fresh provisions from the surrounding country and all supplies of food had to be brought in from Lisbon. The light cavalry was a most important part of the garrison force and was absolutely essential if the besieging Moors were to be kept back from the walls of the town. Without mounted troops any reconnaissance, even on a much less ambitious scale than Teviot's ill-fated excursion, would be impossible. But the price of fodder made any sizeable body of cavalry unsustainable and even by the end there were probably no more than 200 horsemen in the garrison. As early as 1680 Charles threatened to abandon the settlement unless Parliament voted more supplies. The problem was postponed, as we have seen, by the fears and suspicions aroused by the Popish Plot but in the end this may have been the decisive factor in the decision to give up Tangier.

Meanwhile, the garrison and the civilian population made the most of a somewhat uncongenial environment. Social life and amenities gradually improved. Several officers made gardens round their quarters and, although the supply was vulnerable to Moorish interference, water

was brought in by aqueduct and its distribution, especially for irrigation, generally improved. Plays were put on, apparently a popular
pastime for winter afternoons. When the Mole was completed plays
were sometimes performed in a temporary building there, but later a
military storehouse at York Gate was converted. Amateur play-acting
was always, and still is, a popular amusement for the forces abroad and
these may be some of the first recorded garrison performances. Plays
produced by the soldiers included 'The Indian Emperor', 'The Earl of
Essex' and 'The Olde Brother'. Travelling companies came from Spain,
too, and reportedly gave much pleasure. Bowling greens were laid out
and numerous taverns and bawdy houses were opened for the con-
venience of the garrison.

Pepys, who was violently opposed to the continuance of the colony,
especially after his visit as a member of the winding-up party in 1683,
wrote: 'Nothing but vice of all sorts, swearing, drinking and cursing
etc. The women as much as the men.' He added that Dr Balam, the
Recorder, left his estate to his servant on condition that he did not
marry a woman of Tangier, or one who had ever been there. But it was
of course Pepys' business by then to disparage the place in the interests
of his royal master.

About 20 families made up the élite of the colony and even this small
group declined by 1680. Beneath them in the hierarchy came the munic-
ipal dignitaries, the ministers and doctors, schoolmasters and minor
officials, agents, the governor's secretary and the more important merchants. Below these were a few subaltern officers, soldiers, shopkeepers
and 'mole workers'. No doubt this social stratification provided the
pattern for most British overseas settlements for the next two centuries.
In addition of course, though never accepted as part of human society
overseas, there was what was called 'a shifty company of foreigners'.

That the troops were brutal and uncontrolled is quite clear and it is
most unlikely, despite Routh's classification of Tangier life in 1679,
that soldiers were ever admitted to polite society. The 1st Tangier
Regiment, commanded by Colonel Kirke, known in the colony with
some irony as 'Kirke's Lambs' because of the Paschal Lamb which was
depicted on the regimental standard, enjoyed a particularly unsavoury
reputation. After the abandonment of the colony in 1683–84 the two
Tangier Regiments were brought home and quartered in the West
Country. They were in action at the battle of Sedgemoor and the

pacification which followed the Monmouth Rebellion. Both regiments appear to have earned a reputation for great brutality but they were presumably following the wishes of their royal master and the lead given by the notorious Judge Jeffreys. In later life the Tangier Regiment became The Queen's Regiment with the proud position of 2nd Regiment of Foot and is now part of The Queen's Division where its nickname, Kirke's Lambs, is still known and used.

Parliament wanted Charles to exclude his brother James, a practising Catholic, from the succession before agreeing to more financial support for Tangier. James, Duke of York, and the Lords Sutherland and Rochester, the most trusted of Charles's confidential advisers, suggested the recall of the Tangier garrison if necessary, as a support for the monarchy. As the events of the Monmouth rebellion show, even a small body of trained troops could overawe a hostile countryside.

Early in 1683 Charles, rather than allow some other country to have Tangier, decided to 'cast it into the sea'. On 2 July, Lord Dartmouth, considered by Pepys to be a fine sailor but an indecisive leader, as was shown in 1688 when he failed to intercept the invading force of William of Orange, was entrusted by Charles with overseeing the withdrawal. The Portuguese, perhaps at the prompting of Queen Catherine, tried to prevent the abandonment of their 'gift'. But Charles was convinced that no country less powerful than Britain could hold Tangier.

Dartmouth and his fleet set out, ostensibly to succour the garrison but with secret orders to withdraw it completely whilst providing compensation for the merchants and property owners. Even Pepys, who accompanied the expedition as Chief Financial Member, did not know the real purpose of the operation until they were five days out. But it is more than likely that he had an inkling of what was intended and certainly the garrison guessed what was in the wind and started to draft their claims for compensation long before the fleet came into sight. On arrival, Dartmouth ordered a show of strength to discourage a Moorish attack and even landed 1,000 sailors from the fleet, dressing them in the red tunics intended as replacements for the worn-out clothing of the regiments in garrison. Pepys, observing them parade through the streets and, pro-Navy as always, 'thought they made a very good appearance and made with the small shot as good a volley – or better, than the soldiers'.

Not only was Pepys Treasurer to the winding-up expedition but, because of his over 20 years' experience as the main administrator in England of the colony, he acted as Dartmouth's chief adviser and secretary. He had prepared a speech for Dartmouth during the voyage, giving all the arguments for destroying Tangier and the Mole. These included the expense, the ruinous state of Tangier itself, the perpetual alarms and excursions caused by the Moors, the difficulty of provisioning Tangier and the danger of starvation. Finally, and surprisingly, he cited the uselessness of the Mole which had provided so little protection that it had become necessary to remove naval stores to Gibraltar, where with the agreement of the Spanish a depot was formed.

Pepys had procured for his brother-in-law's son, Balthasar St. Michel, who had been employed as Admiralty Agent at Tangier, the post of Agent and Store Keeper. St. Michel became something of an albatross round Pepys's neck, being inefficient, which Pepys certainly was not, a sponger and a whiner. It says a great deal about Pepys's loyalty and concern for his family and kinsmen that he afterwards obtained for 'Balty' the post of Navy Commissioner at Chatham and at Woolwich during his own heyday as Secretary of the Navy. Surprisingly 'Balty' seems to have made a moderate success of these posts through, it was said, sheer energy and brashness. Both Pepys and his relative were forced to resign after the Glorious Revolution of 1688 because of their service to the monarchies of Charles and his brother James.

Apart from his close association with Tangier, Pepys has always been regarded as the maker and preserver of the post-Commonwealth Navy. He shared the views of the senior naval officers of his time on the need for England to look to her 'moat' but he was less gloomy than many of his contemporaries concerning the future after the withdrawal from Tangier. The widespread abuse of 'good voyages' whereby naval captains solicited high value freight such as bullion or plate to be conveyed in the royal ships, often at the expense of legitimate and more urgent naval business, occupied much of his time at the Navy Office. But once this area of corruption had been brought under control he felt much of what had been lost in the Mediterranean could be recovered.

The unfortunate experience of Tangier did not for one moment blind him to the lasting value of an easily accessible and defendable base in the western Mediterranean. There is evidence that even as he sailed away from the settlement his eye fell upon the Rock of Gibraltar. Bryant says that on his voyage back to England Pepys discussed with the engineer Beckmann the possibility of its replacing Tangier. More than any other place, Beckmann said, it would give England command of the Strait; it could be captured without the loss of a single English life and afterwards fortified for a mere trifle against all the fleets and armies in the world. Lest Spain should take fright or any other nation be tempted to act first, Pepys and Beckmann agreed to keep the project to themselves for the time being and they did not even mention it to the King. This reticence was probably very sensible since it is unlikely that Charles would have had much interest in the seizure of Gibraltar, having so recently had his fingers burned in Tangier. However, within 20 years of the final abandonment of Tangier the British captured Gibraltar, and are still there.

On the British withdrawal all the interests in Tangier were compensated at a total cost of £11,243. 17s. 4d. including £600 to the few Portuguese who stayed on after the British took over. It took three months to demolish the Mole and the whole of the winter of 1683–84 to destroy the town and its defences. All the mines were finally sprung on 5 February 1684. Routh suggests, rather fancifully perhaps, that the withdrawing companies, as they rowed out to the waiting ships, sang verses of the Tangier's Lamentation and, in view of the reluctance of soldiers everywhere to leave a familiar location for something conceivably worse, he may be right.

Tangier's Lamentation

> Let the Moors repine, their hopes resign,
> Now the 'Pagan Troops' are cheated,
> Let Foot and Horse disband their force,
> Since Tangier is defeated!
> Alas Tangier, what sudden doom
> Hath wrought this alteration,
> That this thy March should now become
> Thy fatal Lamentation?

The Rock of Gibraltar

In 1684 when Pepys first cast his eye eastwards down the Strait and saw Gibraltar as a substitute for the now ruined and abandoned Tangier, Britain and Spain were in a relationship of uneasy neutrality. Soon, under the imperatives forced upon the Britain of William III by Louis XIV, who had supported the deposed James II, the two countries were in an equally uneasy alliance. This alliance included the unlikely bedfellows of Spain, the Netherlands, Austria and Bavaria, in the Six Years War against France.

From 1689 the British and Dutch fleets engaged in a series of actions against the French, in many of which the French came off best. Off Cape St. Vincent in 1693 a fleet of over 400 merchantmen, escorted by an inadequate naval force under Admiral Sir George Rooke, were outgunned and dispersed by a superior French fleet. Some of the scattered ships, naval and merchantmen, were rallied by Rooke who took them to Gibraltar. The sheltering fleet was bombarded by the French ships and attacked in the harbour by fire ships. The British sailors improvised a defence by mounting guns from their ships on the harbour mole, beating off the French attack and saving what was left of the badly-mauled British fleet. Little had been done to improve the defences of Gibraltar during the 17th Century but the hasty improvisations so successfully made and the spirited action of the British crews impressed Rooke with the importance of Gibraltar as a base, especially after the demise of Tangier. Admiral Rooke returned to Gibraltar 10 years later and this time the British were to stay.

The next stage of the struggle against French domination was the War of the Spanish Succession. Charles II of Spain died childless in 1700. There were two candidates for the Spanish throne, Philip V, a grandson of Louis XIV of France, and the Archduke Charles of Austria (Charles III), a Habsburg. Britain and her allies could not accept the possibility of a union of France and Spain under a Bourbon monarchy and so they went to war in 1702 with the object of placing Archduke Charles on the Spanish throne. There was no open war with Spain but both candidates had their Spanish supporters and inevitably they were drawn into a general conflict.

In February 1704 Charles sailed from England under the protection of a fleet commanded by Admiral Rooke but his army was quickly routed by a French army under the now widely accepted King Philip V. The Catalans, from whom much had been expected, failed to rise and Admiral Rooke began to be fearful of having to return home after yet another débâcle in the Mediterranean. Having failed to find the French fleet, a council of war was held off Ceuta on Rooke's flagship. It was made clear to the Council that a spectacular success was necessary to restore Charles's prestige and Admiral Rooke's reputation. Councils of war have an unhappy record of recommending retreat or at least caution. This time however, knowing that the garrison was weak and the defences not improved since Rooke's successful defensive battle against the French in 1693, it was decided to make an attempt on Gibraltar.

On 1 August 1704 about 2,000 British and Dutch marines landed on the sandy isthmus between the north end of the Rock and the Spanish mainland. Over 15,000 rounds were fired by the fleet and naval assault parties landed on the mole and in Rosia Bay. The party which landed on the mole under the command of Captain Hicks was at first successful but was almost completely destroyed when a magazine blew up beneath them. The second landing party of 200 men under Captain Whitaker landed in Rosia and moved on to positions where they were able to enfilade the defenders of the mole, which was finally captured. Jumpers Bastion the position from which the mole was captured was named after one of the officers who had managed to get ashore and was killed in the earlier assault and the name and location are still commemorated in Gibraltar.

The Prince of Hesse, in command of the attack from the landward side, advanced against the town at the same time as the landings were taking place. The garrison was summoned to surrender but fighting only gradually died away and the Spanish did not finally capitulate until the morning of 4 August. Admiral Sir George Byng was in charge of the landing operations which, despite the early losses on the mole, were a great success.

Unfortunately Byng was less successful in maintaining order in the town after the surrender. Plundering, rape and general violence were the normal consequences of failing to give up a defended town or fortress before a general assault was ordered and Gibraltar was not excepted from the harsh rule. After a few days order was restored – or rather riot had run its course. In the terms of surrender it was stated

16

that all the inhabitants who wished to remain would enjoy the privileges they had always had and that religion should remain unmolested. In the event, the Spanish population departed en masse and settled in San Roque a few miles from Gibraltar. The Convent, almost the only building of any size, had been ransacked by the assault troops and the monks and nuns also departed for Spain. In 1728 the Convent was made the official residence of the Governor and the Convent Chapel became the only place of Protestant worship in the Fortress.

Despite official British policy, Anglo-Spanish suspicions and ill-feeling continued and the War of the Spanish Succession dragged on indecisively for several more years after the capture of the Rock. Animosity continued to be fuelled by memories of the great struggle with Spain in the 16th Century, culminating in the defeat of the Armada, and it was not until 1711 that negotiations began to end the war with Spain and France. The Treaty of Utrecht in 1713 eventually confirmed Britain's possession both of Gibraltar and of Minorca, which had also been captured from the Spanish. Although the British and Dutch had captured the Rock in the name of Archduke Charles, they kept it for Queen Anne, and by 1713 the advantages of having a permanent base in the western Mediterranean were obvious to a new British Government. The Tories had returned to power in 1710 determined to wind up land operations against the French and instead to pursue a maritime strategy.

At first the seizure of Gibraltar was overshadowed by Marlborough's great victory over the French at Blenheim which occurred only four days later, but the Rock was essential for the new British strategy. Although in the early days the British public, remembering the unfortunate and expensive experiences of the Tangier colony, were lukewarm towards the new settlement, it soon became clear that Gibraltar should be regarded in a different light. Suggestions had been made during negotiations for the surrender or exchange of the Rock but too much blood had been spilled and too many old wounds reopened to make any accommodation possible.

The Treaty of Utrecht, whilst it confirmed British possession, unfortunately contained many ambiguities. It did lay down that the Rock was 'to be held and enjoyed absolutely with all manner of rights for ever', but then the difficulties started. There was to be no communication with the surrounding country, allegedly to prevent smuggling; Moors and Jews were not to reside in Gibraltar; the sandy strip between the Rock and Spain was to remain strictly neutral; and there were other conditions all accepted by a powerful and victorious Britain in the confident belief that they could be swept aside whenever it suited. In fact to ignore or avoid the conditions of the Treaty suited both sides from time to time. Smuggling from Gibraltar into Spain soon became a major industry engaged in as much by the Spanish as the inhabitants of the Rock and food and wine have always been imported through the frontier into Gibraltar whenever there was no open war between the two countries. Finally, in the event of war or if war threatened, both sides would attempt to occupy as much 'neutral ground' as possible.

All these uncertainties gave the Spanish some hope that they might eventually recover the Rock but they were given no such encouragement by the British. However, they have provided much of the legal basis for Spain's case, put in modern times to the United Nations, and for the emotional basis of her appeal to many Third World countries. Queen Anne made Gibraltar a Free Port in 1712, even before the Treaty of Utrecht was concluded. General Bland, the then Governor, persuaded the Queen that British influence would be much increased as a result and that the port would then rival Leghorn, the only other Free Port in the Mediterranean at that time. A more practical consideration for the people of Gibraltar was that Morocco would only trade on a reciprocal basis for the food that Gibraltar required from Morocco.

In 1726 the Spanish tried to recapture the Rock. This time, after 20 years of peace, the defences, neglected as much by the British as they had been by the Spanish, were in an even worse state than in 1704. Many of the guns of the Fortress had remained *in situ* from the time of its capture. But great bravery on the Spanish side could not compensate for the incompetence of the Spanish engineers and gunners in what was almost entirely a gunner's war. A Spanish attempt to explode a mine under Willis's Battery at the north end of the Rock failed after a whole year's work; the Spanish guns began to wear out and, most important of all, Spain failed to learn a lesson vital for the future: they were not able to seal off the Rock to prevent reinforcements and supplies coming in by sea. Hostilities ceased but peace negotiations were, as usual, long drawn out. In 1729 The Treaty of Seville confirmed the arrangements made in the Treaty of Utrecht but the ambiguities remained. Despite a war with France in 1756 which brought about the loss of Minorca, Gibraltar enjoyed 50 years of calm until 1779 when the 14th siege, afterwards known as the Great Siege, commenced.

Peace and calm in an overseas garrison in the 18th Century meant squalor, brutality and debauchery for the soldiers and their women, whether legitimately married or not, and idleness, corruption and the quest for 'perquisites' by their officers. Colonel N T St John Williams in his book *Judy O'Grady and the Colonel's Lady* says: 'The first officially recognised wives arrived in Gibraltar in 1710 with the relieving regiments and shivered with them in the bleak winters. Boredom alleviated by drunkenness became so prevalent that flogging featured daily on the morning parade'. Fortescue quotes a soldier's diary from 1728: 'Here is nothing to do nor any news . . . but the harmless diversions of drinking, dancing, whoring, gaming and other innocent debaucheries to pass the time. Sodom and Gomorrah were not half so wicked and profane as this worthy city of Gibraltar.' Camp followers were subject to the Articles of War and could be flogged for drunkenness and 'plunders', which usually meant the receiving and selling of stolen goods. The whirligig, a cage just large enough for one person, which could be spun round so as to induce giddiness and 'landsickness', was usually reserved for 'unruly and lewd women' and is said by St John Williams to have been used often during the sieges to amuse the weary soldiers. The punishment usually went on for an hour. It is reported that during a period of heavy and continuous bombardment during the Great Siege two drunken soldiers found a statue of the Virgin Mary in a ruined chapel and promptly sentenced it to a session in the whirligig.

The officers in the intervals of peace lived well in their messes, holding weekly dances, and giving and receiving hospitality from neighbouring Spanish towns and houses. The more senior officers, from a multiplicity of 'jobs', appointments and straightforward bribes, accumulated considerable wealth. Captain Sayer, in his *History of Gibraltar*, quotes from a pamphlet written about the time of the Treaty of Aix-la-Chapelle, giving the Governor's perquisites in 1729:

From		Spanish Dollars
	5,000 bottles of wine	10,000
	1,000 bottles, brandy & rum	9,765
	1,200 Ships anchorages @ 3 Dols.	3,600
	60 Jewish & Genoese porters	2,160
	Christmas boxes from Jews etc.	1,000
	Permits to enter town	1,000
	Jews, hawkers & pedlars	500
	Wine Licences	600
	Ground rents	10,000
	Medical passes to foreigners	1,000
	Remunerations & squeezings	2,000

As		
	Principal goat keeper	500
	” cow keeper	500
	Head Butcher	4,100
	Head Poulterer	500
	Chief Baker	1,000
	Head Gardener	500
	Master Fisherman	500
	Tallow Chandler	2,000

From		
	Public jobs, wharfage etc.	2,000
	Miscellaneous	600

TOTAL:	53,825 Spanish Dollars

Even allowing for some exaggeration and a degree of 18th Century satire this presents quite a formidable list of opportunities for corruption, making Pepys' somewhat shamefaced gifts and considerations look very modest indeed. The basically decent and honest administration of General Eliott certainly curbed the worst excesses of corruption during the Great Siege, when circumstances were less conducive to jobbery, and profiteering than in the preceding long period of peace with a comparatively open frontier. Nevertheless there is plenty of evidence that hoarding and other anti-social behaviour went on. After the Great

Siege the level of corruption returned to normal and remained high almost until modern times. The staple local industry of smuggling encouraged an attitude of dishonesty and bribery and 'turning a blind eye' spread the profits through the population.

After 1728 and the successful defence of the Rock in the 13th siege it was obvious to the whole Mediterranean that Gibraltar was going to remain a British base. Up till then non-British outsiders were limited to 30 days residence on the Rock. This limitation must have been quite liberally interpreted in the case of traders and artisans who had services to offer but after the siege the ban was completely lifted. A contemporary account says 'Englishmen, foreigners, rich Jews and Moors flocked thither from all quarters. Houses were quickly built by the incomers, led by the Jews, anxious to establish themselves under the protection of a permanent British garrison at one of the important crossroads of Western Europe'. H.W. Howes, who has made a study of the population and trade of Gibraltar from the beginning of the British occupation, gives the following figures for the population in 1753:

Civilian residents:

British	351
Genoese	597
Jews	575
Spaniards	185
Portuguese	25
Total	1733

To this total should be added 83 British nationals employed by the Navy and Victualling Office. This is hardly evidence of 'flocking thither' in the half century following the capture of the Rock but it does suggest that at least the loss of inhabitants as a result of the British arrival was more than made good by the mid-18th Century. Of course there would have been a policy, apart from adequate provisioning and entertainment for the garrison, of keeping the number of mouths to be fed in any new siege to a minimum. There would always have been two infantry regiments in the garrison plus artillerymen to handle the many guns with which the Fortress was furnished. In addition there would be a complement of sappers and miners who, with their tunnels and emplacements in and around the Rock, soon made it peculiarly their own. In time of siege, when this was possible, the garrison would be increased, as it was during the Great Siege, to eight regiments of infantry with an augmented force of artillery and engineers.

Minorca, the Alternative Base

As has been said, Minorca was captured by the British during the War of the Spanish Succession. In 1708 the allied Dutch and English fleets seized Sardinia, which became a rich store for the support of the Austrian claimant to the Spanish throne because of its proximity to Barcelona. In the same year a force of 2,600 men under Major General Stanhope took Minorca. British possession was confirmed at the Peace of Utrecht and it was held without difficulty for almost 50 years until the Seven Years' War.

The Treaty of Utrecht saw the first flowering of British maritime policy in the Mediterranean. After the Treaty and the death of Queen Anne, Britain and Holland were ruled by one king, William III, and virtually by one government. As Mahan says: 'After the Treaty of Utrecht . . . the English government more and more steadily, and with conscious purpose, pushed on the extension of her sea power. While as an open enemy she struck at France upon the sea, so as an artful friend, many at least believed, she sapped the power of Holland afloat. The treaty between the two countries provided that of the sea forces Holland should furnish three-eighths and England five-eighths or nearly double' . . . whilst . . . 'Holland should keep an army of 102,000 against England's 40,000 thus virtually throwing the land war on one and the sea war on the other'. That these may have been the preferred options for both countries was not allowed by Mahan to confuse the point he was making.

The great importance of Minorca to Britain, and indeed to all the naval powers which contested its possession, lay in its enormous natural harbour said by some to be the best in the Mediterranean. Port Mahon lies on an inlet three miles long of deep, sheltered and easily-defended water. It is well placed for fleets blockading Toulon and the French Mediterranean coast, and was used by Nelson during the Napoleonic wars for just this purpose.

In the period immediately after the Peace of Utrecht, Spain, under Cardinal Aberoni and its Queen Elizabeth Farnese, tried to reverse some of its provisions and the English Whigs did consider negotiations which might have meant the surrender or exchange of Minorca for Gibraltar. G.T. Garratt in his book *Gibraltar and the Mediterranean* writes of a long series of courts-martial for cowardice at sea which would seem to provide eloquent proof of the decay of British power at sea until at least the start of the Seven Years War. Minorca, Gibraltar, and to some extent Lisbon, were mutually supporting bases, able to reinforce each other as required. The 13th siege of Gibraltar (1727–28) provides a case in point where Colonel Kane, in command in Minorca, was able to reinforce the Rock at a crucial time. But the security of Gibraltar and the other Mediterranean bases depended entirely upon command of the sea and it was here that Admiral John Byng, son of the Admiral Byng who had so successfully seized Gibraltar, failed with his expedition to succour Minorca, to overcome the French fleet and allowed the base to be captured, bringing down the fatal wrath of George II on his head.

At the start of the Seven Years War in 1756 the Mediterranean was neglected by Britain, partly because she had so many vulnerable points around the world to be protected but also because so many of her seamen were absent in trading vessels carrying on the essential commerce of the country. The French seized the opportunity to make a noisy demonstration in the Channel whilst at the same time equipping 12 ships at Toulon which sailed under the Duke of Richelieu with 15,000 troops. The French army landed on Minorca on 10 April 1756 and quickly invested Port Mahon, whilst the French fleet blockaded the harbour. The garrison, which numbered barely 3,000, with the Governor, all the Colonels of all the regiments in garrison and 35 officers absent on leave, was taken completely by surprise.

Admiral John Byng and his relieving force left Portsmouth only three days before the French left Toulon and reached the vicinity of Port Mahon six weeks later. Although a breach had been opened in the fortress walls, the garrison was still holding out when the British fleet came into sight. The French fleet stood out to bar the entrance to the harbour and an indecisive and confused battle followed. Both fleets withdrew from the action before the outcome was decided, the French to preserve a fleet on which the safety of the investing forces depended and the British to preserve the fleet on which the whole of their Mediterranean strategy rested. Both admirals were accused of incompetence and cowardice but Port Mahon passed to the French on 28 June.

Admiral Byng withdrew his battered fleet to Gibraltar where his ships could be repaired and his many wounded sailors attended to. Byng himself was recalled to England where he was tried by court-martial for cowardice and found guilty on a lesser charge, which nevertheless still carried a mandatory death penalty. His appeal to George II was rejected and he was executed by firing squad on the deck of a warship in Portsmouth Harbour. Voltaire, who had commented on a similar sternness of the Venetian Seigniory in its dealings with galley captains accused of lack of zeal in the 16th Century, refers to the case of Admiral Byng in *Candide*. His hero, Candide, in the course of his travels, arrives at Portsmouth just in time to see the British admiral being shot to death. On enquiring into the circumstances of the execution, Candide is told 'but in this country we find it pays to shoot an admiral from time to time to encourage the others'. Candide was taken aback but perhaps the 'encouragement' worked. In India, Clive's remarkable victory at Plassey followed closely on Byng's tragedy at Minorca, and 1759 brought the famous 'year of victories' – the still celebrated battle of Minden, Wolfe at Quebec, Amherst completing the conquest of Canada and Eyre Coote finally destroying the French in India. By the end of the year Britain had won her Empire, her arms were triumphant in Europe and her navy was supreme on all the oceans of the world. At the time, the loss of Minorca seemed of more consequence than might have been the loss of Gibraltar but, under the 1763 Treaty of Paris, Minorca was returned to Britain.

In 1777 Francis Carter visited Tangier and Gibraltar and made a journey along the coast from the Strait to Malaga. His book, *A Journey From Gibraltar to Malaga*, published in London in the same year is full of recondite information and witty comments on places and people he found along the way. Like most 18th Century records of Grand Tours it is perhaps overfilled with notes of the classic, in this case Roman, antiquities which at that time were in abundance along the Mediterranean coast; sadly, in modern times many have disappeared or been incorporated into more modern buildings. Amongst Carter's comments on Gibraltar is this one on the Convent, the Governor's residence:

It is a plain building more convenient than elegant, but pleasantly situated near the sea, with a large garden; the church of the Convent is kept open for Divine Service, and the only one in the town, all the other chapels and places of worship having been turned into storehouses, to the great scandal of the Spaniards, and the inconvenience of the Protestants: The bells of the tower incommoding the Governor, were, by his order, unhung, so that the inhabitants are forced to repair to church by beat of drum.

Carter, like many travellers of his day, found it necessary to affect a sycophantic style towards his Sovereign and towards the officials and Government representatives on whom he depended for hospitality and assistance during his journey. But he does seem to have gone a little overboard in this description of the Gibraltar Naval Hospital; having stopped on a walk south from the town towards Europa Point he says:

> ... as well to rest the ladies as to admire that noble proof of the beneficient heart of our pious sovereign, who has erected such a princely asylum for those who fall sick in his navy service; a care and attention which are extended all over the British dominions, and are so many monuments of humanity and benevolence that distinguish the English amongst the nations.

But his description of Estepona, the nearest village along the coast from Gibraltar, could not be bettered today, despite the latest Disneyesque developments: 'a poor town and a modern one with nothing worth remarking'.

In his notes on the history of the area, Carter points out that Henry Plantagenet got leave from Edward III to serve under Alonzo XI, the King of Spain, against the Moors in Algeciras. He says this may have been the first siege or battle in Europe in which guns were used. The Moors created great havoc with them, the Spaniards having none. Algeciras surrendered in March 1344 after a siege of 20 months but was recaptured and destroyed by the Moorish King of Granada in 1368.

In the same year that Francis Carter made his tour along the Mediterranean coast from Gibraltar to Malaga, a new governor was appointed to the fortress who was to lead and inspire the garrison in one of its most fateful periods. General George Eliott took up his post before Spain had declared war on Britain or commenced the operations of the 14th siege of Gibraltar. France formally joined the American colonies in their war of independence against Britain in March 1778 and Spain was not long in following the French lead. The Spanish, however, were more concerned with the recovery of Minorca and Gibraltar and their West Indian colonies than with the ultimate fate of the Americans who might in any case have provided a dangerous example to Spain's own colonies in the south Americas. However, the French fleet from Brest had been careful to join the Spanish fleet before the declaration of hostilities, so that together they could accomplish the long-desired invasion of Britain. Although a combined fleet of 66 ships entered the Channel they were eventually driven back by the sickness of the crews and easterly gales, though not before panic had spread along the English coast.

It was obvious to Eliott and the Gibraltar garrison that it could only be a matter of time before the fortress was attacked by Spain and France and as soon as he arrived he did his best to improve the defences which, as usual, had been neglected in the years of peace. Eliott was lucky in that he found on arrival Chief Engineer Colonel William Green, who had been in residence since 1761 and who, besides being a gifted and original engineer, was passionately interested in the defence of the Rock. Green had gone to England in 1769 to try to persuade the government of the day to provide more resources for the defence works but with little success. However by 1772 he had replaced the civilian artificers on contract from England and the continent with a military company of soldier artificers. The civilian artificers, described by Colonel Green as 'indolent, drunken, disorderly and overpaid' could leave the Rock at any time regardless of military need. The new company of artificers, forerunners of the Royal Engineers, were drawn as volunteers from the regiments in garrison, from whom 68 were selected. Sergeant Ince, a name soon to become famous on the Rock, was the senior 'other rank' and the Company soon made an impact on the sapping, mining and construction problems of the fortress.

Green, like his Commander, General Eliott, was a trained gunner as well as an engineer and their compatibility during the siege helped the garrison to sustain itself so successfully against the prolonged assault. Eliott was educated at Edinburgh and Leyden universities and spoke several languages. He was trained as an engineer at the Royal Military Academy, Woolwich, where he also attended a course in gunnery. Wounded at Dettingen but present again at the Battle of Fontenoy, he retired in 1776 but accepted the governorship of Gibraltar when it was offered to him in 1777. He was originally commissioned in the Horse Grenadier Guards (afterwards the 2nd Lifeguards). Eliott was a most experienced and for his day, enlightened officer and it would not have been possible to find a commander better calculated to inspire and encourage his officers and soldiers and their families while at the same time bringing an educated and inventive mind to the problem of defending the colony.

At the beginning of the siege, because of the necessary dispersal of British maritime power, and despite a speech by Lord Chatham in 1770 to the effect that the maintenance of a sufficient force in the Bay of Gibraltar to cover the garrison was a cardinal point of British policy, the Spanish navy was in the ascendancy in the Strait and was able to enforce a blockade. General Eliott waited three months for the Spanish to start a landward attack and then decided to force the action. With typical bravura, the signal for the garrison to start to make life uncomfortable for the investing armies was the playing by military bands of 'Britons Strike Home', written by Henry Purcell for his opera *Bonduca*. At the signal, a gun laid by one of the garrison officers' wives, was fired into the Spanish lines.

The strength of the defences and the battery positions on the north end of the Rock were thought to make an attack on that side almost impossible, and so it proved to be. Colonel Green, in the two years before the siege commenced, had extended the batteries, one above the other, up the scarp of the Rock, and early in the siege a gun had been hauled up to the highest part of the Rock, overlooking the Spanish lines. From here almost all Spanish positions threatening the British from the north could be enfiladed.

By the end of the siege the final problem of firing into the Spanish positions had been overcome by tunnelling into the rockface to make a gallery in the 'Notch', a rock buttress which dominated the whole of the north face. A battery of five heavy guns was placed in the gallery in September 1782 and the new position was distinguished with the name of St. George's Hall. In after years the great gallery became famous as one of the sights of the Rock and visiting dignitaries, including President Theodore Roosevelt, were entertained in the artificial cavern. Today St. George's Hall houses an exhibition depicting the battery as it was during the Great Siege and continues to be a source of wonder to visitors and pride to the British, including the present day Gibraltarian inhabitants of the colony.

In February 1782 the garrison was dismayed to learn that Minorca had fallen to a combined French and Spanish attack. Commanded by the Duke of Crillon, 8,000 Spanish soldiers landed in Minorca and quickly captured Port Mahon. The Spanish brought 100 heavy guns with them for the reduction of Fort St. Philip which dominated the harbour, and there they were joined by 8,000 French troops. The British garrison at the time comprised only two regiments, the 51st and 61st Foot, plus two Hanoverian battalions. A regiment meant to reinforce the garrison had been retained by Eliott at Gibraltar, but some volunteers, including a company of Corsican irregulars, managed to fight their way into the fortress during the siege. The garrison managed to resist all the attacks of the vastly superior investing forces and, despite the local superiority of the Spanish and French fleets, continued to communicate with the outside world by sea.

But what could not be achieved by armed attack was eventually accomplished by disease. Fortescue says that half of General Murray's garrison had lived on salt provisions for three years whilst the other half had had salt rations for an incredible six years. During the siege it was impossible to grow fresh vegetables within the fortress to supplement the rations and scurvy was the inevitable consequence.

After seven weeks during which the plague raged through the fort, only 760 soldiers remained fit for duty whilst guards alone required 415 men each day. Murray capitulated five days later by which time only 600 soldiers could crawl out of the fortress to lay down their arms. In the 18th Century magnanimity and pity could still be shown to a surrendered enemy and both the French and Spanish armies did their best to succour the surviving British soldiers, a gesture, described by Fortescue as the epitome of Spanish generosity and gentleness. But now, with the danger of Minorca removed as a threat to his rear, the Duke of Crillon could turn his attention and 16,000 extra troops to the subjection of Gibraltar.

Early in 1778 Admiral Darby had relieved Gibraltar with a fleet of 100 supply ships, removing the fear of starvation from the fortress for another year. The frustrated Spaniards replied by commencing a continuous bombardment that went on for 13 months. In the first six weeks of the new attack, 56,000 shot and 20,000 shells were fired into the fortress. They seemingly caused little loss of life. Most of the civilians and a few non-essential soldiery were evacuated to the southern end of the Rock. The soldiers and sailors manning the immediate defences were disposed in bomb-proof shelters close to or beneath their alarm positions.

Many civilians and soldiers' families had already been sent back to England; in order to be allowed to stay it was necessary to produce for inspection 250lbs of flour or 360lbs of biscuit. One of the unfortunate consequences of the bombardment was that many hoards of food and wine, hidden by traders and merchants before they moved off to the comparative safety of the south end of the Rock, were uncovered by exploding shells and discovered in the deserted town by the soldiers now in occupation. To assuage their indignation at this hoarding of essential supplies, the soldiers proceeded to make short work of them and had a week-long orgy among the wine casks. Eventually many of them became unmanageable and order was only restored by the application of the cat-of-nine-tails or the gallows.

Miriam Green, wife of the Chief Engineer who was promoted to Major General during the siege, kept a diary whilst she was in garrison which provides some interesting details of life in the town in the time of the heavy bombardment. Paving stones were removed and the streets were ploughed up to reduce the danger from shell splinters. She describes the shortage of food and the onslaught of smallpox which carried off 500 in 1780, including 50 soldiers whose 'poor families were greatly thinned'. The Greens, since they had been on the Rock since 1761, had had a house built south of the town and so were able to move out from their official residence when conditions got too bad, joining many other temporary refugees. But they were better off than most. According to Colonel St. John Williams, Catherine Upton, the wife of an ensign, said of the severe bombardment of 1781: 'That night, my husband and I lay amongst a 100 soldiers screened by a curtain. The "silken sons of ease" in England know not what the army have endured in Gibraltar.'

When the Greens finally left Gibraltar after the siege, they sold their house, Mount Pleasant, to the government. It remains to this day, with some alterations and additions, as The Mount, official residence of the admiral. Miriam Green also tells us in her diary that it became quite fashionable to become a 'watcher' of the Spanish lines so as to be the bearer of good tidings if the investing forces were seen to be marching away; or at the very least an observation might produce something new to gossip about. It was to be some time however before the watchers could actually see the besieging regiments marching away. Miriam Green's journal is reproduced in part in an early edition of *The Royal Engineers Journal* and a copy can be seen in the Gibraltar Garrison library.

No doubt, like all good commanders, Eliott wanted to keep the fighting spirit of his troops high by dominating the 'no-man's land' between the opposing armies. The traditional way to do this was, and still is, by active patrolling, raids and, when conditions are favourable, by large scale attacks and sorties but with necessarily limited objectives. He saw just such an opportunity in November 1781. For some time the siege had deteriorated into a desultory artillery duel and General Eliott noted that the Spaniards tended to retire at night from their forward works, leaving their cannon and battery placements, saps and trenches almost unguarded. On the night of 26 November three columns, containing 824, 620 and 570 men respectively, went out to demolish the enemy works on the North Front. All the columns were successful even though the batteries attacked were three-quarters of a mile from the British lines. The object of the sortie was accomplished in one hour; 10 large mortars and 18 26-pounder guns were spiked and the stores and wooden works burned for several days after the attack.

Captain John Drinkwater, who served with the 72nd Regiment (The Royal Manchester Volunteers) during the siege and returned to serve there later, wrote a classic account of the Great Siege in which he says that the Spanish were bitterly ashamed of their poor showing at the time of the sortie. He also makes the interesting point that the 12th Foot, later the Suffolk Regiment, and later still combined into the 1st Anglian Regiment, was one of the famous Minden regiments. Taking part in the sortie they fought next to Hardenberg's Hanoverian Battalion which had fought shoulder to shoulder with them against the French in the Minden battle.

Another echo from the same historical past was observed during the German airborne invasion of Crete in May 1941 in the Second World War. German parachute casualties captured by the New Zealand forces defending the island were found to be wearing a 'Gibraltar' flash and it transpired that their German Jaeger Battalion was a descendant of the Hanoverian battalions which had fought in the defence of Gibraltar in the Great Siege. Drinkwater gives a breakdown of the garrison at the start of the siege. In 1781 the garrison comprised 209 officers, 59 staff, 313 sergeants, 169 drummers and 4,632 rank and file, a total of 5,382. Allowing for the few reinforcements that may have reached the Rock before his sortie and deducting casualties from disease and combat, it seems that Eliott must have committed over a third of his strength to the raid. It is not surprising that although the commander of the sortie was Brigadier Ross, promoted to Major General soon afterwards, General Eliott could not keep out of the action and appeared amongst the most advanced of the raiding parties.

Casualties amongst the British and Hanoverians were minimal and Drinkwater's figures for casualties to the end of 1781 including those incurred in the sortie are given as: killed and died of wounds, 122 all ranks; permanently disabled, 46 all ranks; wounded, 400 all ranks. Scurvy broke out in the garrison immediately after the sortie but a cargo of lemons from Algiers helped to abate the disease; nevertheless there were 260 deaths from sickness in 1781 alone.

After the fall of Minorca in 1781 the Spanish redoubled their efforts to recapture Gibraltar and, just as the loss of the Balearic base inspired Eliott to strike back in the sortie of November, the shame of the Spanish at the débâcle provided a spur and inspiration to their own efforts. Early in 1782 it was clear to the defenders that a great new offensive was in the offing. One hundred Spanish and 60 French ships brought supplies and reinforcements to the besiegers. New floating batteries were designed by the French military engineer, d'Arcon. The new assault ships were roofed and insulated and fitted with water sprinklers to prevent their being set on fire by red hot shot. Each battery would mount from 10 to 26 guns on one side only and d'Arcon claimed that the special ships were indestructible and unsinkable.

In June 1782 the Duke of Crillon, the victor of Minorca, was given command of the new assault on Gibraltar and his forces were increased to about 40,000 men against the 7,000 soldiers, sailors and marines defending the fortress. On 13 September the floating batteries were brought into position and the assault finally commenced. About 400 guns were in action altogether, the British having about 100 of these. General Eliott was determined to use red-hot shot on the floating batteries and he had every British battery provided with grates over which the shot could be heated. The red-hot shot was tried out against the Spanish land batteries on 8 September, on the orders of Lieutenant General Boyd, the Lieutenant Governor. Many enemy batteries and emplacements were seen to catch fire and this gave the defenders confidence and convinced them that the floating batteries could be defeated.

At first on 13 September the British fire did not seem to be having much effect on the assaulting batteries even though they were anchored at almost point-blank range for the defenders' guns. But by the late afternoon smoke was seen to come from one of the assault ships and by nightfall several of them were burning furiously. During the night most of the attacking ships were seen to be in serious difficulties. General Eliott followed the progress of the artillery duel throughout the night from King's Bastion and by 11.00am next morning five of the attacking batteries had blown up, three were burned to the waterline whilst the remaining two were in flames.

The attack collapsed and British gun-boats, which had been adding to the confusion of the attackers by firing into the burning hulks still afloat, turned to rescuing their wounded, mutilated and shocked crews. The attack was never renewed and the crowd of fashionable visitors which had assembled to see the final subjugation of the Rock drifted away in some chagrin. It is said that the Queen of Spain herself had arrived to see the final assault from a nearby hill and she, too, was disappointed. Certainly the hill from which the Queen is said to have watched, clearly visible from Gibraltar, is known as the Queen of Spain's Chair and is gleefully pointed out to visiting tourists from the summit of the Rock.

Admiral Howe relieved the Rock with a convoy of provisions in October and this, on top of the failure of the meticulously prepared sea-borne assault, marked the end of the last attempt to eject the British from the Rock by force of arms. The blockade dragged on for a little longer until hostilities were finally suspended on 3 February 1783. There could be no doubt that the heroes of the siege were General Sir

George Eliott, whose appointment had come at exactly the right time to inspire and steel the garrison for their epic defence, and all his senior officers including Colonel William Green, who supported him without faction or any but helpful advice during the long trial of strength and determination.

But there were many other officers and soldiers who played an important part in the successful resistance. Sergeant Ince designed and supervised the construction of the rock tunnels and batteries which were eventually able to dominate the North Front of the Rock. Captain Mercier suggested a short fused shell to produce an 'air burst', perhaps inspiring Lieutenant Shrapnel, who was also present during the siege, to invent the devastating munition which still bears his name. Also to be mentioned are the governor's Aide-de-Camp, Lieutenant Koehler, who invented a gun carriage which could be depressed so that it became possible to fire down directly from the higher rock face batteries; and finally, Captain Whitaker who produced a lightweight, hollowed-out shot which could be filled with a flammable substance and had an effect similar to the modern Napalm bomb. A much admired model of Koehler's gun carriage is now mounted in Casemates Square where it serves as a reminder of the inventiveness and ingenuity shown by soldiers under the pressures of siege warfare. A less happy and less successful but none the less ingenious example of invention fathered by the imperatives of war was d'Arcon's floating assault battery.

There must have been many other unsung heroes and heroines of Gibraltar's Great Siege just as there must have been examples of devotion and adaptability which passed unnoticed in the earlier sieges of Malta and Famagusta. More recently Lucknow, Mafeking, and Malta in 1942 must have presented circumstances of abrupt change from what could have been a life of sybaritic idleness and excruciating boredom to one of endeavour, inspiration and self-sacrifice. In Gibraltar, as in other places at other times, the great good fortune of having the right man in pace at the right time was crucial to its successful resistance. General Eliott, as we have said, was not only an educated soldier, but was also what was soon to be called a scientific soldier, trained in the intricacies of military engineering and gunnery to the limits of the knowledge of his day.

Perhaps more important, Eliott was, again within the limits of the age, a man who knew how to get the most out of his officers and men and might in a later century have been labelled a humanitarian. There are records of Eliott buying food and wine from Minorca and Morocco, and later from prize ships brought into harbour by British men-of-war and privateers, which he had distributed to the sick soldiers and their families who could not afford the vastly inflated prices of a town under siege. Ernle Bradford tells us of the governor returning a personal gift of food from the Duke of Crillon, saying that since all food brought into the fortress was sold for the public good there was no point in sending him food which he could not personally enjoy. Eliott was also of course trying to bluff the besieging forces into believing that there was no shortage of fresh food in the garrison. But it was by such gestures that he won the hearts of his men and their families and convinced them that the hardships of the siege really were being shared by all.

After the siege a kind of peace returned to the Rock, but a tumultuous peace it must have been. Very heavy drinking was commonplace in this garrison as in all others and since the men were often paid only at two-monthly intervals, it was necessary to abandon all parades except for the guard until the money ran out. Regiments had to be paid at different times so that the whole garrison would not be drunk at the same time. Riot and mutiny were frequent occurrences.

In 1801 reports on the state of affairs in Gibraltar reached England and a very popular governor, General O'Hara, was succeeded on his death by the Duke of Kent, a not very bright soldier but a strong disciplinarian who was sent out with instructions from his brother, the Duke of York, to impose order on the seeming chaos. O'Hara was reputed to have received an annual income of £7,000 from licensing the 90 taverns within the fortress walls in which the garrison regularly got drunk. This was something of an improvement on the meagre 500 dollars from licensing shown in the governor's perquisites for 1729 but O'Hara entertained lavishly, was very well liked and enjoyed his nickname of the 'Cock of the Rock'. Although the garrison was flattered to be given a royal governor, the old easygoing ways of O'Hara were preferred. He had finally succumbed in Gibraltar to wounds received whilst fighting the French revolutionary armies and the young Napoleon Bonaparte in Toulon, where he was captured but eventually exchanged for a French general. He returned to Gibraltar where he had previously served as Lieutenant Governor, for the last few years of his life.

The Duke of Kent succeeded in quelling the disorders in the garrison but only at the expense of provoking a more serious mutiny which was only finally put down by the execution of three of the mutineers and the transportation to Australia of nine others. To his surprise and anger the Duke was recalled to England to answer the criticisms which his actions had provoked, and he did not return. Before he left Gibraltar he presented the officers of the 54th Regiment with a piece of plate to commemorate their loyalty and that of their men during the mutiny. It was said that the local wine merchants who had lost much money when the Duke closed their taverns, and some army officers who were out of sympathy with their royal commander, had intrigued to have him removed.

The wars against revolutionary France had commenced in 1793 and, although British sea power preserved Gibraltar from yet another siege, the Rock was partly blockaded. There were two sea battles in the Bay, in both of which British ships triumphed. Sarah Fyers, like her predecessor Miriam Green, was also an 'enemy watcher' and she witnessed one of the sea fights. Sarah was the daughter of another sapper family. Her father was Chief Engineer on the Rock, having arrived with his family in 1787, a few years after the Greens had departed for England.

We pick up Sarah's story as an English squadron sails into Gibraltar Bay to engage a French fleet which was sheltering under the friendly guns of Algeciras:

> . . . it certainly was a beautiful sight to see those magnificent ships, their white sails shining in the sun and following each other at intervals. The breakfast room was soon deserted as we hastened to an eminence near the pluviometer, whence we had a perfect view of the town of Algeciras opposite and the whole of the coast on that side of the bay.
>
> The day was beautifully clear and fine. We were presently joined by several officers of the Royal Engineers . . . Mr. Mann, Mr. Jones, and others. We were not kept long in suspense as to the intention of the British Squadron, for the ships began firing against the French ships and the Spanish defences including the little island opposite the town of Algeciras. With what interest was the scene watched from our side of the Bay. Every soul in the place seemed to have congregated either on the Line Wall or on the heights, and the murmur of so many voices came to us like the sound of the sea waves.

Sarah's colourful description of the action gives little hint of the anxiety that she and the other onlookers must have felt, for they would have been only too well aware of the serious consequences of a British failure for the garrison and its families. Fortunately, throughout the revolutionary wars and the Napoleonic wars which were to follow, the Rock was never directly attacked. Sarah married Lieutenant Cornelius Mann who had watched the battle with her from 'near the pluviometer'. Soon after the attack they were married in Engineer House and General O'Hara gave the bride away. She made an excellent army wife and Cornelius went on to become a Major General and to fight in the Napoleonic wars which are the subject of our next Chapter.

CHAPTER II

The Mediterranean and the Napoleonic Wars

The capture of Gibraltar marked the beginning of the permanent occupation of British bases in the Mediterranean area and the inevitable and inexorable expansion eastward. The revolutionary wars, and especially the French successes in Italy, brought about a temporary withdrawal of British naval and military forces into the Atlantic whence they could serve as a shield against French invasion attempts on Ireland and the English Channel coast. Although Nelson was back in the Mediterranean with a reconnaissance squadron by 1798, after an absence of two years, the damage was done. Napoleon was able to slip out of Toulon, capture Malta and land a full-sale invasion force in Egypt without being intercepted.

However, the French fleet was caught and destroyed in Aboukir Bay by Nelson, changing the whole balance of power in the Mediterranean to Britain's advantage. The Battle of the Nile also led directly to a native Maltese rising against the French occupiers of their islands and the ultimate role of Britain as the protecting power. This sudden opening up of the Mediterranean brought the British into action in many of the littoral countries and prescribed the kind of warfare that is typical of a situation where a nation with superior sea power is at war with a country weak at sea but with large and seemingly invulnerable armies.

A link between the 18th Century bases of Gibraltar and Minorca and further expansion eastward, triggered by Napoleon's design to seize

Egypt as a stepping stone, is provided by General O'Hara whom we met as governor of Gibraltar in the previous Chapter. Before becoming governor of the Rock in 1795, he was as the deputy governor, involved in the plan to send a British force to Toulon to support the French royalists against the revolutionary army that was investing the town and port. The town had declared for the royalist cause as a result of the execution of Louis XVI and the excesses of the revolutionary terror in Paris, Lyons and the Vendée.

Britain had another interest in Toulon in the still powerful elements of the French Mediterranean fleet that had taken refuge in the harbour and inner basin, constituting a serious threat to allied naval superiority. Major General Lord Mulgrave was appointed to command the allied forces composed of Spanish, Neapolitan, Corsican and British troops aided by French royalist volunteers. The main aim of the force was to defend the town, harbour, dockyard and arsenal but for the British preventing the French fleet from falling into the hands of the revolutionary forces was paramount.

Despite a spirited defence of the forts and batteries covering the town the arrival of the young Napoleon Bonaparte to command the revolutionary artillery investing the town provided a new impetus for the attack of the French revolutionaries. Lord Mulgrave was relieved of his post by General O'Hara from Gibraltar. O'Hara brought with him from the Rock two regiments of foot and some artillery but these merely replaced and did not reinforce the allied troops under siege. By the end of October 1793 the attacking army outnumbered the allies by a wide margin. The defenders' situation was made worse by the lack of co-operation of the Spanish and Neapolitan troops who refused to accept the overall command of the British. Disaster under these circumstances was inevitable, given the newly-encouraged aggressive sprit of the French.

The occasion of the disaster was a well-mounted and initially successful attack on one of the French batteries investing the town. The sortie, carried out by combined force of which 400 were British, took its first objective with ease, but was then turned into a rout when the British troops, who had played a crucial part in the attack, pursued the retreating enemy too far, as they were often to do in the Peninsular War, and could not be rallied in the face of a determined counter attack. The British were forced back, losing all they had gained and 200 British troops were lost to the French. To complete the débâcle, General O'Hara who had hurried forward to help to stem the retreat, was himself seriously wounded and captured by the French. Toulon was abandoned amidst scenes of chaos and mutual recrimination during the night of 19 December 1793.

It had been planned to destroy the French fleet and arsenal before the withdrawal but the Spanish troops charged with the responsibility for the destruction of the fleet failed to carry out the task. Several warships were left intact, the arsenal was not destroyed and some British ships were damaged when, contrary to orders, two French powder ships were blown up instead of being sunk at their moorings as was intended. Sir Sidney Smith, a British naval captain whom we shall hear of again, took a completely unauthorised part in the attempt to neutralise the French ships. While Smith claimed complete success for his personal intervention, the Spanish were able to suggest that without his officious interference they might well have achieved the complete destruction of the enemy fleet. Significantly, once the extent of the failure to destroy the French ships became apparent, Smith lost interest in his own account of the misadventure. Nelson never forgave Smith for what he saw as an attempt at self-aggrandisement and vain display.

Smith was not the only officer to appear, for the first time, on the world stage at Toulon. Apart from the already acclaimed 'immortals', Nelson and Napoleon, and the brave and congenial O'Hara from Gibraltar, John Moore, as yet only a Brigadier, was nearby; and General David Dundas, brother of the incompetent and much loathed Minister for War, took part in the failed sortie and subsequent abandonment of Toulon, brought about in part by the failure of the minister to supply sufficient troops. Major Koehler, the engineer officer who had made an important contribution to the successful holding of Gibraltar as a lieutenant during the Great Siege, enhanced his reputation during the withdrawal from Toulon by personally spiking all the guns in Fort La Malgue whilst under heavy fire. He was also the last allied soldier to leave the French shore. Not least among many others was a Scotsman, Sir Thomas Graham.

Graham had no reason to love the French. While he and his young wife, with whom he was passionately in love, were travelling in Italy, she died from the plague. He set out to bring her body back to England and attempted to enter France through Marseilles. The coffin, sealed in Italy, was broken into by officious and brutal French customs officers. Graham never recovered from the experience and he retained his hatred of the French until the end of his life. He offered himself as a gentleman volunteer with the British forces at Toulon and was taken as an honorary aide-de-camp by the commander, Lord Mulgrave. He performed with outstanding valour, personally leading one column in an attack on the French. Mulgrave's favourable opinion of him persuaded him to return to England after the fall of Toulon in order to raise a regiment at his own expense with the hope that he would be taken on to the permanent British military establishment. He could not persuade the Duke of York to grant him a permanent commission in the army because of his age and comparative lack of military experience, but he had the right to command the regiment he himself had raised, which afterwards became the Cameronians. When General O'Hara returned to Gibraltar as governor in 1795, Graham followed, to take command of his regiment.

After the withdrawal from Toulon the situation of the allies in the Mediterranean continued to deteriorate. Napoleon's 'whiff of grapeshot' in October 1795 scattered the last revolutionary mob in Paris and set him off on his bid to conquer the world. His series of great victories started in the Italian Alps and rapidly spread down into southern Italy, hustling the Bourbons out of Naples and eventually forcing the British out of the Mediterranean, at least for the time being. By the end of 1796 the British bases on Corsica and Elba had been evacuated, the French had regained Sardinia and the Neapolitan Royal House, now confined to Sicily, withdrew their ships and their co-operation from the British fleet. Gibraltar was the only remaining British base in the Mediterranean and no British ship moved east from the Rock until May 1798 when Nelson took a reconnaissance squadron of two battleships and three frigates back in search of information about French movements and intentions. He quickly learned that the French fleet had broken out of Toulon and that Malta had surrendered to Napoleon.

The British Occupation of Malta

In one sense the French capture of Malta was only incidental to Napoleon's grand design for a descent upon Egypt, to be followed, once the way had been opened, by the even more ambitious expulsion of the British from India and its incorporation into a French-dominated world state stretching from the Atlantic to the Indian and Pacific Oceans. Napoleon's fantastic plan was ended by British naval supremacy after the Battle of Trafalgar in 1805 but he continued to cling to this grandiose scheme. Even as late as 1812 he was suggesting that after the still-to-be-achieved capture of Moscow and the assured defeat of the Russians, his armies could march on and invade India from the North.

However, before the French landed in Malta they had been intriguing there for some time. By the last quarter of the 18th Century the position and prestige of the once proud Order of St John, the hereditary rulers of Malta since the 16th Century, had been seriously eroded. Internationally its influence had almost ceased to exist and internally the native Maltese including the clergy were becoming increasingly disillusioned with the oligarchic and élitest rule of the self-perpetuating Order of Knights. The success of the French revolution brought increasing pressure to bear on the Knights. The Order owned many estates in France and derived much of its income from them. Even before the revolution the French had begun to question the value of the Order in terms of its benefits to the safety of coastal towns and trade, once secured by the operations of its much reduced war fleet. The egalitarian and democratic ideas of the revolution were in opposition to the aristocratic and absolutist government of the Knights, and in 1792 the Order's possessions in France were confiscated. When France severed its links with the Order the Knights began to search through the palaces of Europe for an equally wealthy and powerful protector.

As the revolutionary wars dragged on through the period of the Directory a new ambitious and aggressive star appeared in the firmament in the shape of Napoleon Bonaparte. The strategic importance of Malta suddenly re-emerged for the first time since the Turkish war fleets had rampaged in the central Mediterranean 200 years earlier. Austria, Russia and Britain showed a belated interest in the future of the island. The Kingdom of the Two Sicilies insisted that the island should revert to them since Sicily was the donor of the original gift through Charles V. The Knights, showing a previously unsuspected gift of prescience, proposed unsuccessfully an alliance between Malta and the newly-established United States of America. France worked away quietly at its subversion within the island. The Grand Master of the Order was promised a pension and French Knights, the majority in the

Order, were offered pensions and the right of domicile in France.

In 1797 the Directory accepted Napoleon's plan for the invasion of Egypt as a preliminary to the descent on British India. He was also authorised to take over Malta to prevent it from falling into the hands of France's enemies. Napoleon sailed for Egypt via Malta on 19 May 1798, his heavily-laden invasion fleet narrowly evading Nelson as he sailed out of Toulon. The French arrived off Malta on 9 June and the island capitulated within three days.

The native Maltese, although at first prepared to welcome their new masters, believed that the island had been handed over through the treachery of the French Knights. The present-day Maltese point out with some irony that the coat of arms of the last Grand Master, Ferdinand von Hompesch, features what could be taken for a double cross. After the French take-over the Knights were bundled out of Malta, allowed to take with them only a few of the possessions and treasures of the Order which were taken under the protection of the Czar of Russia who hoped by this means to extend Russian influence into the central and western Mediterranean. The Knights never returned to Malta and although the Order still exists, with headquarters in Rome and representatives and hospitals in many parts of the world, it never recovered its former illustrious position in the affairs of the Mediterranean.

The French fleet sailed on to Egypt leaving a small garrison on the supposedly friendly island of Malta and carrying with it a mountain of loot from the treasury and vaults of the Order. The Maltese were not sorry to see the Knights depart and for a short time all went well; but as so often happens, the newcomers, through greed and insensitivity to local religious and social customs, soon aroused the anger of the islanders. The looting of the treasures and trophies of the Order may have been acceptable but when the churches were profaned and sacked anger quickly turned to riot. When news of Nelson's destruction of the French fleet in Aboukir Bay reached Malta riot turned to insurrection. Small bodies of unsupported French troops were massacred in risings across the island and eventually the small French garrison was concentrated in the more easily defended town of Valletta. The massive defensive works around the town, built at tremendous cost after the Great Siege by the Turks in the 16th Century, were now put to use for the first time. It was clear to the Maltese investing Valletta that it could not be reduced without outside help and an appeal was made to the British, the new masters of the Mediterranean, for troops, guns and supplies.

It was hoped at first that a blockade of the French, cutting off supplies from France, would be sufficient to persuade the besieged garrison to surrender. To this end Nelson sent a squadron under Captain Alexander Ball who was later to become the first Civil Commissioner of the island. Ball was drawn increasingly into the affairs of the island, at first in mediating and reconciling the divergent views of the three native Maltese leaders, the notary Emmanuele Vitale, Canon, later Bishop, Caruana and Vincenzo Borg. Ball persuaded these three to co-operate with each other and with the British. He so won their confidence with his understanding and sympathetic handling of the people and their local problems that he was soon recognised as Civil Commissioner and accepted as the authentic voice of the native interests in the island. This was not always to his benefit in regard to the government at home.

Graham from Toulon, the one-time ADC to Lord Mulgrave, had meanwhile raised his Regiment of Foot, and took part in the British recapture of Minorca, for the third time. He was then sent to Malta in temporary command of two regiments to co-ordinate military operations against the French still holding out in Valletta. Graham's forces included some inferior troops from the Kingdom of the Two Sicilies and some Maltese companies with British officers who bore the brunt of the fighting. The Czar had agreed that Russian troops would join the British in their occupation of Malta, and his assumption of the rôle of Grand Master of the Order of St. John and Protector of the island would have gained credence from their presence. Russian troops did move slowly down the west coast of Italy from Naples to Messina but on 11 January 1800 they were withdrawn to the island of Corfu as the Czar prepared to abandon the second coalition against the French. In leaving the coalition the Russians gave up all their claims and ambitions in Malta, as the British were to point out at an appropriate time a little later.

Apart from being a brave soldier, as he demonstrated on many occasions, Graham had something of the courtier and statesman about him. He must also have possessed much personal charm since he received a letter from Lady Hamilton congratulating him on his part in the recovery of Minorca. Graham quickly realised that his force was inadequate to capture the strongly-fortified town of Valletta and it was not until more British and Neapolitan troops arrived early in 1800 that serious negotiations for a French capitulation were begun. Graham agreed to provide ships to take the French garrison to the French mainland and, more controversially, allowed them to take with them all the portable loot they had collected on the island.

Two years earlier Napoleon's army, when it sailed on to Egypt, was reputed to have taken over one million pounds worth of looted treasure in its baggage. The French insisted that it had all been lost in the burning ships sunk in Aboukir Bay, but what better way to divert public treasure into private pockets? The armies of Napoleon, in an age of rapacity that was common to all the European armies, were acknowledged to be the most efficient at pillage as well as the most dashing in their military accomplishments. Certainly one prize item that did reach France was the sword of Grand Master Valette who had provided the inspiration and leadership to hold out against the Turks during the Great Siege of Malta in 1565; it is now in the Louvre in Paris.

Britain was uncertain at first about what its future relations with Malta should be. The government could see no advantage in remaining on the island and an uncharacteristically sycophantic Nelson provided support by publicly stating that Malta was useless as a base and that Minorca or Corsica were preferable because of their comparative closeness to Toulon and the French coast. The Maltese people very much wanted Britain to remain as the Protecting Power and Alexander Ball strongly advocated this course, whilst encouraging the islanders to take a larger part in their own government than had been allowed under the Knights. Ball upset the British government by his strongly voiced opposition to withdrawal and even more to the idea of handing the island to the Russians, who would reinstall the Knights.

At the short-lived Peace of Amiens in 1802 it was agreed that in return for a French withdrawal from some occupied territories Britain would leave Malta and the Knights would return under Russian control. But this arrangement quickly came to nothing. Britain came belatedly to realise that Malta could control the whole of the central Mediterranean and that it would be madness to allow any other major power to possess its port and dockyard facilities. The lack of progress in the French evacuation of southern Italy provided a ready-made excuse for the retention of Malta and although Captain Ball went back to sea in 1801 he returned in triumph as Commissioner in 1802 having achieved a knighthood and the rank of Rear Admiral. He stayed until 1809. Russian claims on the island were dismissed on the grounds that she had played no part in its capture and should therefore have no part in its disposal.

When Sir Alexander Ball returned to Malta as Commissioner in 1802 some of his earlier problems had been resolved. The French had gone from the island and even with the resumption of hostilities in 1803 British naval superiority in the Mediterranean, established at the Battle of the Nile and confirmed at Trafalgar in 1805, guaranteed a trouble-free period as far as the major powers were concerned. However there were matters to be settled between Malta and the newly-established United States of America on the one hand and the petty pirate states of the North African littoral on the other.

The United States, barely 20 years old and with a very small navy, nevertheless had a fast growing overseas trade. The Bashaw of Tripoli regarded the seemingly unprotected American ships as fair game. A small American squadron had very little success against Tripoli and unfortunately had to abandon a well-armed and modern frigate in Tripoli harbour, much to the horror of the other nations trading in the Mediterranean. A new and larger American squadron under Commodore Preble arrived and included amongst its young officers the soon-to-be legendary Stephen Decatur, who led a raiding party into Tripoli harbour where the abandoned frigate, *Philadelphia*, was captured, run aground and blown up. Eventually an even larger American squadron forced the Corsairs to release the crew of the *Philadelphia* after the payment of a ransom.

An American squadron had been operating from Malta even before the British took over the island, which perhaps suggested an alliance with America when the Knights were looking for a substitute for the support withdrawn by the French in 1792. As the traditional enemy of the Corsairs and Barbary pirates, the British continued to co-operate with the Americans. Ball had similar problems with the ruler of Algiers who would not acknowledge the validity of the passports Ball handed out on a rather liberal basis and which sometimes it must be admitted got into the wrong hands. Ball achieved through diplomacy, no doubt backed by the persuasive power of the British navy, rather more than the Americans who were not yet able to 'speak softly, but carry a big stick'. The North African situation was not entirely resolved until the 1830s with the French occupation of what we now know as Tunisia and Algeria.

As has been said, even before the breakdown of the Peace of Amiens, Nelson and Britain were beginning to have second thoughts about the importance of Malta. Ball was soon told to slow down the preparations for the British evacuation of the island and it became accepted that Malta was too well placed strategically to allow any other naval power to have it. Napoleon himself used the question of Malta as a *casus belli* for forcing the renewal of hostilities in 1803. Both Britain and France were equally determined not to allow a hostile power to establish itself in Malta. Napoleon went so far as to say that he would rather lose a *Département* of France than abandon his design on Malta. But, to the delight of the Maltese, Britain remained in strength and under the Treaty of Paris in May 1814 became the sole and undisputed ruler of the island.

After 1803 hostilities resumed between France and Britain. Sir Alexander Ball wanted to develop Malta as a great entrepôt and to supplant Leghorn as the port most used by British traders in the Mediterranean. The Maltese, under the direction of the Knights and through their own hard work had transformed their rocky soil into fertile fields in which they planted cotton, unfortunately at the expense of cereal crops so that the adequate provision of grain became a perennial problem – a problem which, as Braudel has pointed out, was common to all the Mediterranean islands with an aristocratic or absentee landlord class. Silk and sugar-cane were also crops which appealed to those landholders and proprietors requiring a quick cash return from their land.

Ball was determined to set up a grain store that would hold two years' supply of corn. The underground granaries which he utilised were still there to be used in the Second World War and remain on the tourist itinerary of Valletta. To fill the granaries it was necessary to scour Europe for supplies and Ball had to send one of his assistant secretaries, Chapman, as a special agent to Odessa on the Black Sea to obtain supplies. For all their autocratic ways and their insensitive oppression of the native Maltese, the Order of St. John left the island in a far better state economically and agriculturally than when they arrived and Ball had a good base on which to build. Compared to the other Mediterranean islands in the early 19th Century Malta was prosperous and contented.

The British occupation of Malta had one unforeseen consequence which led to the opening up of the Mediterranean as an area for leisurely travel and sight-seeing, ultimately encouraging the growth of the tourist industry and its most recent manifestation the package-tour. The numbers going on the Grand Tour in the 18th Century, mainly a British practice, declined abruptly as a result of the French revolution and almost completely ceased with the activities of Napoleon Bonaparte. Napoleon's successful Italian mainland campaign of 1797 and subsequent occupation of Italy cut out the usual travel routes to the classical antiquities and art treasures of southern Europe, but the more affluent members of the British public undeterred, began to look for other ways of indulging their appetite for the educational pleasures and exotic delights of southern and eastern Europe. With British domination of the seas assured, especially after Nelson's victory at Trafalgar, the way was open for adventurous sprits to sail into the Mediterranean and approach their classical sites and chosen areas for exploration from the southern flank. The Rock of Gibraltar was an object of pride and fascination to Britons and the events of the Great Siege were recent enough to attract the patriotic and well-connected visitors who used it as their first port-of-call on their voyage into the Middle sea. As we have explained, adequate social connections were essential for access to what were still primitive and scarce facilities. Invitations to stay with or be fed by governors or commissioners, accommodation in officers' messes, free travel on one of His Majesty's ships of war, and the not inconsiderable perquisite involved in the franking of private mail apparently without limit on distance or bulk, were much sought after. Letters of introduction to friends, and friends of friends, in posts overseas smoothed the way for the comparatively small number of travellers from the close-knit, aristocratic community.

The 'Romantic Movement' was already well under way in Britain and elsewhere and many of its followers including Samuel Taylor Coleridge, already celebrated as the author of *The Rime of the Ancient Mariner*, journeyed to the Mediterranean for inspiration and food for their various muses. Coleridge also hoped to improve his precarious finances by obtaining a post with the governor of Malta. The story of

Coleridge's brief sojourn in the Mediterranean, even though it be slightly out of sequence, will provide a description of both Gibraltar and Malta after the resumption of hostilities in 1803, following the collapse of the Treaty of Amiens. Coleridge was at a low ebb in his social and family life. He had already received acclaim for his writing, especially for his work with William Wordsworth published jointly as *The Lyrical Ballads,* which included his *Ancient Mariner*, *Kubla Khan* and the first part of *Christabel*. He was still very much lauded at the fashionable gatherings in London's literary drawing-rooms at the time of his departure from England. Like Wordsworth he quickly became disillusioned with the French revolution and its slide into the 'Terror'.

In December 1783 he had given up his studies at Cambridge, travelled to London and, under the influence of drink, enlisted in the 15th Dragoons. After two miserable months he was bought out of the army on the grounds of insanity. His narrow escape from what would have been for him a hatefully uncongenial life seemed to sober him up and he resumed his place at Cambridge. At this time he met Robert Southey and in 1795 they married two sisters, Sara and Edith Fricker. Although Coleridge appeared to be devoted to his wife Sara and to his family, he became hopelessly involved in a kind of cerebral love affair with Wordsworth's sister-in-law. His life became, to the horror of his friends, increasingly unstable and he started to take drugs to alleviate the depression from which he now suffered. He developed an addiction from which he was never again entirely free. He was also deeply in debt to his many benefactors and friends. Not unnaturally the idea of a journey abroad, to the Mediterranean, became attractive. Apart from escaping from his increasingly irksome family ties, he had an acquaintance in Malta through whom he had some hope of gaining paid employment for long enough to improve his financial position. He obtained letters of introduction to government officials and officers in the garrisons of Gibraltar and Malta and, more importantly in his straitened circumstances, he obtained a free passage on one of His Majesty's ships.

Coleridge sailed for Malta in the Spring of 1804. At that time, Spring, being the best season for a passage, the transit time for a Brig was about three weeks. Because of bad weather his voyage took 40 days including a respite of six days in Gibraltar. Being in a convoy with a naval escort provided some security but Coleridge confessed that he and the other passengers lived in abject fear of being captured by the French or by Algerian privateers. Despite the presence of French frigates and a sizeable British fleet in the western Mediterranean, the North African coast and the Greek archipelago were still infested with pirates. Because of the weather Coleridge had to spend much of his time below deck. Strangely, for the author of *The Ancient Mariner*, his previous sea experience was limited to a return journey to the Isle of Man. Now in the light of his new-found nautical knowledge and with time at his disposal he was able to revise some lines of the *Mariner*, which had been published six years earlier.

The poet went ashore at Gibraltar, one imagines thankfully, on 20 April. He found 'a town of all nations and languages'. He went first to Griffiths' Hotel, which he describes as the social centre. This hotel was used by Disraeli on his tour of the Mediterranean almost 30 years later, and by George Borrow later still, but sadly it has now disappeared and there is scant knowledge of its original location. Coleridge delivered two letters of recommendation in Gibraltar, one to the Garrison Chaplain, a Mr. Frome, and another to a Major Adye, author of a standard work on gunnery. He does not appear to have met the governor or been invited to dine but he did make friends among the more intellectual officers, usually the engineer officers some of whom he met again in Malta and who were able to provide the entrée to comfortable facilities in the messes in both garrisons. Coleridge describes Europa Point, the southernmost part of Gibraltar, as 'full of gardens and pleasant trees, broom, geranium and prickly pear. There were aspen popular trees all in rich foliage with corn knee-high'. He visited St. Michael's Caves 'full of massy pillars and stalactites'. Like the patriotic Englishman abroad which he obviously was, he was scandalised to find the common opinion among Gibraltarians and most other Mediterranean people that they preferred the French because of their manners.

Coleridge left the Rock on 27 April in a convoy escorted by the 32-gun frigate *Maidstone* and they arrived off Sardinia after 18 days sailing, much of it against contrary winds. Malta was finally sighted on 18 May. Coleridge went ashore at once to find the Casa di san Poix, the house of his friend Dr (later Sir John) Stoddart, who held the office of King's and Admiralty advocate. The poet lived with the Stoddarts until he was able to move into an apartment offered him by Sir Alexander Ball when he was able to give him a temporary post in his administration. Coleridge had had a letter of introduction to Ball but he had not been very sanguine of obtaining a situation. However, of Ball's three assistant secretaries one, his Public (1st) Secretary, Macauley, was taken up with routine administrative matters, the second, Laing, was about to depart for Scotland on leave and the third, Chapman, was, as we have seen, in Odessa negotiating for corn, a business which seems to have been unduly protracted. Ball was at loggerheads with the military commander of the garrison, General Villettes, whom Coleridge described as the leader of the 'old fogeys' who were alleged to be anti-jacobin and anti-democratic. The general was against the employment of native Maltese as officers in the Malta Regiment or in government service. In the battle of words, or rather letters, with the government at home, Ball felt that he needed someone of Coleridge's obvious literary talent to 'dress' his letters. He offered Coleridge the post of temporary assistant secretary, on salary and with a suite of rooms in his Palace, for a period of two months but the tenure was extended and eventually he was being paid as Public Secretary whilst Chapman was absent.

It is obvious that Coleridge was good at his job and was well thought of by Ball and by Mrs. Ball who was clearly pleased to have a 'literary lion' on her husband's staff. Coleridge reciprocated their feelings and although he cavilled at the paper work he was a loyal and devoted assistant to Ball, and partisan in his support in later years in England in his writing and public statements. In due course he became Ball's memorialist.

His work in Malta was concerned with most matters of public interest. He wrote much of Ball's correspondence with Nelson and completed or corrected many of his letters to London concerning the intrigue going on between the Bey of Algiers and the French. He enjoyed living in the suite of rooms which had been part of the Grand Master's Palace but he never regarded his stay as more than temporary. The Palace had been taken over as the Civil Commission and although the reputation of the Order had reached its nadir after its surrender of the island to Napoleon, Coleridge and his military friends had a great respect for the architectural achievements of the Knights. He described the architecture of Valletta as southern baroque and the works of art as predominantly religious with a strong Neapolitan flavour. The Civil Commission overlooked what is now Queen's Square. In front of the

Commission Buildings is another large square which was intended to be the site for the library but in Coleridge's time it was used as the garrison mess and ball-room. Malta's splendid library is now housed in Queen's Square and the old mess and ball-room provide accommodation for what the Libyans call their Cultural Institute.

At the time of Coleridge's stay about 40,000 people lived in the city area whilst about 70,000 lived in the countryside and the small towns. The language spoken commonly in Malta was, and still is, a dialect of Arabic with a strong admixture of Italian. After 150 years of the British presence English is now spoken widely but in the early 19th Century Italian was the language of education and of the public notices. Ball tried to reserve most government posts for the Maltese as he had for officers in the Malta Regiment but patronage continued and many posts were filled from Britain by the nominees of the home government. The Maltese enjoyed a reputation for being honest, hard-working and frugal, and unlike the Sicilians who were usually represented as lazy, they had turned their rocks into good soil for the cultivation of their staple crop, cotton. The thread was exported to Spain and brought in half a million pounds sterling annually. There were few other exports except oranges which were particularly good and were distributed round Europe as presents, first by the Knights and later by the British governors and senior officers. The large-scale cultivation of cotton meant that only four months' supply of corn could be grown in a year. This was particularly dangerous in time of war and the handling of all grain on the islands was in the hands of a government monopoly, a corporation called the *Universita*. As we have said, Ball was determined to lay in two years' supply when war was renewed in 1803, at a cost to the government of £200,000.

It was the policy of British governments for 166 years not to interfere in the religion of the inhabitants. Every attempt was made to cultivate good relations with the Maltese and the desire for popularity on the part of the British as well as the dictates of common sense supported this policy. However there were difficulties from time to time. The British officers and officials were solidly Protestant and occasionally an evangelical zeal would appear in the garrison. Usually this was kept within bounds but when a religious movement like the Army Movement gained some influence, as it did around the middle of the 19th Century, there was a danger of overt proselytism and a somewhat wilful misunderstanding of the Catholic faith and way of life. On one occasion a distaste for the Catholic (although hardly religious) rites of carnival provoked rioting and in 1846, the 'jostling' of some Highlanders.

Amongst Coleridge's friends in Malta was Captain John Burgoyne of the Royal Engineers, afterwards to become one of the most famous military engineers of the century, an Inspector of Fortifications and a Field Marshal. Wherever he went Coleridge found lasting friends among the younger and better educated officers who, because of their training at the Royal Military Academy at Woolwich, tended to be gunners or engineers. Chapman finally returned to Malta and Coleridge was able to leave towards the end of September. His few months in Malta seem to have turned a profit as he was able to send money home to his wife and to pay for his passage to England. According to the *Oxford Companion to English Literature* Coleridge returned to England 'broken in health and a prey to the use of opium'. There is plenty of evidence that he was very well-acquainted with opium before he left England although the cheapness and easy availability of the drug in the Mediterranean may have fed his habit. Coleridge was one of the most notorious hypochondriacs in 19th Century letters but he managed to live for a further 30 years after his return, although it is possible that he had written his best work before he left England.

Meanwhile events in the Mediterranean had moved forward. After Nelson's victory of the Nile, Napoleon, thought to be impotent in Egypt without his fleet, successfully consolidated his hold on the country so that he was able to contemplate the elimination of the forces of the Ottoman Porte where the Sultan had become an ally of Britain. Early in 1799 Napoleon moved north along the coast, capturing Jaffa and sending his siege train in small ships along the coast of Syria. Off Cape Carmel the French flotilla was surprised by the British warship *Tigre* and after a chase Napoleon's train of heavy artillery was captured.

The *Tigre* was commanded by Sir Sidney Smith, the same officer who had incurred Nelson's disdain at Toulon. After Toulon Smith had been engaged in several small naval actions in the Channel in one of which he had been captured by the French. Eventually he managed to escape from his prison in Paris and make his way back to England. His jailers may have been quite glad to see the back of him but at home he became something of a popular hero. He was given command of the

80-gun *Tigre* and a somewhat ambiguous mission in the Eastern Mediterranean. His brother was envoy to the Sultan and Sir Sidney construed his orders to imply that he was also the head of a diplomatic mission to the Sublime Porte which gave him a command independent of Lord St. Vincent, Commander-in-Chief in the Mediterranean, and also of Nelson who was St. Vincent's trusted assistant and second in command. This presumption of Sidney Smith's earned him a rebuke from the British government but his self-esteem was such that this did not deter him from his chosen course of action. That he was self-opinionated and vain cannot be doubted but he was also a brave and daring officer determined to achieve glory at almost any cost. Here was one more example of the right man appearing at the right time and place to ensure a great and important victory.

Smith certainly exploited the victory for his own ends but the victory was real enough. The town of Acre, perhaps the most important bastion between Egypt and Turkey, fought over on many occasions by the Crusaders, was vital to Napoleon's plan to strike at the Turks. Smith arrived there just in time to prevent it being taken by the French. He threw sailors and marines into the town and reorganised the defences, mounting guns captured from Napoleon's siege train on the walls. The defensive works around the town were strengthened under the expert supervision of a talented French royalist engineer called Phélippeaux who had been imprisoned in Paris with Sidney Smith and escaped with him to England. He joined Smith's eastern Mediterranean cruise as a volunteer. The Turkish army defending Acre was strengthened materially and in its resolve by the English presence and by the leadership of Smith. After several attempts on the town during 60 days of siege the French were finally driven off and retired back along the coast to Egypt. This was the first time that a French army under Napoleon's direct control was beaten in the field. Realising that he had reached an impasse in Egypt, Napoleon abandoned his army and sailed for France, evading the British fleet and disembarking in France on 7 October 1799.

After Trafalgar with Nelson dead Sidney Smith was unequivocally in command of the British naval forces in the central Mediterranean. Action at sea and on the coast of Italy took on that exciting but small-scale character in which the British seem to excel. Under the direct control of Sir Sidney, as he now was, Captain Hoste, a gifted protégé of

Nelson's, carried out a series of raids on the western Italian coast culminating in the Battle of Maida in which a small British and partisan force decisively defeated a larger French army on the European mainland for the first time in the Napoleonic wars. The district of Maida Vale in London was named after the victory.

Smith captured Capri and although he lost the Neapolitan fortress of Gaeta, alleged to be as impregnable as Gibraltar, through a failure to get food to the starving garrison, the British position in the south of Italy improved. Hoste was now able to take his ship the *Amphion* into the Adriatic, the 'lion's mouth', to raid French shipping. At first his activities were still confined to small coastal raids which produced several 'prizes', very welcome to Hoste as to all naval captains. Until 1808 the Captain's share of a prize was just under half the assessed value of the captured ship and cargo. After 1808 the share was reduced by nearly half, without any noticeable effect on the aggressive spirit of the navy. Until 1801 ships captured anywhere in the Mediterranean had to be escorted to Gibraltar to the Prize Court, but a Prize Court was set up in Malta in that year and this was also used by the Americans for the valuation and disposal of prizes captured from the Barbary pirates. Coleridge's post as Public Secretary in Malta meant that he was a permanent member of the Court. By 1810 Hoste was in command of a squadron with a roving commission in the Adriatic. The French held Corfu in strength but were isolated there and not strong enough at sea to prevent the British from snapping up the other Ionian islands; but they, in turn, were not strong enough to tackle the French bases on the Dalmatian coast which had been taken over from the Venetians.

Hoste finally got his big chance in a fleet action against the French at the battle of Lissa. This battle was regarded as a miniature Trafalgar in Britain and was conducted by Hoste according to Nelson's precepts. When the French frigate fleet, stronger for once than the British, was within range Hoste hoisted the signal 'Remember Nelson'. But the French Admiral Dubourdieu had also remembered Nelson and the 'pell-mell' battle that he had advocated. The battle of Lissa was as bloody and unrelenting a combat as any of the earlier great fleet actions. British seamanship and gunnery won the day and the French were decisively defeated. All but two of the combined French and Venetian fleet were captured or destroyed and British domination of the Adriatic was assured. Hoste returned to Britain in 1811. Before sailing for home the fleet gathered at Malta where they picked up the best known of all the Mediterranean Romantics, Byron, who had had a long sojourn in Greece and the Aegean. In a style flamboyant enough to have pleased Sir Sidney Smith the poet penned his *Farewell to Malta*. It may be noted that the poet is not altogether impartial in his praise of the ladies of the island nor in his preference for 'those triumphant sons of truest blue' over the 'red faced' military.

> *Farewell to Malta*
> Adieu you females fraught with graces;
> Adieu, red coats, and redder faces;
> Adieu, the supercilious air
> Of all that strut 'en militaire';
> . . .
> Farewell to these, but not adieu,
> Triumphant sons of truest blue;
> While either Adriatic shore,
> And fallen chiefs, and fleets no more,
> And nightly smiles and daily dinners,
> Proclaim you war and women's winners.

Byron's *Farewell to Malta* was prophetic for him and for Hoste. Both returned almost at once to the Mediterranean. As naval commander in the Adriatic, Hoste operated from the island of Lissa, now Vis, which officially became a British base in 1811. It was garrisoned by two companies of the 35th Foot, 260 Swiss mercenaries, 280 Corsicans and 300 Italians of the Calabrian Corps who proudly wore the battle honour 'Maida' on their caps as recognition of the part they took in that famous victory. Napoleon was by now so heavily committed to his invasion of Russia that there were great opportunities to be seized in the Adriatic. Hoste organised and took part in the capture of the Dalmatian fortress towns of Cattaro and Ragusa, now Dubrovnik. In 1814, with the fall of Napoleon, Corfu surrendered. It became, with the other Ionian islands, the United States of the Ionian Islands, under direct British protection with a British high commissioner. The British remained happily in Corfu for the next 50 years. Hoste became a baronet in July 1814 and was awarded a KCB. He died in 1828, without ever becoming an admiral. Byron returned to Greece to fight in the war of Independence. He became increasingly disillusioned with the corrupt and indecisive military leaders around him and horrified by the brutality of both Greeks and Turks. He was not to see Greek independence, dying of cholera at Missolonghi in April 1824.

When the British returned in force to the Mediterranean in 1798, a vital task was the recapture of Minorca. The island had been lost to the French and Spanish in 1781 but its importance as a base from which to observe the French coast and as a haven to shelter the storm-tossed fleets blockading Toulon when they could safely abandon their vigil for a few hours, was paramount. Under the Peace of Amiens in 1802 the island was handed back to Spain and Britain never occupied it again although frequent use was made of the facilities of Port Mahon, the island's great natural harbour, especially during the Peninsular War. The island had been in British hands for almost 70 years in its three periods of occupation and might well have become a permanent British colony. It had been suggested on several occasions that it might be exchanged for Gibraltar but nothing came of the idea, and once the prospect of lasting peace with the French seemed a reality in 1815, the island lost its attraction to the Navy.

In 1830 the French took over Hospital Island in the middle of Port Mahon, as a coaling station and depot during their invasion of Algeria, but gave up their facilities after 10 years. Even the Americans established a base on Minorca in 1822 by treaty with the Spanish. Ostensibly they used it for ship maintenance and the training of their midshipmen but the importance of sea power was already well understood and the young republic was already anticipating a rôle outside its immediate territorial waters. Although one of the Balearic islands, Minorca considers itself to be – and is to some extent – apart and different from Majorca. During the Spanish civil war Minorca remained loyal to the Madrid government whilst Majorca sided with Franco and his fascist régime. The Francoists in Majorca bombed the government troops in Minorca continuously during the civil war and this is partly the cause of the rivalry and distrust between the islands.

Even after Trafalgar, Sir Sidney Smith habitually sheltered his fleet at Port Mahon during bad weather in the Gulf of Lions. The regaining of maritime supremacy in the Mediterranean by the British and their allies, and especially after the overwhelming victory of Trafalgar, while not removing the necessity for the island bases, brought the action of the war against Napoleonic France right up to the shores of the European mainland, and in some cases into the interior.

The most immediate effect of the French decline at sea was a characteristically aggressive gesture of defiance from Napoleon. In 1806 he promulgated the Berlin decrees which sought to ban all British goods and ships from the whole of the continent of Europe. But the decrees rebounded on their perpetrator. At first Gibraltar and the Portuguese ports were used by those intent on flouting the ban as profitable entrepôts, but the invasion of Portugal by France and Spain closed the loopholes for a short time. The British replied by carrying off the Portuguese Royal Family to exile in Brazil and, for good measure, seizing the Portuguese fleet to prevent it falling into the hands of the French. But the heaviest British involvement in Europe after Trafalgar came about not as a result of the invasion and partition of Portugal but because of a crass attempt by the French to usurp the Spanish throne, and the wholly unexpected and violent reaction of the Spanish people. The spontaneous rising of the people against the French 'bringers of liberty', shocked and heartened Europe and presented Britain with a unique opportunity to use her maritime supremacy to land and support a substantial army on the European mainland.

The Peninsular War

Once it was clear that a serious revolt was taking place in Spain the British government determined to send an expeditionary force to support what it was hoped would be a strong and sustained challenge to French power. Money, weapons and a small well-armed but above all mobile British army would back-up the growing armies of regular and guerrilla Spanish forces. Spanish reactions were not quite what the British had hoped for. Money and weapons were welcome in unlimited quantities but local jealousies and suspicions opposed the landing of British troops in Spain and in many of the coastal towns there was a fear, perhaps not unreasonable, of going the way of Gibraltar.

The Portuguese had also risen against the French and since the only remaining potentially hostile fleet of any size, the Russian Mediterranean squadron of nine ships of the line and two frigates, was sheltering at Lisbon, protected by French guns in the Tagus forts,

Portugal was an obvious target. Sir Arthur Wellesley, later the Duke of Wellington, was given command of the British force over the heads of four more senior generals and left Cork with an army of 9,000 men. He landed at Montego Bay, north of the Tagus, on 1 August 1808. He was quickly reinforced by Spencer with 6,000 men from the Mediterranean. Junot, the French commander in Portugal, had his headquarters in Lisbon and set his troops in motion as soon as he was aware of the British landing. Wellington pressed forward towards Lisbon to win a brisk action at Rolica on 17 August and a more serious battle at Vimeiro on 21 August. Vimeiro was Wellington's first battle against the French in the Peninsular War and it set the pattern for the next six years. It also destroyed the myth of French invincibility and confirmed Wellington's faith in his soldiers and theirs in him. The way to Lisbon was open and Junot, in the Convention of Cintra, agreed to vacate Portugal, leaving the Russian fleet to be taken over and neutralised for the remainder of the war by the British who now manned the Tagus forts, dominating the harbour and anchorage.

These preliminary operations were, of course, on the Atlantic coast as were the supporting measures undertaken, once Spanish reluctance had been overcome, to provide a British reinforcement for the garrison hastily thrown into Cadiz. But from Cadiz operations lapped over onto the Mediterranean shores. Sir Hew Dalrymple, governor of Gibraltar, was in close contact with the Spanish generals in Andalusia and was able to provide them with arms and ammunition even before Wellington had arrived off the Portuguese coast. Once Cadiz was invested by the French and it was realised how important it was to hold Spain's main naval base and arsenal, the governor mounted a series of small raids along the Mediterranean coast and into the immediate interior. Their aim was to threaten the French supply lines and to encourage the many Spanish guerrilla bands which were already becoming an important factor in the war, rivalling the regular troops in their courage and effectiveness.

The British troops engaged in harassing the French were provided from a force commanded by General Brent Spencer, who had been sent off from England with no very clear idea of whether he was to attack Lisbon, land at Cadiz or make an attempt on the Spanish North African base of Ceuta. He solved the problem by attempting none of these over-ambitious schemes. Instead, half his force went on to reinforce the Neapolitans and British in Sicily and half were retained in Gibraltar as a reserve. It was thought that a French army was on the way to attack Gibraltar and possibly also Ceuta. The attacks did not materialise so Dalrymple organised raids on Ronda and the ports of Marbella, Fuengirola and Huelva. An expedition in October 1810 was notorious for being composed of five nationalities; 340 men of the 81st, 500 German, Polish and Italian deserters from the French army and a Spanish regiment from Ceuta. A force of 1,400 men speaking five languages could attempt very little and when it was brought into action near Marbella, in the hope that the town of Malaga would rise against the occupying French, the motley deserters in the ranks all fled back to the French. Nevertheless it was felt that the efforts from Gibraltar had had some effect in unsettling the French and had relieved the pressure on Cadiz.

General Graham, who eight years previously had arranged the surrender of Valletta, took command of the British troops in Cadiz. Graham had despaired of ever being granted a regular commission in the army but having met Sir John Moore, campaigning in the Mediterranean and in Gibraltar, he accompanied him as an honorary ADC on his ill-fated march into the interior of Spain. Graham was with Moore at Corunna when the latter was struck fatally by a French cannon ball. It seems that Moore had praised Graham's soldierly qualities in his despatches to such good effect that it was finally decided that he had earned his place in the regular army list. He had the rank of Colonel because of the regiment he had raised (The 90th Foot) in 1794, but he did not receive his commission until he was 47 years old. Happily his commission was back-dated to take account of all his previous service and he was promoted to the rank of Major General immediately.

This was not by any means the end of his military career and like that other stormy petrel of the Mediterranean, Sidney Smith, he had a habit of turning up wherever honour and glory were likely to be found. Unlike Smith however, Graham was not a man for self-aggrandisement and his actions were usually left to speak for themselves. He soon found himself commanding the British component of a force from Cadiz which was landed near Gibraltar and marched to attack the rear of the French forces investing Cadiz. His British forces were smaller than the Spanish contingent so he unselfishly placed himself under the orders of the Spanish General Lapena, known significantly to his men as 'Donna Manuela'. The management of the approach march to the outskirts of Cadiz was a farce. The force was allowed to become strung out along the beach so that the British, as the rear-guard, came under attack by a large part of General Victor's army. Graham had his men well in hand and was able to turn them around and, attacking up hill, achieve a bloody but very decisive little victory over the French. Had Lapena's Spanish troops been brought into action the victory would have been complete and it is possible that Victor would have had to lift the siege of Cadiz for a time at least. But Graham had his day, and at a time when Wellington's army was secure but unexcitingly idle behind the Lines of Torres Vedras. The Battle of Barossa in 1811 was made much of; Graham was quickly promoted and made Wellington's second-in-command.

Before the arrival of British troops in Cadiz, and whilst the Spanish were still not prepared to admit them into the port, General Spencer had landed a small force made up of three battalions and some light companies at Puerto de Santa Maria, at the head of Cadiz Bay. He marched them to Jerez in the hope encouraging the Spanish to hold Seville but even before he reached his goal he heard that the capital of Andalusia had fallen so he could only withdraw and embark his troops.

At the same time Lord Cochrane in the frigate *Impérieuse* landed 5,000 troops from the Balearics to blockade the French in Barcelona. He also harried the French driven out of Gerona by the Spanish as they straggled along the coast road to Barcelona. Later he assisted the Spanish at Valencia. Cochrane only disposed of two frigates, and a larger British naval and military force might have been able to encourage the Spanish to more decisive action against the highly vulnerable road which ran beside the Mediterranean for more than 100 miles. Almost every attempt to aid the Spanish irregulars against the French along the Mediterranean littoral failed, despite British superiority at sea, largely because of petty rivalries between the guerrilla bands, disputes over jurisdiction between district and provincial juntas and, especially at first, suspicion of British motives. At the least the Navy was able to give the guerrillas some degree of mobility and the heavy gun support that they would not otherwise have had.

Gibraltar continued to play an important part in the Peninsular War, but mainly as a base for the British fleet and as a depot for the supply of arms and ammunition for the Spanish armies and guerrillas operating in the south of Spain. The fortress also provided an impregnable haven for the insurgents when they were pressed too closely by the French. On more than one occasion they were flushed out of the Sierra de Ronda and forced to take shelter under the guns of the Rock, but not once during the whole of the war in Spain did the French attempt to capture Gibraltar although they advanced as far as San Roque and attacked the Spanish and British garrison in the walled town of Tarifa across the bay. The Spanish had held out in Tarifa despite strong French attacks and the British reinforcement of the garrison helped the town to hold out until the French finally withdrew.

The conduct of the British at Tarifa and Graham's victory at Barossa were very worthy examples of small scale actions calling for bravery and military skills that were often overlooked in the great set piece battles of the Peninsula. A reminder of both these actions can be found in King's Chapel in Gibraltar. A tablet in the garrison church reads:

To the memory of
Lieutenants Joseph Bennett and John Light
of the Light Infantry and Grenadier Companies of the 28th Regt.
commanded by Lieutenant Colonel Belson, which together with the
Flank Companies of the Garrison were detached to Tarifa, where a
Force was assembled by Lieutenant General Graham to attack in
conjunction with the Spanish Army, the French before Cadiz.

At the memorable Battle of Barossa fought on 5 March 1811,
those two promising young officers, at the head of their respective
Companies (their Captains having both quitted the field
from shots early in the action) received their mortal wounds.

This tablet is erected by their brother officers.

After Wellington broke out from his fortified encampment behind the Lines of Torres Vedras, his axis of supply moved first from the south away from the Mediterranean to Oporto and then, after the Battle of Vitoria and the capture of San Sebastian, to the Biscay ports.

At the end of the war, Britain held Gibraltar, Malta and the Ionian island of Corfu. Gibraltar had already been held for over 100 years and Malta would be held for over a century and a half. Corfu and the other Ionian islands were put under British protection at the Congress of Vienna in 1815 and remained an important British base for 50 years. By the end of the Napoleonic Wars, attention was already shifting again towards the East. Britain's interests in India and elsewhere in the countries bordering on the Indian Ocean made the safeguarding of the route through the eastern Mediterranean and across the isthmus of Suez into the Red Sea of vital importance. Events in Greece and the long-standing enmity between Russia and Turkey called for a British presence if communications over the short land-link to India were to be maintained. Even before the Suez Canal linking the Mediterranean and the Red Sea was completed, a railway had been constructed along the route but the opening of the waterway cut the travelling time to the East by the Cape Route by half. Later, the cutting of the canal and the discovery of oil in the Middle East and its transportation, would make that short strip of land one of the most closely-watched, closely-guarded and valuable in the world.

The one sure thing that the Congress of Vienna achieved was a peace between the major powers of Europe that lasted for more than 40 years. There were clashes and disturbances that spilled over and so involved the great powers but there was no large-scale war. The new focus was upon the emerging nations in the old Turkish Empire, most of which arose in the Mediterranean littoral where Britain remained the dominant naval power. She was able to protect her gains and was in a position to further both her own interests and those of her close allies and client states once Napoleon was safely isolated on the island of St. Helena.

CHAPTER III

From the Peninsula to the Crimea

Nevertheless, the 40-year peace resulting from the Congress of Vienna only looked backward to pre-Napoleonic Europe, and to that extent was reactionary and obscurantist, steadfastly continuing the policies and philosophy of the *Ancien Régime*. The policy gave rise to what was to be called the 'Metternich System'. The great powers of Europe guaranteed the status quo of the reaffirmed, and in some cases resurrected, monarchies and agreed to intervene if necessary to keep the royal houses of the treaty signatories on their thrones. Furthermore they agreed to assist in the task of bringing back under control any of their territories and colonies actively seeking independence. This policy was to be applied not only in Europe but also in South America, where the doctrines of the French revolution, still highly regarded in some quarters even in Europe, were reinforced by the new notions of nationalism and self-determination. In the Americas, Metternich's system received a mortal blow when the American President Monroe in 1822 made clear, in a message to Congress, those principles of United States policy which were to become known as the Monroe Doctrine. Europe was warned off interfering in the affairs of the western hemisphere and prevented from attempting to extend its colonies or influence in that area.

In Europe, Britain soon had problems in Spain where the return of Ferdinand VII had been supported against the liberal and Jacobin opposition. France was in favour of the granting of a constitution. The British intervention was half-hearted and confused because of another overriding principal of Metternich, the 'legitimacy of established government'. Before liberal nationalism attained the status of government policy in Britain, the concept of legitimacy caused much heart-searching and confusion, particularly in the case of the many and ill-defined areas of the Turkish Empire. The island of Corfu was one of these areas of high strategic value but of confused sovereignty. Corfu had never been subject to Turkey but its position adjacent to the Turkish-held mainland of Greece made it impossible to hold or control except by agreement with a powerful maritime nation, capable of defending the island against the importunate and usually conflicting claims of neighbouring states.

The Occupation of Corfu

The ideas of the French Revolution quickly took root in Corfu, as they had in the Spanish Americas. The island had first been given to Venice as its part of the loot after the Fourth Crusade (1202–04), and the sack of Constantinople, when the conquerors shared out the newly-won Christian Byzantine territories. Corfu was divided into 10 fiefs each of which was given to a Venetian nobleman. For a few years only, from 1204 to 1214, Corfu remained in Venetian hands and then for the next 172 years it was handed around from one European royal house to another, sometimes as part of a dowry, sometimes as the spoils of conquest. Finally in 1402, after 16 years of *de facto* possession, Venice regained the island from the Kingdom of Naples for the sum of 30,000 gold ducats. The Venetians ruled the island for a further 400 years and left their clear mark on its administration.

In return for the protection of Venice the inhabitants of Corfu were expected to give absolute obedience and loyalty. Being so close to the Turkish-held mainland of Greece, the island was under constant threat of invasion, especially when, at the height of their power at the middle of the 16th Century, the Turkish galley fleets roamed at will through the eastern and central Mediterranean. The defences of the island were continually improved, and although this was done at the expense of the inhabitants, they were at least spared the oppression and brutal treatment endured by the Greeks on the nearby mainland. Unlike Cyprus, the Venetians were able to hold Corfu against the constant pressure of the Turks. Genoa, the constant and unremitting enemy of Venice, twice raided Corfu and the other Ionian islands which were also under Venetian rule, but did not attempt to settle permanently.

The wars with Turkey gradually wore out the Serenissima Republic and by the end of the 18th Century Venice was no longer a great maritime power in the Levant. Britain, France and Russia, rivals for power in the Mediterranean, were becoming increasingly interested in the Ionian islands because of their strategic position at the entrance to the Adriatic. In 1797 Napoleon's successful campaign in north Italy brought about the downfall of Venice. The teachings of the revolution were eagerly embraced by the peasants of Corfu and a French fleet was sent to take possession of the island.

As elsewhere, the French were first welcomed as liberators but as the discrepancies between the ideals of the 'Enlightenment' and their practical application in Napoleon's military dictatorship became apparent, it was clear that one kind of repression had been replaced by another. Even the administration, when the island had become a full *Département* of France, was largely carried on by the old island nobility. Under the new rule, all citizens were to enjoy equal civil rights, but it quickly became clear that some citizens were more equal than others. New impositions of taxes and compulsory levies by the French added to the outraged feelings over the bad behaviour of the unpaid French troops. As in Malta, the plundering of the churches by the soldiers finally turned the people against France.

Meanwhile, Russia and Turkey, in an unlikely alliance, had been trying to persuade the Corfiots to rise against the French garrison. After several months of fighting the French were obliged to surrender to the commanders of the two allied fleets. But once again the Corfiots were disappointed in their hopes for a more representative régime. At first there was hope of a democratic constitution but the draft was rejected by Russia and Russian control of Corfu and the other Ionian islands was recognised in the constitution of 1806.

However, the Russian grasp of the Ionian islands was short-lived. On 14 June 1807, they were decisively beaten at Friedland – if a Russian defeat can ever be so described. The French victory led to the famous meeting between Napoleon and Czar Alexander on a raft at Tilsit on the Nieman river. As part of the Tilsit settlement Russia gave up Cattaro on the eastern shore of the Adriatic and the Septinsular Republic of the Ionian Islands to the French.

During the second French occupation of the islands the French were careful to create a better impression than on their first stay. The Ionian Islands were declared a *Département* of France and a French general was installed as governor general with instructions from Napoleon to defend Corfu at all costs in the event of a British attack. As we have seen, the British Navy was increasingly active in the Adriatic after Trafalgar, and Captain Hoste, at first with only one ship but later in command of a small fleet, harried the shipping of France and its allies along both shores of the Adriatic sea. The Ionian islands fell one by one to the British, Corfu to General Campbell in 1814, after the garrison had been weakened not only by the earlier withdrawal of troops needed in Russia and elsewhere but also by their reduction to near starvation as a consequence of Britain's complete domination at sea.

The British Protectorate of the Ionian Islands (1814–64)

The departure of the French still did not bring independence to the Ionian islands. The Russians, having lost control of them, proposed to the Congress of Vienna that the islands should be given their independence but this was rejected by the other victorious powers, Austria, Prussia and Great Britain. In 1815, the Treaty of Paris did recognise the islands as an independent state, to be known as the United States of the Ionian Islands. Britain, as the occupying power and with overwhelming strength in the Mediterranean was named as the sole protecting power. The islands were administered by a Lord High Commissioner and the first of these was the erstwhile commander-in-chief of the British forces in the Mediterranean and governor of Malta, Lord Maitland, who was installed as high commissioner in 1816. He appears to have learnt very little from his experience as governor of Malta and soon made clear that British 'protection' meant absolute British rule.

Nevertheless, much was accomplished in the Ionian islands in the establishment of local government and a free press. Major public works were inaugurated, roads built and an aqueduct constructed to bring water into Corfu town. In general the economy prospered under British rule. However, British achievements were set against a lack of independence and the frustration of the islanders' desire to join in the Greek War of Independence which started in 1821. But it was not until 1848, 'the year of revolutions' following a further revision of the constitution, that the Corfiots were able to call openly for union with Greece.

Disraeli's attitude towards Greek independence was entirely consistent with the Tory policy of supporting the Sultan and preserving the integrity of his dominions. He saw the Greek insurgents as no better than their Turkish oppressors. Certainly their record of atrocities and massacres was no less lurid or horrifying. Perhaps, in the end, the Philhellenes' attitude towards the Greeks was brought about by a confusion between the past glories of classical Greece and the semi-barbaric and haphazard state which was to emerge with independence.

In Corfu, 50 years of British rule seemed to have made as little impact on the British as it did on the islanders. It is almost as if, compared with Gibraltar or Malta, or of course India, the British uncharacteristically believed themselves to be in the islands temporarily and with no desire to enter into friendly or close relations with the inhabitants. One is left with the feeling that sadly the British left little of value in the islands. Cricket is still played by the Corfiots and a bizarre, lingering passion for ginger-beer strikes a 'tuck shop' note. The rather splendid memorial to High Commissioner Maitland is now covered with graffiti and the British lager-louts have arrived in force, having moved on from Spain and Majorca.

The declining years of the British occupation might have been cheered up a bit by the presence of Edward Lear, the Victorian humorist and artist, who visited Corfu and stayed there from 1860 until the British left in 1864. But even the honest Lear, who learned to love the island, was scathing about the British destruction of their forts and other military facilities when they left. The fit of pique was no doubt reminiscent of the disgruntled English leaving Tangier almost 200 years earlier, when, as we saw in Chapter I, they destroyed the newly-built mole and fortifications so that no one else should have them.

British rule in the Ionian Islands was ended in the same way as it had begun, through expediency. Pressure on the British to allow union with Greece never abated and it poisoned relations at home and in Europe. A face-saving compromise presented itself in 1864 when, in return for the 'election' of the British-sponsored candidate for the Greek throne, the Danish Prince who became King George I of the Hellenes, the Ionian islands were ceded to Greece. The British treaty ceding the islands stipulated that they should remain strictly neutral and for a while this was possible, but in the 20th Century they were drawn into the First World War. British, French and Italian forces used the island of Corfu as a base and, after the defeat of Serbia at the end of 1916, the Serbian government and what remained of the Serbian army were transferred to Corfu. In 1922, Corfu was bombarded and then temporarily occupied by the Italians in retaliation for the assassination of members of a commission delineating the Albanian-Greek border. At the outbreak of the Greek-Italian war in 1940 Corfu was again occupied by the Italians who had hoped to establish a separate Ionian state. The Italians, when they re-entered the war on the Allied side in 1943 resisted the Germans and fighting took place on the island in which many of the older buildings were destroyed.

The Rock in the First Half of the 19th Century

When Disraeli arrived in Corfu in 1830 and took a firm line against Greek independence he had, in the course of his Mediterranean Grand Tour, already visited Gibraltar and Malta. Like Coleridge and others before him, he used the Rock as a place to recuperate after a rather tiresome voyage from Britain. By 1830, Gibraltar had lost some of the 'wild west' reputation for which is was notorious throughout the 18th Century. The brief tour of the Duke of Kent as governor from 1801 to 1803 had done much to tighten up discipline in the fortress. The imposition of a Code of Conduct, the closing down of most of the drinking dens and the imposition of an almost Prussian régime began the clean-up of what had been regarded as the lowest and most dissolute garrison of the British army. Whilst some abuses and outrages were amenable to change, others were not.

Like his royal brothers in England and many governors before him in Gibraltar, the Duke had a mistress, Mme. St. Laurent, whom he established in nearby Spain, in an old house a mile north of San Roque, still known as the Duke of Kent's farm. As least he was fairly discreet in his arrangements, unlike the flamboyant O'Hara before him who was reputed to keep one mistress in the town and one at Governor's Cottage at the southern end of the Rock, exchanging them regularly on Sundays and Wednesdays. As in all garrison towns, brothels were an unmistakable and substantial part of the local scene. It was not until 1918, with the arrival of Sir Horace Smith-Dorrien, 'who closed some of the lower grade brothels', that much was done to tackle that particular social and hygienic problem. One is left wondering about the 'higher grade' brothels.

Gibraltar was also known, until at least the middle of the 19th Century, as one of the unhealthiest stations for the army in Europe, and perhaps anywhere. Yellow fever and the plague were prevalent. A virulent fever epidemic in 1804 led to the establishment of what is now known as the Trafalgar Cemetery, where the sailors wounded in that battle and afterwards dying in Gibraltar were buried alongside the victims of disease. The cemetery is situated just outside the town wall at South Port. The outbreaks of fever, lumped together with other prevalent and often fatal diseases under the general description of 'Rock fever', continued and as late as 1865 an outbreak of cholera, which became the scourge of Gibraltar, caused the deaths of 578 soldiers and civilians. When it became clear that cholera had no respect for wealth or social class, its eradication was at last tackled systematically. This led to the setting up of Sanitary Commissions in both Britain and Gibraltar, though in the latter case not until late in the century.

Disraeli, accompanied by his friend William Meredith, arrived in Gibraltar in mid-June 1830 to find a town that had changed little since the 18th Century and would have been instantly recognisable to Coleridge. The friends stayed, as had Coleridge, at Griffiths' Hotel. As befitted a published, although not as yet a very successful or widely-read author, he visited the Merchants' Library and Club which used to stand at the east end of what is now Macintosh Square. (Merchants were not allowed into the magnificent Garrison Library which was for the exclusive use of officers and their families.) Disraeli was pleased to find in the Merchants' Library all the books written by his antiquarian father, Isaac, and lost no time in writing home to tease his father about his literary fame. The Merchants' Library no longer exists and sadly, the Garrison Library, whilst it is still standing and still stocked with its valuable collection of books, has fallen upon hard times, like so many of the old buildings and facilities of the Services, and awaits restoration to its former glory.

As with so many of his aristocratic contemporaries, Disraeli's path to and through the Mediterranean had been smoothed by his connections who procured for him a passage on HMS *Messenger* and a letter of introduction to the Assistant Inspector of Health in Gibraltar, Doctor Alexander Broadfoot. In his turn, Broadfoot was able to introduce the friends to the Lieutenant Governor, General Sir George Don, whom Disraeli describes in his correspondence with his father as 'a very fine old gentleman of the Windsor Terrace School'. Sir George was Lieutenant Governor in name but acted as Governor from 1814 to 1831, during the absence of the Duke of Kent who, although not allowed to return to the Rock after his mishandling of the mutinies early in the century, clung stubbornly to his appointment until 1830. He was also acting Governor during the nominal appointment of the Earl of Chatham, who only spent a few months in Gibraltar.

Disraeli obviously made quite a hit with Lady Don who showed the travellers the Convent, the Governor's 'Palace' and its garden. As a vain and egotistical young man, Disraeli was clearly much pleased with the attention he received. The Convent was said by Disraeli to be 'one of the most delightful residences I know, with a garden under the superintendence of Lady Don full of rare exotics with a beautiful terrace over the sea . . .'. He adds: 'Besides this Sir Geo has a delightful pavilion modestly called the Cottage at the extreme point of the Rock, and a villa at San Roque in Spain about 10 miles off.'

The Lieutenant Governor was very hospitable to Disraeli and Meredith, suggesting excursions into Spain including the by-now-obligatory mini-tour of Andalusia. They visited Cadiz, Seville and Granada and Disraeli was overwhelmed by the evidence of Moorish culture still remaining from the old Kingdom of Granada, which was just beginning to be popularised by Washington Irving's books. *The Conquest of Granada* was published in 1829 and *Legends of the Alhambra* in 1832. Disraeli recommended Washington Irving's works to his father and commented that his own first novel, *Vivian Gray*, published in 1827, was well regarded in Gibraltar although it had had little success at home and in truth was not thought much of by the author himself.

Disraeli was fascinated by the Jewish community in Gibraltar and this, together with his first acquaintance with Moorish culture, may have led to the reaffirmation of his Mediterranean origins and his life-long interest in the Near East. It may also account for his lack of sympathy for the cause of Greek independence. His new-found interest in the oriental and exotic encouraged him to indulge his taste, recently becoming prevalent among the young rich, especially young officers from the fashionable regiments, in dandified dress. He obtained what he called an Andalusian costume which, from the description he sent his father, sounds more like a bullfighter's 'suit of lights'. He wore the costume around the garrison to the amusement of the other dandies on the Rock, all of whom according to Disraeli were subaltern officers. Later, in Malta, where he also wore his exotic clothes, he appeared to be vainly pleased with the raffish figure he cut despite being subject to some contempt and hauteur. But even with his vanity and colourful manner, he and Meredith made many friends in the garrison and were invited to the various messes and clubs and to numerous private parties. Disraeli, although in debt over his writings, was the recipient of much generosity from his father and this must have helped him with his social contacts. Like Coleridge before him, his charm, genuine interest in what he was seeing for the first time, as well as his polished manners and wit, helped to ease his way. Again, as for Coleridge, his Gibraltar contacts and friendships provided a ready entrée into British society in Malta.

George Borrow, a traveller of a very different stamp from Disraeli but, in his own way, as well-known in mid-century Britain, visited Gibraltar in the course of his travels in Spain. He was born in 1803, the son of an army recruiting officer and spent much of his early life in garrison in Edinburgh Castle. In 1835, he was commissioned by the British and Foreign Bible Society 'to travel through Spain and take stock of the condition of the people and to distribute the Bible there'. One would have thought that he was being sent to darkest Africa, but no matter. As a result he published *The Gypsies in Spain* in 1841 and, perhaps his most famous book, *The Bible in Spain* in 1842. In the latter he describes his visit to Gibraltar by boat from across the bay and his meeting with the legendary Griffiths of the hotel of that name. His picture of the Rock would have pleased and been confirmed by Coleridge and Dizzy.

Before us lay the impregnable hill; on our right, the African continent, with its grey Gibil Muza, and the crag of Ceuta, to which last a solitary bark seemed steering its way; behind us the town we had just quitted, with its mountain wall; on our left the coast of Spain . . . There, at the base of the mountain, and covering a small portion of its side, lay the city, with its ramparts garnished with black guns pointing significantly at its moles and harbours; above, seemingly on every crag that could be made available for the purpose of defence or destruction, peered batteries, pale and sepulchral looking . . .

I now proceeded up the principal street, which runs with a gentle ascent along the base of the hill. Accustomed for some months past to the melancholy silence of Seville, I was almost deafened by the noise and bustle which reigned around. It was Sunday night, and of course no business was going on, but here were throngs of people passing up and down. Here was a military guard proceeding along; here walked a group of officers, there a knot of soldiers stood talking and laughing. The greater part of the civilians appeared to be Spaniards, but there was a sprinkling of Jews in the dress of those of Barbary, and here and there a turbaned Moor. There were gangs of sailors likewise, Genoese, judging from the patois they were speaking, although I occasionally distinguished the sound of 'tou logou sas', by which I knew there were Greeks at hand . . .

He describes his meeting with Griffiths:

Close beside me stood my excellent friend Griffiths the jolly ostler . . . Let those who know him not figure to themselves a man of about fifty, at least six feet in height and weighing some eighteen stone, an extremely florid countenance and good features, eyes full of quickness and shrewdness, but at the same time beaming with good nature . . .

A visitor who did not have to stay at Griffiths' hostelry was the Duke of Cambridge. He arrived in Gibraltar in January of 1838 on his tour of the British military establishments in the Mediterranean as part of his education and training for high office. He hunted twice a week in Spain, presumably with the Calpe Hunt, which was reputed to have been formed from hounds left behind by the Duke of Wellington which enjoyed joint ownership and joint Spanish and British Masters. The hunt, although it provided much pleasure over the years, was often a cause of friction between the Spanish and British members and , on one occasion, almost brought about the downfall of at least one governor of the Rock. The Duke went on shooting trips into the nearby Sierra north of Gibraltar and, on one occasion, camped with some British companions in the Cork Woods for a few days.

Allan Andrews points out in his book *Proud Fortress* that by the 1850s the long years of peace since the Battle of Waterloo had led to a great increase in the merchant community in Gibraltar and this, rather more seriously than the contretemps over the Calpe Hunt, brought about the impeachment and dismissal of a governor. By mid-century the population of the Rock had grown to about 20,000 people. The Governor, General Sir Robert Gardiner, tried to suppress the ever-active smugglers but the merchants of Gibraltar needed the smuggling trade to get their goods into a strongly trade-protected Spain. Gardiner countered by claiming that a civilian population of 20,000 was a danger in time of war and became involved in a number of unconstitutional acts, culminating in an attempt to censor the local newspapers. Andrews says that the situation in Gibraltar was not unlike that in Tangier under British administration in the 17th Century, when the merchants and the military were bitter enemies. The military won in Tangier but the world had changed and the Governor could not understand the position he found himself in. Gibraltar was ruled ultimately by the elected British Parliament and Lancashire MPs were not prepared to lose their profitable Spanish market for cotton goods which passed illegally through Gibraltar. Gardiner had to go.

Malta Becomes a Crown Colony

We now move on to Malta, following the Grand Tourists, soldiers of fortune, romantic poets and Princes. Malta was a very different colony from Gibraltar and had a much larger population, its own language, history and culture. The Gibraltar garrison had, in a sense, brought their civilian population with them and attracted new residents from all over the Mediterranean. The religion of Gibraltar was predominantly Catholic but not aggressively so and the last thing Gibraltarians wanted was an independence that would leave them without British protection or British trade. In the almost three centuries during which Britain has occupied the Rock, that particular aspect of Gibraltarian hopes and ambitions has not changed in the smallest degree.

In Malta, on the other hand, the population is indigenous, proud and independent-minded. It is not so concerned with trade although the great expansion of the dockyard provided welcome work and technical training at a time of great population growth. Finally, as with most colonised peoples, the Maltese preferred to rule themselves rather than be ruled by an alien Northern European race with religious and cultural differences however efficient and benign as administrators and managers they might profess to be.

When Coleridge was working for Sir Alexander Ball in Malta, with the Napoleonic wars still in progress and Trafalgar not yet fought and won, the future status of the Maltese islands was, as we have said, very much in doubt. At first it was intended that the Knights of St. John, bustled out of Malta by the French, should return and that Malta would be protected and preserved as a pro-allied, neutral state. Even before Trafalgar, with British power and confidence growing in the Mediterranean, it became clear that as in Gibraltar, the British had arrived to stay. By the time that Lady Hester Stanhope arrived in Malta in 1810, there was little doubt that the island would become a permanent British base. Like Coleridge before her and Disraeli later, she travelled from England in a warship, stopping on the way at Gibraltar where, thanks to her illustrious but now deceased uncle, William Pitt, she was treated royally by the Governor and accommodated at the Convent. She expected no less. When at first she received a frosty answer to her request for a passage on one of His Majesty's ships, she wrote at once to General Sir Richard Grenville, First Lord of the Admiralty at the time, who also happened to be her first cousin:

> If after Mr P [Pitt] has added during his administration 600 ships (line of B & Frigate) to the Naval force of this country, a relation or even a friend of his cannot be accommodated with a passage in one of them it is rather hard, & if they do not chuse to do the thing handsomely they may let it alone. I am much too ill to be worried. I will give you no further trouble on this subject for I will ask nothing more and refuse every offer I don't like with the contempt it deserves.

She got her passage on the frigate *Jason*. She travelled to Gibraltar and on to Malta, the Ionian islands and Constantinople into her self-imposed and permanent exile. Early on her journey she sailed close under the cliffs of Corunna where her brother, Charles, and Sir John Moore, said by some to be her only true love, had died in Moore's last battle before his battered army embarked for England. On the second leg of her journey from Gibraltar to Malta, sailing on HMS *Cerberus*, the ship dropped anchor at Port Mahon in Minorca and she was able to see the town captured by her ancestor the 1st Earl of Stanhope in 1708.

Lady Hester was no snob, however short her tongue, and on arriving in Malta she graciously refused the accommodation offered by the Governor, General Oakes, staying instead with the Commissary-General, Mr Fernandez, whose wife was the sister of her maid, Mrs Elizabeth Williams. She had been very much affected by her brother's and Moore's deaths, but she had embarked on an ill-starred romance with a much younger man, Michael Bruce, whom she met during his Grand Tour in Gibraltar. She soon renounced him to save him embarrassment and the possibility of being disowned by his father. It is probable that this was what finally persuaded her never to return to England. She died quite alone in Syria in 1839.

Unlike Lady Hester, Disraeli was definitely a snob. His reputation had preceded him from Gibraltar but it seems that in Malta, too, his wit compensated for his brashness. He and Meredith were made temporary members of the Union Club and the Malta Sporting Club and he was able to flaunt his 'Andalusian costume' to what Disraeli was convinced was the admiration of his young military friends. He observed that 'the society at Malta is very superior indeed for a colony'. Although he had no letter of introduction he called upon the Governor, Sir Frederick Ponsonby, and insists that 'having given full play to his wit, had him rolling on his sofa in risible contortions'.

Unlike Gibraltar and the Strait, which he compared favourably to 'our beloved and leafy Bucks', he has very little to say about the islands or indeed the Knights' classical architectural design of Valletta, except to make the point that the Union Club was housed in the old Palace of the Knights of St. John of Provence. He was still under the spell of the more exotic Moorish styles which he had seen recently in Granada and Seville.

In Malta, Disraeli met James Clay, whom he had known at

Winchester and Oxford. Clay was the quintessential British, upper class rake whose whole Grand Tour was one round of seduction and debauchery. Disraeli took to Clay and, despite Meredith's obvious dislike of him, accepted him as his close companion for the rest of his tour. Clay had hired a yacht in which to cruise through the eastern Mediterranean and Disraeli and Meredith joined him as paying guests. No doubt Clay's example contributed to Disraeli's extravagance and it was not until he returned to England and his very concerned family that he reverted to a more sober style, there to begin his life's work in building up and safeguarding an Empire, not least in the eastern Mediterranean.

In 1836, a commission was sent from England, in part because of concern over the dreadful economic state of the rural areas of Malta. To the disappointment of the inhabitants, because of the fear that the liberal and nationalistic ideas circulating freely in Italy might take root in Malta, thereafter providing a haven from which the Italian subversives and agitators could operate, there was no proposal to allow an elected assembly. One positive gain from the commission, however, was that a free press was eventually established.

When the Duke of Cambridge arrived in Malta in 1839, during his 'educational tour', he was naturally made much of by the garrison and island government. He remarked on the enormously strong fortifications, the large stone houses and the luxury enjoyed by the Knights before their expulsion. He inspected the 47th Foot with the Governor, Sir Henry Bouverie, and remarked that the Maltese Regiment manoeuvred well. He also heard a complaint, commonplace in peacetime, that the fortifications were too extensive and therefore too expensive to keep up.

The Duke sailed on to Corfu in a steamer on 16 May to continue the same routine of inspections, receptions and sight-seeing tours. But this was a useful and necessary preamble to his return as commander of the garrison in 1843 and later when he became Commander-in-Chief of the British Army.

Another well-known visitor followed the Duke of Cambridge to Malta the following year. William Makepeace Thackeray records his Mediterranean journey in *Notes of a Journey From Cornhill to Grand Cairo*, published in 1846, under the pseudonym of M.A. Tidmarsh. His book of travels is really quite remarkably dull and one can only be surprised that he went on to write *The Snobs of England* in 1847 and *Vanity Fair* in 1847–48. It is to be hoped that his characters were not drawn from the civil and military society encountered on his travels. One of his comments however, makes up for much of the tedium; on being shown the sword of the dreaded Corsair Chief Dragut, a leader of the Turks in their 16th Century siege of Malta, he described it as 'a most truculent little scimitar'.

In the first half of the 19th Century, only a very few governors made their mark as contributing something distinctive to Malta. Sir Thomas Maitland, the first Governor appointed after a Commission of Inquiry in 1813, arrived in the middle of an outbreak of plague. Through stern but efficient administration, he got the epidemic under control within a year but at the expense of his popularity. He abolished the old *Universita*, which as we saw in Chapter II operated the corn monopoly including its import and distribution, allegedly because of its inefficiency but probably also because of its corruption. He also reformed some of the practices of the courts and promoted a wider use of the English language throughout the islands. He was never a popular governor and declined to take up the suggestion to make use of an Advisory Council of Maltese citizens. When he left Malta to become the first High Commissioner of the Ionian Islands, he took with him the name 'King Thumb' because of his autocratic manner.

Richard More O'Ferrall, appointed in 1847 and William Reid, who followed him, were both fortunate to serve at a time when the British government was becoming interested in the reform of its Home and Overseas departments. Both Governors were anxious to introduce civil reforms in Malta and both were concerned to involve more Maltese in the running of the island's affairs. Another Governor, Lieutenant-General Sir John Gaspard Le Marchant, had been in trouble with the Horse Guards for his bullying and martinet manner with his regiment in Ireland before the Crimean War. But such were the vagaries of promotion and preference at the time that, like his fellow officer Cardigan, who was given command of the Light Brigade in the Crimea despite an appalling record, he was given the much sought after post of Governor of Malta in 1858 and completed his full tour in 1864. Marchant may have adopted a milder manner in Malta but his military recalcitrance was very useful in his governorship, since he was able to establish a clear line of demarcation between civil and military control very much to the benefit of the Maltese people.

Perhaps it was just as well that Marchant was not governor of Malta until well after 1848, 'the year of revolutions'. The islands were already harbouring hundreds of political refugees from Italy and there was much support for them locally and from liberals in Britain. Republican movements across Europe found an echo in Malta and there was an extraordinary feeling of fear and lack of confidence in Britain and her overseas possessions. This was all the more strange since the British had done more to encourage independence and constitutional reform than any other country in Europe.

Despite this, Britons at home were terrified by the prospect of a Chartist-led revolution and at the same time were bracing themselves to meet a non-existent threat of invasion by the French from across the Channel. There was even a rumour that there was to be an attack on the Valletta defences launched from within the walls. The Duke of Wellington showed the Chartist threat to be wildly exaggerated and it took only a short time to dispose of the myth of French invasion, which seems to have been fostered by the military in the hope of getting an expansion in the armed forces. The reaction to the Malta scare was to encourage liberal-minded governors like O'Ferrall and Reid to increase local participation in government.

In the 1850s Malta, and the whole of the Mediterranean including Gibraltar, felt the effect of two events which shook the military and political administration of Britain to their foundations, a shock which shook the British and their overseas Empire out of the lethargy that had prevailed since the defeat of Napoleon.

The first of these two cataclysmic events was the outbreak of the Crimean War in 1854. Pursuing her traditional policy of supporting Turkey, the 'sick man of Europe', against expansionist Russia, Britain and her allies decided that the main land operation of the war should be directed against the Crimea, with the object of capturing the great Russian naval base and arsenal at Sevastopol. There is a difference of opinion as to whether the Black Sea and its immediate hinterland should be regarded as part of the Mediterranean, but in any case, the Crimean War affected the whole of the Mediterranean area and especially those possessions and bases already held by Britain. All the troops sent to the war by Britain, and all their supplies, had perforce to sail the whole length of the Mediterranean and then into the northern Black Sea where, in winter especially, the weather was very much more severe than in the Aegean.

In Malta, and to a lesser extent in Gibraltar, the effect of the war in increased spending, and in the demand for stores and services, was immediately apparent. There were many more soldiers and sailors ashore with money in their pockets. It was said that in Malta the demand for personal services had driven prices up to London levels. This led to an acute shortage of berths for shipping in Malta and a search in the main creeks of Grand Harbour for room to extend the naval dockyard facilities. The problem was eventually solved by the Navy's taking over French Creek next to Dockyard Creek in Grand Harbour. The Navy compensated local interests for this by aiding financially the development of Marsa Creek as berths in a new basin for civilian shipping.

Apart from the financial and commercial effects of the Crimean War, the appalling conditions in which the troops were fighting in the winter of 1854–55 brought reforms not only in the army and the Commissariat Department but also in the general running of the Civil Service at home as well as in the Colonial Service. A new spirit of self-criticism emerged which, over a period of time, allowed Britain to move forward into an era when education, self-government and a reasonable provision for the poorest section of the community became accepted as an ideal towards which all civilised countries should progress. Even in the second half of the century, movement towards this goal was hardly rapid and reforms overseas lagged behind those taking place in Britain, but a start had been made. The 'white man's burden' was about to be taken up enthusiastically by enlightened administrators everywhere and the new reforms were needed and welcomed in the Mediterranean as elsewhere.

The second shattering event of the mid-19th Century for Britain and her Mediterranean possessions was the outbreak of the Indian Mutiny in 1857. At the time of the Mutiny, work on the Suez Canal had not yet started and there was not even a railway across the isthmus. But the importance of the short route to India was already recognised and it was realised, in some quarters at least, that the difference in travelling time between the Cape route and the route through a canal would result in a journey of only 6,280 miles as against the longer route of

10,800 miles. In time of war, or indeed serious mutiny, the difference could be crucial. Conditions in Gibraltar and Malta and the whole Mediterranean basin were changed as much by the Mutiny as by the Crimean War. Once people at home in Britain had had time to reflect on events in India, a new approach to native peoples came about which affected the Mediterranean as much as Asia and Africa.

CHAPTER IV

The Canal, Cyprus and the High Tide of Empire

When the Indian Mutiny broke out in 1857 it could still take a battalion of troops from England up to nine months to reach India by the Cape route. It was not until the next year that a railway was opened across the isthmus of Suez linking the fast route to Egypt through the Mediterranean, with the P&O steamers sailing regularly through the Red Sea to Bombay. Another 10 years would pass before the much-discussed Suez Canal would be opened. Even then, and despite the isolated position of India made obvious by the Mutiny, official opinion in Britain was opposed to the building of the canal, and much scientific and engineering support was mobilised against it. The government was worried lest it allow the French too much influence and power in an area vital to British interests, and its opponents produced some extraordinary and strangely unscientific evidence to convince the public that a canal would not be practical.

The noted engineer, Robert Stephenson called at Malta on his way back from Egypt where he had been supervising the building of the isthmus railway link, and was asked to advise on the building of a canal to link Grand Harbour with Marsamexett. The scheme was never proceeded with, mainly because of the objections of the army commander who thought that any changes would weaken the defences. There was also some concern at the cost of Stephenson's plan. There was certainly money available, however, and military expenditure in the

81

island went up from about £200,000 p.a. in the 1840s to over £400,000 in 1854 and £800,000 in 1856. This was still well before the naval expansion programme which began with the opening of the enormous Somerset Dock in French Creek in 1871. The new Hamilton Dock was not opened until 1892 and the new harbour works and breakwater at the entrance to Grand Harbour were only completed in 1907–09. When the Somerset Dock became operational it was larger than any dock available to the Royal Navy at Portsmouth.

Financial aid for economic development could not keep pace with the staggering amounts spent on improving the naval and military facilities, but expenditure on the armed forces in Malta boosted the economy and provided work for the rapidly-growing population. There was a recession after the Crimean War, but activity in Malta in shipping and general trade boomed once the canal was opened and there was a continuing benefit from the much-increased trade through the Mediterranean.

Malta was much more fortunate than Gibraltar in this respect. The advent of ever larger steamships meant that Gibraltar could be bypassed, and Malta became the site of the largest coaling station in the Mediterranean. But once the canal was open, the vast increase in shipping passing through the Mediterranean did benefit the Rock and more ships called there again. The naval base and dockyard at Gibraltar was sadly neglected, however, in the inevitable move towards the east. Malta had become the main fleet base in the Mediterranean because of its central position. Aden had been acquired in 1838 in the course of a local dispute with its Arab ruler and so the entrance to the Red Sea and the southern end of the short route to India were secure.

There was very little economic development in Gibraltar or Malta during the 19th Century but Malta especially gained from the increase in military expenditure. The construction of Victoria Lines, a great defensive work built right across the island along a series of scarps known as the Great Fault, brought the greater part of the island within its defensive system and provided much needed work in the 1870s. With the decline of the cotton growing and weaving industries in the islands, when the United States of America re-emerged as a cotton exporter after the Civil War, many Maltese were forced to emigrate and by the end of the century over 50,000 Maltese were scattered round the Mediterranean littoral.

Relations with the Catholic Church in Gibraltar and Malta were the subject of some concern on the part of the authorities. In Gibraltar this was no real problem. The Rock housed a mixture of races and religions of which the Catholic community was the largest and until recently, was dominated by the Irish Catholic teaching orders which on the whole, had a tradition of tolerance and co-operation towards their fellow-countrymen of other religious persuasions. The Roman Catholic Bishop of Gibraltar has usually, though not always, been of Irish origin.

In Malta the situation is somewhat different. The Catholic Church had a long-established and powerful following and its Bishops were exclusively of Maltese origin, with a tradition of successful resistance to Islam. It was necessary to tread more carefully than in Gibraltar. Even in Malta, treading carefully was not too much of a problem except on those fairly rare occasions when British officers with strong non-conformist principles tried a little proselytism. Senior officers were usually quick to discourage this kind of excess, but as we saw in Chapter II a more difficult situation arose in 1846 when a strict sab-batarian Governor tried to ban the Catholic celebration of Carnival on a Sunday. On that occasion there was some friction between civilians and, significantly one supposes, soldiers from a Scottish regiment. No one was seriously injured even though the Scotsmen drew their dirks. Thirty-five Maltese were arrested, the cases of all but three were dismissed by the local courts. Of the three remanded, one got 15 days imprisonment and the other two were sentenced to six days. All three were released on payment of a fine of eight shillings and four pence. Apparently there were no protests either of injustice or undue leniency. Sadly, those days are gone. Perhaps now the Maltese look back with some nostalgia to the British régime and its tolerance. Under the present constitution, only one of Malta's political parties is strongly Catholic and governments can be elected which are violently opposed to the interference of the church in secular matters.

Britain in 1875, represented by the same Disraeli who would have fought for the Turks, at last bought shares in the Suez Canal Company from the Kedive, allegedly at a bargain price, thus ensuring that she would be committed to the preservation of Turkey in the interests of stability in the Near East and the Canal Zone in particular. The canal had already demonstrated its commercial success and control of the Suez link was all that was missing from an 'all-red route to India'.

Complete control would have to wait a little longer but meanwhile the tide of Empire was at the flood. The canal and the route to India had to be protected from the Russian Bear, still with a sore head from the defeat in the Crimea and still anxious to advance into the warm waters of the Mediterranean. Even more, the British feared the direct intervention of the Russians across the northern borders of India and the mixture of diplomatic intrigue, spying and subterfuge, which came to be known as 'the Great Game', was begun. At the other end of the Mediterranean, in Gibraltar, there was little excitement or intrigue except perhaps among the members of the Calpe Hunt; but their extraordinary behaviour as we shall see, did not come to a head until the next century.

The Sanitary Commission set up in Gibraltar in 1865 in response to a cholera epidemic which claimed 572 lives, took over some local government responsibilities but it was very late on the scene; pestilence had been common for over 100 years by then. Gibraltar was a convict station from 1842 to 1875 and the convicts were housed along the water front in the most unsanitary situation on the Rock. They were used to scarp the Rock, scraping away the soil and undergrowth so as to make the rock faces steeper and to remove vegetation which might provide cover or combustible material in the event of an attack. Eventually all the convicts were repatriated or sent to other penal colonies. The inundations along the western side of the Rock were reclaimed and the connection between dirty drains and the periodic outbreaks of plague was at last accepted.

In the 1860s the Exchange Committee, a kind of Chamber of Commerce, was officially recognised as representing the views of the merchants but their deliberations and recommendations were only advisory and remained so until the next century. With the growing importance of Malta the dockyard at Gibraltar had suffered from neglect. By the 1880s there was no dock adequate to receive modern ships and no equipment available to cope with engineering or structural repairs of any complexity.

At last, in 1895, when commercial and naval competition from Germany was beginning to alarm the British government, a five million pound scheme was inaugurated. Quarries were dug to yield rock to reclaim the waterfront and build moles and a sheltering breakwater. Electrification and the provision of distilleries with underground reservoirs was begun. A transverse tunnel was excavated inside the Rock. But the new installations and the renovations had been too long delayed and by the time of their first use, in the First World War, they were already very much out of date.

Unlike Malta, there was no surplus population waiting for work and most of the labouring tasks in the new constructions were carried out by Spaniards from across the frontier. By 1880 the development of long-range artillery led to the conclusion that Gibraltar was also vulnerable to attack from the landward side and that the previous reliance on naval domination of the Strait to preserve the Rock was no longer sufficient. Although Spain was not actively hostile to Britain, the invasion of the Iberian peninsular by a powerful foreign state was always a possibility. Spain would have preferred to see Britain established on the other side of the Strait in Morocco, as a counterweight to the French. To this end conversations aimed at exchanging Gibraltar for the Spanish base at Ceuta were begun but nothing came of them. The largely sentimental attachment to the Rock of the British public made any political exchange impossible.

The Mediterranean fleet was permanently based at Malta, and despite a massive German naval building programme, the central Mediterranean base received the lion's share of an inadequate defence budget. Politically little had changed in Malta. But to anticipate events a little, after the British had taken over Cyprus in 1878 it was planned to settle Maltese peasants there, under the supervision of the Maltese government. It seems likely that the scheme would have worked quite well, at least for a time. Unfortunately, a private settlement scheme that looked suspiciously like an indentured labour plan came in for some bad publicity at the same time and the official scheme had to be abandoned. Malta still had no form of elected representative government but heated local opinion, fanned by a free press, could certainly bring pressure to bear on the British government.

The visit of Garibaldi to the island in 1864 provided adequate proof of this. The colonial government was wary of Garibaldi with his heroic image as a fighter for Italian nationhood and unity and his plainly-expressed democratic sentiments. They would have preferred him to bypass Malta on his way to England, but the people of Malta thought otherwise. He stayed at the Imperial Hotel in Valletta for 36 hours and received many visitors including some British officers of the garrison.

He was heckled by a group of pro-Bourbon refugees from Sicily who had gathered outside his window but they were quickly silenced by Garibaldi's Maltese sympathisers. The Maltese remembered the many liberal refugees from Sicily and the Italian mainland who had been protected and supported in Malta on many occasions even before 1848. Troops of the 25th Foot joined in the cheering on his departure via Gibraltar for England, where he was met by great enthusiasm.

The *Malta Times* published a welcoming poem in its issue of 23 March 1864, which concluded thus:-

> Hail, venerable Chieftain Freedom's stay!
> Lift thy sword on high – let not vain alarm
> Deter thee in thy course – for victory waits
> To crown the trophies of thy daring arms.
> Take, then, our humble welcome to this isle!
> May peace and honour always be thy due,
> And blessings wait thee in our 'father land'
> As freemen gratefully we welcome you.
> (Signed) G.

Gibraltar could not offer anything so grand as the welcome extended to Garibaldi in Malta; not indeed would it be true to say that the Rock attracted poets and writers to the same extent, except as a short respite on the voyage to Malta and on to the east. Byron, Coleridge and Disraeli all wrote about Malta and incorporated their experiences there and elsewhere in the Mediterranean in their writings. But it is unlikely that for the modern taste they can compare with the fictional adventures of James Joyce's heroine, Molly Bloom. Joyce lived on the Adriatic from 1905 to 1915 but there is no record of his having been in Gibraltar although the evidence of his novel *Ulysses* suggests that he visited the Rock on at least one occasion. Joyce made three trips to Dublin whilst he was living in Trieste, and a call at Gibraltar would not have been unusual. Joyce sets Molly Bloom's birth in Gibraltar towards the end of the 19th Century. In her famous soliloquy whilst seated on the WC, which makes up the last section of the book, she gives many details of Gibraltar, and La Linea, just across the border in Spain. The topographical details of the Rock, the streets of the town, local food, religion and relations between Gibraltarians and Spaniards all suggest a more than casual knowledge on the part of her originator. She comments, in the less steamy parts of her reminiscences, on the visit of General Ulysses S. Grant, (another Ulysses!) and on the arrival of the *Marie Céleste* in the harbour. She looks out towards Morocco, Tangier and the Atlas Mountains and, for anyone who has lived in Gibraltar, the descriptions have an authentic feel. This may just be a manifestation of Joyce's genius, but his long sojourn in the Adriatic must have given him a feeling for the Mediterranean and have directed his interest towards the *Odyssey* of Homer, providing a framework for Bloom's epic travels round Dublin.

The Great Game in the Eastern Mediterranean

War broke out between Turkey and Russia on 24 April 1877. The Russians declared war ostensibly to protect the Balkan Christians who were for the most part Eastern Orthodox, but the conflict was exacerbated by the nationalist risings of pro-Slavs in Serbia and elsewhere. The rivalry between Russia and Austria in the Balkans made a settlement much more difficult and tended to encourage the revolutionaries there, still under the nominal suzerainty of the Porte, to continue with their insurrection. In the end a tacit alliance between Russia and Austria in support of the risings brought about the withdrawal of Turkey from much of the western Balkans.

Britain became alarmed as Turkey came under pressure and Disraeli persuaded the Cabinet and the British Parliament to send a fleet to the Dardanelles to protect Constantinople. At the Congress of Berlin in June 1878 Austria and Britain both became convinced that Turkey was now a spent force and the restraint of Russia and the protection of British interests in the Near East must be achieved by other means, if necessary at the expense of Turkish interests and territory. Britain was no longer sure that Turkey could close the Straits to a Russian fleet but by now the defence of the Suez Canal and the safeguarding of Egypt had become the cornerstone of British policy in the Mediterranean. As part of the spoils from the Berlin Congress, Britain acquired Cyprus as a base from which to keep an eye on Russian activities and to provide a flank-guard against a possible move to the south by the increasingly ambitious Russians.

The arrival of the British in Cyprus, therefore, was based upon the assumption that Turkey had become an unreliable ally, but despite this the British presence was rather an ambiguous and uncertain affair. Turkey was to receive the revenue collected under British arrangements, less the cost of administration as calculated by the Turks. In 1880, the Turkish impost amounted to £96,000 a year. Without this impost Cyprus, unlike most other British colonies, could have paid its way, and some modest improvements made to the communications, flood control and land usage on the island without recourse to subventions from the British exchequer.

Travellers in Cyprus, and there were many once Britain could guarantee their safety if not their comfort whilst on the island, complained continuously about the bad bargain over the impost. Sir Sam White Baker, in his *Cyprus as I saw it in 1879*, probably the first book in a new genre, and a scoop worthy of today's instant journalism, exploring and popularising the new 'bit of red' on the map, says quite bluntly that 'the English government were hoodwinked in their hasty bargain'. The expectations of the inhabitants were disappointed. He goes on to give his estimate of the importance of Cyprus to Britain's imperial ambitions. His opinions, which give no hint of being influenced by notions of morality, certainly reflect the views of many British 'Empire-builders' of the time.

> There can be no doubt that Cyprus or Crete was requisite to England as the missing link in the chain of our communications with Egypt . . . Cyprus must be represented by Famagusta without which it would be useless for the ostensible purpose of its occupation . . . Without Famagusta the island would be worthless as a naval station; with it as a first class harbour and arsenal we should dominate the eastern portion of the Mediterranean, entirely command the approaches to Egypt and keep open our communications with the canal and the consequent route to India . . . but all these advantages will be neutralised unless Famagusta shall represent the power of England like Malta and Gibraltar.

Baker continually emphasises the connection between the many swamps and bad drainage with the prevalence of malaria, but he was not aware of the mosquito as the intermediary. He gives a consistent picture of neglect and decay brought about by three centuries of Turkish misrule since the siege of Famagusta and the capture of the island in 1571. Right up to the British occupation the lack of any system of irrigation added to the misery and shortage of food. The peasants' diet consisted almost exclusively of raw vegetable matter.

The British government had already endorsed Baker's view of the strategic importance of the island by appointing Major General Sir Garnet Wolseley to be the first High Commissioner. Wolseley would have preferred an appointment more in the public eye, but he was prepared to make the best of it for the present. He understood very clearly that the key to success in Cyprus was the imposition of a new revenue system and this necessitated a new and large-scale survey of the island. These tasks were usually undertaken by a survey section of the Royal Engineers. It so happened that a young sapper subaltern, Herbert Kitchener, had just completed work on a map of Palestine for which he was congratulated by the Palestine Exploration Fund and commended to the Commander-in-Chief, Field-Marshal HRH The Duke of Cambridge. He was appointed to 'Survey and Triangulate the Island of Cyprus'.

Kitchener expected to take up to three years on the survey and here he came into immediate conflict with Wolseley. Kitchener was employed by the Foreign Office and he told the High Commissioner that his map was to be published under his own name after about three years' work; that it would be a model of its kind and that future scholars and archaeologists would be placed permanently in his debt. This was the wrong way to tackle Wolseley, who was not impressed. He and Kitchener, although widely separated by rank and experience, were not dissimilar in temperament. They were both bullies and wanted their own way but since one was a general and the other a subaltern there could be no doubt which would come out on top. Wolseley, after clearing the ground with the government, told Kitchener that his requirements called only for a rough survey for revenue purposes, which could be pieced together anonymously within a few weeks. To complete his control of Kitchener and his work Wolseley arranged that the cost of the survey would be defrayed from the Cyprus revenues rather than from the Foreign Office vote. Kitchener was no doubt relieved when Wolseley accepted a command in South Africa in 1879, less than one year after arriving in Cyprus, but like the High

Commissioner he too was already looking for a new and more glamorous appointment.

The early occupation of Cyprus was regarded as something of a costly failure by the British public which was alarmed by stories of disease and bad living conditions in the popular press. Kitchener wrote two articles for *Blackwood's Magazine* in 1879, partly as a geographical description of the island but also as a vehicle for his ideas on its future and its role in the imperial destiny of Britain. In the first article he responds to what he said had been the 'Cyprus Fiasco', saying that inexperienced troops had been sent out to hold a country which might prove to be Britain's most important possession from a political point of view. He insisted that the climate was no worse than Malta with its ague or Gibraltar with its Rock fever. He put forward a set of rules which look naive by modern standards but which provided the first real guide lines for healthy living in a semi-tropical environment.

His other priorities for Cyprus were the construction of roads, especially in the mountains; the building of camps at the more healthy altitude of 3–4,000 feet and the planting and preservation of trees. Before he left, Wolseley at least made a start on this list. Kitchener recommended that the swamps should be drained and the old system of water storage with aqueducts and cisterns renewed. He believed that the unhealthiness of the island had been exaggerated and that the prevalent sickness was largely due to ignorance. Finally, before he left, he drew attention to the Cyprus climate: there was usually a cool western breeze blowing from the sea: the dew was refreshing at night and there was a natural dryness in the climate. The modern visitor would not necessarily agree with all Kitchener's observations but they did provide a useful starting point for the army.

When Wolseley left Cyprus for South Africa he was succeeded by Major General Sir Robert Bidulph, who persuaded Kitchener to return to his work on the island by offering him a doubled salary and a better status. Kitchener enjoyed his second stay in Cyprus much more. He organised archaeological excavations and became Curator and Honorary Secretary of the Cyprus Museum when it was founded in 1882. He is still honoured in Cyprus for his archaeological work which is commemorated, apart from his work on the museum collections, by a rather mysterious sundial which was erected – no one seems to know when – on the terrace in front of the Archaeological Museum in

Limassol. The 1st Battalion of the 20th Foot (The East Devons) was encamped at Polymidhia on the outskirts of Limassol where the sundial was apparently found in 1879 and their title and badge appears on the side of the dial with the regimental motto *OMNIA AUDAX*. The Blue Guide to Cyprus insists that the sundial once belonged to Kitchener but there seems no evidence for this and it is not the kind of *objet d'art* that Kitchener was later renowned for collecting. The Regimental Secretary of the Lancashire Fusiliers, with whom the East Devons were amalgamated in 1881, says there has been much interest in the sundial but no hard facts. He would welcome any information that might come to light.

When Wolseley took up his post as High Commissioner in Nicosia a residence, Government House, was built for him to the south-west of the town. Sir Samuel White Baker, stayed with the Wolseleys twice on his tour of Cyprus and found them and the officers of the garrison extremely hospitable. It cannot have been easy to provide hospitality at such short notice but it was expected and remains a cross that Governors, Commissioners and Garrison Commanders have to bear stoically. Taking Kitchener's advice, Wolseley soon set up a summer camp for the troops in the Troodos Mountains and the second High Commissioner, Sir Robert Bidulph had a summer residence built close by.

The Troodos Range, situated roughly in the middle of the island, rises to a height of just under 2,000 metres and is situated entirely within the Greek-Cypriot portion of the now divided Republic, and Wolseley's summer camp is now very much a tourist attraction with good roads and hotels. In winter it has been developed as a ski resort, started by the British troops, but now used increasingly by local civilians and tourists. Cyprus's second mountain area, the Kyrenia Range, lies to the north of Nicosia and runs parallel to the north coast along the whole of the north side of the island. The mountains are only half the height of the Troodos but since they rise directly from the coastal plain they present a more dramatic prospect than the rounded, mainly wooded hills of the more southerly range. The northern range is within the area today controlled by Turkish troops and it is difficult to visit from the south although access is made easy for tourists through mainland Turkey. Between the two ranges lies what used to be a swampy, malarial plain which, having been drained in winter and irrigated in summer, is now comparatively fertile. From north-east to south-west, the island is about 130 miles long and from north to south at the widest part about 60 miles. From a total land area of 3,572 square miles, the two British Sovereign Bases now together occupy 99 square miles.

The religion of the Greek Cypriots is Eastern Orthodox and generally it was not interfered with by the Turks. The Orthodox hierarchy enjoyed a completely independent status and the Bishops were regarded by the Turks and the Greeks as the legitimate leaders and voice of the Greek community. This meant that they were held responsible for the behaviour of their religious flock and, since the Bishops themselves were often the instigators of civil disobedience, the non-payment of taxes and the occasional riot, the Orthodox leaders were often chastised, imprisoned and sometimes worse. When the Greek intelligentsia in Cyprus attempted to conspire with the mainland Greeks against their Turkish overlords in 1821, the Turks struck first, massacring the Cypriot Archbishop and many of his senior colleagues. Sir Harry Luke in his *Cyprus Under the Turks, 1571–1878* says that the massacre of the Greeks in 1821 was the hierarchy paying for its abuse of power. Even after the British arrived and relieved the Orthodox Church of its subordination to the Muslim Turks, the hierarchy continued to plague the administration with its constant misuse of financial privileges. The Orthodox Church was exempt from taxation on its property and revenues but this was on the understanding that it provided educational facilities and some other services for the community. But no accounts were kept, or if they were they were not available for inspection, and very little was done to educate the children in the villages.

The Ladies Visit Cyprus

By the time the British came to occupy Cyprus female travellers rather different from the 'blue stocking' Lady Hester Stanhope had begun to appear around the shores of the Mediterranean and indeed in much more remote parts of the globe now so conveniently civilised by the British presence. Lady Hester visited Cyprus but she had little to say about it under Turkish rule, of which in any case she approved. The only apparent recognition she afforded the island was in the use she made of the British Consul to send her letters and packages, some of which were quite large, home to England at the expense of HM government. Few of the other lady travellers had quite Lady Hester's cachet but many of them were sufficiently distinguished to rate an introduction to the High Commissioner and if they were connected to the higher echelons of the military or government service they might be accommodated at Government House for part of their stay. Two intrepid ladies wrote books about their travels in the island, the first in 1893 and the second in 1937. Both are worth quoting at length and the contrast between the impressions gained at the end of the 19th Century and those of the period just before the Second World War are quite revealing.

Mrs. Lewis, who wrote *A Lady's Impressions of Cyprus* in 1893, was a little given to the purple passages: 'Cyprus, that ancient Queendom of Aphrodite, that fruitful garden now submitted to our rule', she writes in her introduction. The garrison would probably not have recognised their surroundings from her eulogy. She also seems a little vague about the purpose of the British troops on the island. Describing the camp at Polymidhia she says:

> The camp is four miles distant from the town. Probably if the officers' predilections were consulted they would prefer to be quartered at Nicosia where at present only one company is stationed and Nicosia would be glad to have them . . . [in order to] . . . form a more brilliant social centre. But Limassol, from its proximity to the sea is considered a more convenient station for the troops.

She describes the problems in having too many visitors that would be familiar to many modern travellers, and their hosts as well:

> The cooks come down overnight to Limassol, to be ready at morning dawn to pounce on the pick of the market . . . and as is everywhere the case where many English congregate, the prices are raised and provisions for both men and horses are dearer at Limassol than anywhere else in Cyprus.

Wolseley, as High Commissioner, took over the old Turkish Districts and appointed British Chief Commissioners to each of them, their headquarters being at Lefkosia (Nicosia), Limassol, Larnaca, Famagusta and Baffo (Paphos). In the early days all commissioners were military officers and they obviously lived in some style. Mrs Lewis says that after a long and tiring ride from Limassol, about 45 miles on horse back, they were welcomed by the Commissioner at his home at Ktima, near Paphos. In his drawing-room there was

> a magnificent and courteous tabby cat crouched before a brilliant coal fire and there were any amount of books and newspapers . . . Somehow hearing that Paphos was a poor and out-of-the-way place . . . one had not remembered or realised that the English insist upon perfect appoint-ments . . . so we were not quite prepared to find awaiting us a bright and beautiful English house, with all the charms of the 'genius loci' super-added.

One supposes she meant gardens and a glorious view. On a visit in 1989 the author was kindly shown over the quarter of the garrison Sergeant-Major. It is magnificently positioned on a bluff overlooking the seaward end of what is known locally as Happy Valley and it had a garden which was obviously the great pride of the Sergeant-Major and his wife, and which would have graced the pages of *Homes and Gardens* or any illustration of colourful English cottage gardens.

Bidulph, Wolseley's successor, had formalised the arrangement whereby most of the government and as many troops as could be spared moved to a tented camp in the Troodos during the hottest months of the summer, a move obviously inspired by Simla and the other Indian hill stations. Mrs. Lewis notes with approval 'the pleasant social footing . . . the impromptu tea parties under the trees; the tennis courts; the presence of the whole military staff and their excellent band playing at the afternoon receptions at Government Cottage'. She goes on to say 'it has its drawbacks tho' not to be of sufficient moment to be worthy of serious complaint'. However she cannot resist saying 'the ride up Olympus is trying for the ladies'. The 'season' in the Troodos lasted from about the beginning of May until the Autumn. There were full dress dinners and dances, concerts and theatricals, all of which had to be attended on horseback unless one lived near enough to walk. The ladies and children all lived in tents.

Another institution taken over from the Turks was their system of policing, which must have irritated the Greek majority of the population. The Zaptiehs, a horsed police militia, were organised rather like the Indian irregular cavalry. In the Sillidari system each trooper provided his own horse and usually produced any recruits from his own family or village. The British in Cyprus, as elsewhere in the eastern Mediterranean and Asia Minor, were incorrigibly prejudiced in favour of the Turks. Kitchener, in his articles for *Blackwood's Magazine*, had advocated the raising of a Turkish regiment in Cyprus which could be a model for similar regiments in Syria and Asia Minor. Baker, before him, had suggested that the Anatolians and the Turks from Asia Minor would make very good soldiers if led by British officers whom, he said rather optimistically, they would follow anywhere.

Attending a Regimental Sports Meeting, Mrs. Lewis saw a tug-of-war team from the Connaught Rangers pull over a team of Zaptiehs. The Turkish team was very popular and was given three cheers for its effort. It was very pleasant, she commented, to see the cordiality existing between the British and native forces. She was not so impressed with the 'menageries race'; cats and hens, being pulled along by a string tied to their legs.

She also comments unfavourably on the roads as she found them four years after the British arrived. Many were still unmade and the British attempts to build or improve them are compared to their disfavour with the French efforts in Algeria. She seems to forget that the French had been in North Africa for over 50 years by the time she visited the Mediterranean. The French in North Africa also enjoyed a lavish supply of labour derived from their internees and prisoners-of-war resulting from their almost continuous wars of pacification in Algeria and Morocco. The one exception to the network of bad roads was one built through the mountainous grape-vine district by the English Wine Company, which she describes as good – though she says nothing about the local wine. As was common at the time, she attributes the prevalence of malaria to the drying out of the salt lake near Limassol in the summer and hence the exodus to the Troodos mountains. Mosquitoes were still not connected with the disease. The British had provided hospitals at Paphos, Larnaca, Kyrenia and Nicosia but it was extremely difficult to get the islanders, especially the Turks, to use them and the women of both races were particularly reluctant.

In 1893, Mrs. Lewis describes Episkopi, now a British Sovereign Base area, as a picturesque village. The district was fertile, producing oranges, lemons, figs, pomegranates, mulberries, apricots and palm dates. There were many finely-shaped stones and carvings strengthening the usual sun-dried brick buildings and these were brought in from the 'ancient and now dead city of Curium'. Kourion, in the Greek form, is now at least partly restored. The theatre, superbly sited on a scarped hillside looking south towards the Mediterranean, was first excavated in 1949–50 and was partly reconstructed in 1961. It is now again used for public performances. The British Forces Armistice Day Service is held there and the forces combine with local groups to stage plays and concerts of music. The complex of Greek, Roman and Byzantine sites in Cyprus is unique.

When Olive Murray Chapman visited the island and wrote *Across Cyprus* in 1937 she had been told that all roads around Cyprus, near the coast, were excellent, which is more than can be said for them now. She bought a bicycle for £2.10s. but later finding she could hire a car for twopence a mile, travelled in more style. She found a commemorative tablet to Kitchener in Nicosia. 'Here lived Captain H.H. Kitchener, Director of Survey and Land Registry Office, 1880–1883 . . . who constructed the many good roads which on his arrival were non-existent'. She says, 'In recent years still more roads have been and still are being made in Cyprus and it is now possible to motor almost anywhere in the vicinity of Nicosia. Personally, I chose to take a mule'. She was obviously better served than Mrs. Lewis who had no alternative but to ride on horseback.

The Governor and his staff and the troops still moved up into the Troodos in 1937 but by then there was a good hotel amongst the trees. Olive Murray Chapman gathered that many visitors preferred to stay in tents and wooden chalets, 'for as at Kashmir, there are several well-run visitors' camps at the Troodos'. She mentions the *Survey of Cyprus Motor Map* from which she took the spelling of all place names. In her *Hints for Travellers*, she points out that Cyprus could be reached comfortably from London in seven days.

The state of the roads in Cyprus was a perennial topic amongst old Cyprus travellers. One ingenious visitor, after consulting the experts, had a caravan constructed of very sturdy wood and shipped it to Cyprus where his intention was that a team of mules should draw him and his lady around Cyprus in great comfort and security. Sadly, when he arrived in Cyprus, early in the present century, the rain had reduced what few tracks there were to deep bogs. His vehicle was far too heavy for the team of mules and the wheel rims were too thin to provide traction on the soft ground. The two visitors completed their tour on horseback. But even by the time that Mrs. Lewis arrived in Cyprus, and long before Olive Murray Chapman travelled so easily in those parts of the island that she chose to visit, the island had become something of a military and strategic backwater.

Egypt and the Canal

When the Suez Canal was finally opened in 1869 it had been the subject of discussion and speculation for at least 80 years. Napoleon's canal planned in conjunction with the French occupation of Egypt in 1798 involved a survey strangely full of errors, the worst of which was the statement that the waters of the Red Sea were 32½ feet above those of the Mediterranean. The results of the survey were published in Napoleon's enormous study, *Description d'Egypte*, and were made use of by all the denigrators of the canal project, including Britain. Britain's main objection was simply that the idea was a French one which, if it succeeded, would increase French influence in Egypt. It was thought this would lead to the establishment of a French enclave across British communications with India and encourage Egypt to break away from her nominal suzerain in Turkey, which was still, more or less, under British protection. Palmerston, faced by some enthusiasm from British commercial interests, supported the idea of a railway from Alexandria to Cairo and thence eastwards to Suez. The advantages of this plan for Britain were, first, that it would keep the French out, secondly, that it would be built by British engineers and thirdly that it would improve communications with India in the transit of letters, dispatches and light goods.

A series of crises and alarms in the Middle East put off for a while any further consideration of a link between the Mediterranean and the Red Sea. But when, by 1847, a certain amount of stability had returned to the area, the Pasha formed a semi-official commission to investigate a link between the two seas. Britain was represented by the great railway engineer, Robert Stephenson, who came down firmly on the side of a rail link as opposed to a canal. Not only was he a railway enthusiast but he was clearly influenced by the known predilections of the British government. When he finally had to agree with the other members of the commission that the Red was not almost 33 feet higher than the Mediterranean, he said that he had favoured a canal whilst it was thought that there was a height difference because this would cause a current through the canal which would keep it clear, but that with no height difference it would become a stagnant ditch.

Since the Porte, prompted by Britain, would not agree to the canal plans no European country, including France the major protagonist of the scheme, would put up any money for the project. The Khedive supported the idea of a canal and gave Ferdinand de Lesseps, the genius behind the whole enterprise, all possible assistance, short of actual cash. Finally, he allowed de Lesseps to raise the money by issuing shares in France. Three-quarters of the shares were snapped up at once in France and only a small proportion, reserved for investors in Britain and elsewhere, were not immediately taken up. The shares sold brought in almost three-quarters of the two hundred million francs required for the construction.

One of the selling points in France for the 400,000 shares at 500 francs each was that Britain was so strongly and openly opposed to the canal. De Lesseps tells of a Frenchman who approached him with a desire to purchase shares in 'the railway of the island of Sweden'. When it was explained to him that the enterprise was a canal not a railway, not on an island but on an isthmus, and not in Sweden but in Suez, the would-be investor was not in the least put out but said that it did not matter as long as the project was against the English. But despite the enthusiasm of the investors, for whatever reason, work did not begin on the canal until April 1859. Even after construction had commenced the Porte, encouraged by Britain, still attempted to prevent its completion. France, explained Britain to the Porte, was constructing a fortified ditch behind which the Khedive could assert his independence of Turkey; and in any case there was no need for a canal now that the railway was completed.

The impression, strongly held in Britain and elsewhere in Europe, that Napoleon III was a strong man was eventually shown to be mistaken but by then the Porte and even a grudging Britain had swung reluctantly into acceptance of the canal. It was triumphantly opened on 17 November 1869 and the inaugural procession through the 'second Bosphorus' included royalty and representatives from every European country including Britain. Significantly, the first commercial vessel to pass through the canal was British.

By the time the canal had opened it was generally accepted that it was a great international waterway and that no one nation would have proprietorial rights in its operation. This formula allowed Britain to welcome the completion of the canal and to send congratulations to de Lesseps amid only a small whiff of hypocrisy. Once the canal was seen to be working reasonably efficiently Britain's interest became more positive. Even if France was no longer a threat, after her defeat in the Franco-Prussian War of 1870, Russia was still lowering on the northern horizon and Turkey looked less and less capable of acting as a barrier to Russian ambitions.

For a while Cyprus benefited from this situation, as the early enthusiasts had forecast. But there were intrinsic drawbacks to Cyprus as the main defender of the canal route to India. It did not control the land routes from the north towards Egypt and even as a naval base left much to be desired. To build up the facilities on the island to the level of those in Malta or even Gibraltar, given the absence of a reasonable sea port, would have been excessively expensive. Even so, something might have been attempted. Disraeli had acquired the Khedive's shares in the canal in 1875, before the British troops arrived in Cyprus, but from then on successive British governments sought for a way to make their hold over the canal indisputable. The agreement with the Porte over the British occupation of Cyprus was, of course, in pursuance of this policy but it was regarded by most British politicians as only a stopgap. By the 1880s the 'grab for Africa' and elsewhere fed an insatiable appetite for any corners of the globe, regardless of their strategic or commercial value, as long as they could be painted red on the map.

Despite selling his canal shares and taking various other measures calculated to prop up his tottering finances, the Khedive Ismaïl could not extricate himself from bankruptcy. In 1877 he was forced to accept a Board of Commissioners representing Great Britain, France and other interested nations, to examine the general state of his finances. As a result of the report of the Commission in 1878 the Khedive was compelled to appoint British and French experts to some of his more important ministerial offices. Despite this he continued his grossly extravagant life style and in 1879 the newly-appointed ministers resigned.

It was expected that Britain and France would now intervene but before they could do so, Germany, flexing her newly-developed muscles, entered the fray in a brash and blustering manner that was soon to be regarded as typical of German 'realpolitik'. Bismarck issued an ultimatum demanding of the Porte the immediate deposition of Ismaïl, with the threat that Germany would intervene actively in the affairs of Egypt if this was not done. When Britain and France had recovered their respective breaths, they hastened to join Germany in her demands and the Porte could only agree. Ismail was replaced by his son Tewfik as Khedive and the Egyptian army was reduced from 45,000 to 18,000 men, leaving a large number of disaffected officers and soldiers open to sedition. Chief of these was an officer, Ahmed Arabi, heavily addicted to plotting and extremely unpopular with the Egyptian government.

Ahmed Arabi was involved in several confrontations with Ismaïl and later with Tewfik. By 1882 army disaffection had turned to riot and they foolishly chose the foreign communities in Alexandria and Cairo as scape-goats for their troubles. The Turkish government failed to restore order and the French, perhaps with a better understanding of the consequences, withdrew. As the situation deteriorated Admiral Seymour, in command of the British fleet already at hand, bombarded the Egyptian forts round Alexandria, thus committing Britain to future responsibility for the condition of Egypt, a responsibility which may not have been altogether uncongenial.

Within a week plans were well advanced for a British force to intervene. As a preliminary step to eliminating the Egyptian forces from the scene, the canal was seized without reference to the Canal Company or de Lesseps. British transports were taken through the waterway and troops were landed at Ismailia. With the punctilio reminiscent of an Ealing Studios comedy, all the canal dues were paid in full. Sir Garnet Wolseley commanded the British Expeditionary Force which brought the Egyptian army to battle at Tel-el-Kebir in August, losing 459 British killed and wounded but inflicting four times as many casualties on the enemy. Egypt was completely broken, her finances in ruins. Only Britain was in any position, or had the immediate interest, to rebuild what was destroyed.

Kitchener, as well as Wolseley, was involved in the little war with Egypt. He was coming to the end of his second tour in Cyprus when he heard about the situation in Alexandria and, like Wolseley, could not resist getting involved. Unfortunately, as with his early troubles, when generals and junior officers fall out, the junior who refuses to give way is in some peril. Kitchener left Cyprus unofficially and got himself on to Admiral Seymour's flagship from where he observed the bombardment. He says that he took part in a rather hazardous reconnaissance of Alexandria harbour, and on that basis applied for the Egyptian Medal of 1882. The request was turned down by Wolseley in 1884, by which time he was Adjutant General, on the grounds that Kitchener, ostensibly on leave, had worn mufti.

The only communication that Kitchener received from Wolseley was apparently a letter demanding to know why the famous map of Cyprus, over which there had been so much fuss, was still not completed. This seems to have been a fair, if somewhat sly, comment and showed that all was not yet forgiven. The map was published by Edward Stanford in April 1885 and contained much information unusual for the time, to the public credit of Kitchener, as the former Director of Survey for Cyprus. It included plans of the principal towns and villages and showed them as Christian or Moslem, giving place names in Greek as well as Turkish script. Aqueducts, springs, wells, monasteries and ruins were all identified on the map as well as the known ancient sites.

In 1883, the Sudan, previously under Turco-Egyptian rule, came under the control of the Mahdi, a Muslim religious fanatic, and it became necessary for British forces to pacify the country in order to safeguard Egypt. The expedition to the Sudan was poorly managed by a British administration which only half-believed in what it was doing. The British army withdrew from the Sudan having arrived too late in Khartoum to save General Gordon who had been allowed to stay on until it was too late to rescue him. The situation in the Sudan became the excuse for staying in Egypt and eventually the British presence became self-justifying. If the British left Egypt some other power would have to come in, and what would then happen to the canal?

In 1888 the Congress of Constantinople declared that the canal should 'always be free and open, in time of war as in time of peace, to every vessel of commerce or of war, without distinction of flag'. To no-one's surprise this left Britain firmly in control of the canal. Major General Evelyn Wood VC became the first British Sirdar, or Commander-in-Chief of the Egyptian armed forces and virtually ruler of Egypt. Kitchener was accepted as one of his seconded officers by

Evelyn Wood who set out to retrain the Egyptian army; a task particularly congenial to young officers like Kitchener.

The unforeseen result of the British occupation was the intensifica-
tion of 'the grab for Africa'. Britain had now provided the example and
the moral justification for the French annexation of Tunis whilst
German ambitions in other parts of Africa were favoured with a blind
eye. Even Russian expansion in northern Persia and eastern Asia was
accepted. But the Nile Basin and the Suez isthmus were now firmly
under British control and almost any sacrifice or artifice seemed worthwhile to secure that last link in the all-red route through the
Mediterranean from Britain to India.

Even before the British takeover of Egypt and the canal area, tourists
had been arriving in the eastern Mediterranean in ever increasing numbers. Although the traffic did not begin to approach what we know
today, it was enough to cause concern in some quarters. As early as
1840, as many as 100,000 Britons out of a total population of 26 million
travelled to continental Europe every year. Thackeray, who has so little
to say about Malta, could still attack his fellow travellers: 'That brutal,
peevish bully of an Englishman is showing himself in every city in
Europe'. It was mainly the social class of the travellers and not their
overwhelming numbers that seemed to horrify their critics. Piers
Brendon in his invaluable *Thomas Cook, 150 Years of Popular Tourism*,
says the commentators expressed their hostility by referring to 'Cook's
Circus', 'Cook's Hordes' and 'Cook's Vandals'. There can be no doubt
that an innate English snobbery contributed much to the dislike of the
travelling masses. Brendon quotes from the *Pall Mall Gazette*, a new
evening newspaper, in 1865: 'Cook's tourist system . . . encouraged
people to travel above their station, to climb socially by climbing the
Alps . . .'.

The founders of Cook's travel organisation, although they put a
brave face on it, were obviously affected by the criticism, and consciously tried to move up-market as the century wore on. Nevertheless,
in 1878, the year of Britain's acquisition, John Cook was already inves-
tigating Cyprus as a potential holiday resort. But Cook's greatest
triumphs were to come in the British occupation of Egypt. Well before
Wolseley and Kitchener had appeared on the scene, Cook's had become
the acknowledged experts on Egypt as a resort and on Nile travel.
Furthermore they had cornered the market in Nile steamers.

In 1882, after Wolseley had crushed the army of Ahmed Arabi at Tel-el-Kebir, John Cook took the British wounded from Cairo to Alexandria at cost and arranged trips on Nile steamers for the General and his staff, and for some of the soldiers convalescing from enteric fever. When it was finally decided, too late, to launch the expedition to rescue General Gordon besieged in Khartoum, Cook's were consulted about navigation and transport on the Nile. Cook's tendered to move the whole expedition from Alexandria to Wadi Halfa and their offer was immediately accepted. The contract initially called for the transport of 6,000 men and 10,000 tons of stores. In the end 18,000 British and Egyptian troops were moved, together with 130,000 tons of stores. John Cook's 16 years of invaluable experience of Nile travel contributed enormously to the success, if that is what it should be called, of the expedition. But it is also true that many senior army officers would not have accepted the novel methods of transporting an army, and had it not been for Wolseley, the 'modern Major General', advantage might not have been taken of Cook's offer.

CHAPTER V

Into the 20th Century

By the turn of the century British bases, garrisons and colonies had spread through almost the whole of the Mediterranean; only the shores at the extreme eastern end of the sea were as yet unoccupied. The coast, from Egypt up through Palestine to the Anatolian provinces of Turkey in Asia Minor, across the narrow sea from Cyprus, was still in the hands of the increasingly decrepit and ineffectual Turkish Sultan in Constantinople. The importance of the Suez Canal became more obvious from year to year. Not only was general commerce through the canal increasing, most of it British or carried in British ships, but its importance in the transport of oil, the 'wonder fuel' of the future, was beginning to make an impact on politicians and soldiers alike. As the safeguarding of the route to India became less of a problem with the decline of Russian ambitions in the Mediterranean, new enemies began to loom over a stormy horizon. The French, who had been bought off for their acquiescence in the British takeover of Egypt and the canal by being given what was virtually a free hand in North Africa and other areas of the continent further to the south, finally over-reached themselves at Fashoda in 1898.

The Sudan had been reconquered in the campaign of 1896–98, by which time Herbert Kitchener had become Sirdar, the Commander-in-Chief in Egypt. John Mason Cook, son and partner of Thomas Cook, and the real presiding genius of the Egyptian and Nile travel trade, found Kitchener a very different man from the relaxed and urbane Wolseley who in 1885 had paid very large sums to the travel firm for his river transport in the abortive Gordon Relief Expedition. Brendon, in his history of Thomas Cook's, says that Kitchener had to beat John Cook as well as the Khalifa in order to win back the Sudan, and he was successful on both counts. Sir George Newnes wrote:

> Egypt is now in the hands of two armies of occupation. One is composed of British soldiers, and the other of the men of Thomas Cook & Sons. The latter's Generals have certainly taken possession of the Nile but elsewhere they were worsted with severe loss.

Kitchener was a hard man but he also had to contend with a tight budget and Cook's palmy days of being a monopoly supplier of river transport cut no ice with the new Sirdar, who requisitioned what he required and left the payment until later.

The Upper Nile having been pacified, a small French party under Captain Jean-Baptiste Marchand which had established itself on the Upper Nile, about one week's steaming above Omdurman, after a remarkable and courageous march eastward across Africa, was confronted by Kitchener himself. In an unusual mixture of charm and firmness, not always typical of his manner, the French party was persuaded to withdraw from what was obviously, to the British at least, part of the British sphere of influence in East Africa and the Nile Valley. For once, honour was preserved on both sides and although there was something of a crisis in the affairs of France and Britain, common sense prevailed. The French did not again challenge the British presence in Egypt or the Sudan. In fact the lowering of the French flag at Fashoda marked the beginning of a better understanding between the two countries and opened the way a few years later for the *Entente Cordiale* as an alliance for mutual support in the face of Germany's growing strength.

The New Rival – Imperial Germany

Germany had shown in 1879, in its virtual ultimatum to the Porte, which brought about Ismaïl's demise, that it was prepared and more than willing to play a part in Mediterranean affairs. She was not only flexing her muscles in that area but was fast becoming one of the most prosperous trading nations in the world with a large and growing merchant fleet. By the end of the century, not content with sabre rattling, she had a navy deliberately designed to challenge British supremacy on every ocean of the world. It is not surprising that she began to look for markets, spheres of influence and colonies to match those of the older European powers. Being a brash newcomer, albeit with the power in 1870 to defeat France, until then thought to have the strongest army in Europe, she caused Britain (and especially her naval chiefs) to look with suspicion and some alarm at the new German Empire. Lord Fisher, First Sea Lord at the beginning of the 20th Century, was typical of, if somewhat blunter than, the many naval and military men who could foresee the coming conflict. As Commander-in-Chief in the Mediterranean in 1900 his notes for his regular lectures to his officers included the following comment on British naval ship-building:

> You want sufficiency of battleships left over, intact after settling with the first hostile combination, (i.e. France and Russia) as to be ready to deal with, say, our German cousin, who has kept neutral so as to bag the booty.

Fisher was convinced that as soon as the Kiel Canal enlargements and improvements, then underway, were completed, Britain would come under attack.

The more affluent of the British holidaying public, having had their nautical interest sparked off by the international naval arms race, took up cruising. The popularity of the cruises they offered encouraged Cook's to aim at 'the smartest of the smart'. The American office of Cook's arranged to charter the 12,000 ton luxury liner the SS *Moltke* for a Mediterranean cruise and this was so successful that an additional ship had to be chartered. The passengers were almost all American and it is unlikely that at that time (1902–3) a ship with such a well-known German name would have attracted many British tourists.

In 1908, still more ships were launched for the Nile trade and the river and Egypt could still be sold as an experience for the élite. Again, according to Brendon, in mid-Edwardian times the travel agents made a calculated appeal to 'men of the world'. Pandering more blatantly than ever to snobbery, the firm encouraged its patrons to take their vacations in the most exclusive fashion they could afford. For the first time *The Travellers' Gazette* advertised the 'gay and improper' as attractions, not least because of the oriental settings. But tourists in the Edwardian heyday, apart from avoiding anything unpatriotic, were not really aware of a German threat to their pleasures.

The Algeciras Conference in 1906, held just across the bay from Gibraltar, which was filled to capacity by the combined British Mediterranean and Home Fleets consciously assembled to impress the participants, settled the immediate claims of France and Germany in Africa, as well as those of Spain, which was feeling more under threat in Morocco. A year before, the irrepressible Admiral Fisher had told the Conservative government that the British and French fleets were one and could seize the Kiel Canal in a fortnight. The newly-formed British General Staff was already holding talks with its French counterpart in anticipation of joint action against any common enemy that might emerge. At the conference Britain and France presented a united front against Germany, and the *Entente Cordiale* was born.

The Entente was joined by Russia, forming a 'Triple Entente' and leaving Germany with only the Austro-Hungarian Empire as an ally. In 1911 the Germans sent the gunboat *Panther* to the Atlantic coast Moroccan port of Agadir with the intention of landing troops to dispute France's seizure of Morocco. Britain offered verbal support to the French, but nothing more practical, and the French did not feel sufficiently confident in their own strength to take on Imperial Germany on their own so a compromise had reluctantly to be agreed. France and Belgium handed over some of their Congo territories in exchange for recognition of the French Protectorate in Morocco. The compromise satisfied neither side. The battle lines were now drawn in Europe and the next few years could only be regarded by the Great Powers as a period of frantic preparation for war.

The tensions and threats in Europe in the decade before the First World War had their repercussions on the British in the Mediterranean. But just as the period before that war in Britain at least, and judging from contemporary memoirs, novels and diaries, was noted for its halcyon days, typified by great country house parties, and on a large scale for the first time, trips to the 'sea-side' for the lower classes, the

Mediterranean was also *en fête*. However, beneath the surface gaiety there was a rather harsher reality.

Although there was absolutely no call for independence or union with any other country by the 25,000 Gibraltarians, the future of the Rock was still in doubt. Improvements in artillery meant that the base had become increasingly vulnerable. The harbour and docks on the west side of the Rock were exposed to gunfire from concealed batteries on the other side of the bay and from everywhere on a great arc to the west, north and east of Gibraltar. A committee had recommended in 1902 that a completely new dock should be constructed on the east side of the Rock. The plan was rejected mainly on grounds of cost but Admiral Fisher pointed out, from his extensive knowledge of the Mediterranean, that the east side of the Rock would be just as much exposed as the west side and, since the prevailing bad weather came from the east, ships would be exposed to gunfire and at the same time be on a lee shore.

For Gibraltar to be accepted as a viable base it became more and more necessary to assume Spanish neutrality in any future war. But Spain's continuing claims on Gibraltar made that neutrality open to question. There were contingency plans to seize a large area of Spanish territory round the Rock in the event of hostilities so as to keep the Spanish batteries back out of range. It was still possible to contemplate this kind of action before the First World War but even then it was estimated that at least 50,000 troops would be necessary to seize enough Spanish territory to make the Rock safe from enemy gunfire.

In the circumstances it was not surprising that voices were raised in Britain in favour of exchanging Gibraltar for Ceuta, the Spanish colony in North Africa, across the Strait from the Rock. Spain was said to favour the idea and would certainly have welcomed a British presence in Morocco as a counterweight to the French. In retrospect, in addition to the sentimental reasons for retaining Gibraltar, we can now see that an exchange would have been an embarrassing and possibly dangerous mistake. By the end of the 19th Century over 50,000 Spaniards lived in Ceuta and a British occupation, however willing the Spanish government, would have been likely to lead to a Spanish 'enosis' situation. The influential Spanish military leader, Primo de Riviera, was a strong proponent of the exchange plan but in the end, in the face of a strong British lobby whose main plank was the sentimental notion that 'too much blood had been spilled in the defence of Gibraltar to give it up now', any idea of an exchange was providentially dropped.

Primo de Riviera, a man of vision, also put forward a plan for a tunnel under the Strait of Gibraltar to link Africa and Europe. Unfortunately, a tunnel would have had to be 2,000 feet below the surface of the Strait for geological reasons and this would have meant an inordinately long approach tunnel of some 22 miles so the plan was rejected on grounds of expense before any detailed scientific study could be made.

The future of Tangier was another matter where no progress was made. Britain insisted on Tangier being given international status in the Franco-Spanish Treaty of 1912, which was intended to sort out border and sovereignty problems in Morocco, but neither France nor Spain would agree and the question was still in abeyance when the 1914 war broke out. Tangier did not achieve international status until 1923.

Armageddon in the Mediterranean

Despite Russia's having joined the Triple Entente in 1907, her relations with Britain had not improved, except in so far as the two countries' separate spheres of influence in Persia had now been clearly, if not very sincerely, defined. Turkey, defeated by a Balkan alliance in 1913, and feeling increasingly isolated and at the mercy of Russia, asked the Germans to send another military mission to Constantinople. Sensing the desperation of the Turks, the German government insisted that the head of the mission, Lieutenant Colonel Otto Liman von Sanders, should be seconded to the Turkish General Staff and that he should be given command of the Turkish 1st Army Corps which garrisoned the area around Constantinople. The last straw for the allies was a demand from the Germans to control the Straits between the Black Sea and the Mediterranean. The Russians protested violently and persuaded their French and British allies to sign a note of protest, but no further action was taken.

One immediate result of Turkey's abandoning Britain, her traditional supporter, and joining the Central Powers was the British annexation of Cyprus. The island was now no longer held for Turkey and certainly no surplus revenue would be handed over. Cyprus remained a British Crown Colony until well after the Second World War. Considering its important strategic position, situated just off the south coast of Turkey, it played a relatively minor rôle in both world wars.

In the First World War the strength of the Royal Navy and the primitive state of military aviation made Cyprus relatively secure. By the time aircraft or seaplanes were used in more than individual sorties, they could be flown from the Aegean islands of Mudros and Imbros, even if their bomb load was restricted to bombs of less than 100 lbs. weight. The Aegean islands were, of course, much closer than Cyprus to the Dardanelles and the Bosphorus and to capture the entrance to the Black Sea and open up communications with Russia through one of its warm water ports was one of the overriding strategic aims of the war against Turkey. However, Cyprus was a constant threat to the Turks and their German senior partners.

But when the great diversionary attack was launched it was not from Cyprus. At that time there was considerable doubt about Cyprus as a permanent British possession. In January 1915, the British Foreign Secretary, Sir Edward Grey told Kitchener, who opposed a plan to cede Cyprus to Greece, that giving up the island, of which the Admiralty had never been able to make proper use, would be a small price to pay for Greek intervention on the allied side. Lord Fisher, whom Churchill had brought back to the Admiralty as his First Sea Lord in October 1914, urged Kitchener not to worry about Cyprus. 'We don't want a barren island', he wrote. Both Kitchener and Fisher, and probably Winston Churchill too, saw Alexandretta as a much more useful prize after a successful war against Turkey. Kitchener was only persuaded away from the idea of annexing Alexandretta by the promise of Haifa instead.

In the event, Anatolia and the eastern Mediterranean coasts were bypassed in favour of a direct attack on the shores of the narrow straits of the Dardanelles and the Bosphorus leading into the Black Sea. Against Kitchener's advice a naval force tried to rush the Dardanelles in March 1915. This was a complete failure and merely alerted the Turks to their danger. What was meant to be a 'surprise' amphibious attack did not take place until almost three months later, a time used by the Turks, under the direction of their German advisers, to prepare strong points and construct defences which proved to be virtually impregnable. Contrary to expectations, the Turks fought bravely and skilfully under von Sanders and the Turkish General Mustafa Kemal, who afterwards took the name of Ataturk.

By August, General Sir Ian Hamilton had nine British, two French and two Anzac divisions under his command but they could achieve nothing. After several attempts to break through to Constantinople had failed, it was decided to evacuate the peninsula and the troops were withdrawn, with few additional losses, by the end of 1915. The casualties in the campaign had been very high and almost 60,000 had been taken to Malta during the nine months of the allied operations. The remaining troops were taken first to Egypt and then to France where they were sorely needed. Kitchener, who was made the scapegoat for the débâcle, was by now completely exhausted and was forced to accept Sir William Robertson as Chief of the General Staff with direct access to the War Cabinet. Hitherto, Kitchener had insisted on acting as his own Chief of Staff. Robertson was free from subordination to Kitchener who was still, if only temporarily, Secretary of State for War.

Cyprus was not used as a staging post for the attack on the Dardanelles, the forces used having come from Egypt or southern France, and they were withdrawn in the same way. Malta, on the other hand, made a most positive contribution to the campaign. Many Maltese men fought and died taking part in the invasion. Two Maltese officers were awarded the Military Cross and several were Mentioned in Despatches for their part in the fighting. The labour battalions with the Anzac forces were filled with Maltese. In addition, in Malta there were 28 hospitals and convalescent camps treating 2,500 officers and 55,000 other rank casualties from the Dardanelles. Malta, with some justice, protested at not being invited to the 75th anniversary ceremonies, held in Turkey in 1990.

Because of its undeveloped naval facilities Cyprus proved of only limited value, even for naval operations. But it was not ceded to Greece or any other nation although both France and Italy were also interested in its acquisition. The renewal of British interest in the island arose in part from the transformation of Mustafa Kemal, the only successful Turkish general in the Mediterranean War, into Ataturk, the dynamic leader of a group of young, strongly nationalistic Turks, violently opposed to the peace settlement which aimed at dismembering the old Ottoman Empire. There was also a desire on the part of Britain to maintain a base from which a wary eye could be kept on the resurgent navy of the Soviet Union in its Black Sea bases.

Elsewhere in the Mediterranean, the British had been involved in naval actions but on a smaller scale than they were to see in the Second World War. There was constant submarine activity in the Mediterranean, as there was to be in 1939–45, with Gibraltar and Malta playing a full part in anti-submarine warfare. Despite the anti-submarine patrols in the Strait of Gibraltar many U-boats slipped through into the Mediterranean.

In the First World War few Mediterranean ports were open to the Central Powers; the Austo-Hungarian ports at the head of the Adriatic could not be used without attracting the attention of Italian, French or British warships which would have made every effort to bottle them up in the Adriatic or destroy them as they tried to break out. However it was still possible for submarines to pass in and out of the Adriatic and five U-boats were based on Cattaro. Even though the Straits of Taranto were closed with a barrage of nets, sinkings continued, and it was not until the convoy system, first used by the British in the Mediterranean in the 16th Century, was reintroduced in May 1917 that merchant shipping losses were reduced to less than 100,000 tons per month.

Because of the difficulties of getting through the Strait of Gibraltar, U-Boats were brought overland in sections from Germany and assembled at the Austrian base of Pola, where the Austrians built their own warships. The same system was used to get German submarines into the Mediterranean in the Second World War when they were brought in sections to the Rhône and then carried down to Marseilles where they were assembled.

Despite the heavy shipping losses early in the First World War, there appear to have been no threats of starvation or shortage in Malta, where all the surrounding countries were friendly to Britain. In the Second World War with France, Italy, Greece and much of North Africa under Axis control the defence of Malta and communications through the Mediterranean became a much more expensive and deadly business.

The decade preceding the First World War in Gibraltar was a period of quiet consolidation in both its military defences and in social and political life. The smooth-bore guns defending the Rock, with their range limited to about 4,000 yards, were gradually replaced by more up-to-date ordnance and the modernising process was hurried along by the knowledge that the Spanish batteries on the surrounding hills and around Algeciras were armed with the latest weapons from Krupp's factory at Essen in the Ruhr. Spain remained neutral during the war and the Rock continued to be supplied with food from across the frontier. The dockyard was still manned by Spanish workers who crossed the border every day and who, even if they had wanted to, could not afford to give up almost the only non-agricultural employment available in southern Andalusia. The Rock provided a valuable base for the anti-submarine patrols in the Mediterranean and the Atlantic, as an assembly point for convoys and as a contraband inspection station. Once the United States entered the war, it became to all intents and purposes an American base.

At the other end of the Mediterranean, two further campaigns against the outlying provinces of the Ottoman Empire were to have a significant bearing on the British position at the peace conference after the war. In 1914 a small force was sent from India to protect the British oil interests in Mesopotamia. It remained happily on the lower Euphrates until the Turks came into the war on the German side and, in 1915, began to constitute a threat to the Ahwaz-Abadan pipeline. The imperial troops in Mesopotamia were reinforced to divisional strength and thereupon fell prey to delusions of grandeur. The little army advanced up the Euphrates to Basra without too much trouble and conceived the notion of going on to capture Baghdad – an early, and classic example of 'A Bridge Too Far'. The force was too small and too badly organised to carry through its over-ambitious plan and, after a painful siege at Kut el Amara and a gallant defence, in which hunger and disease played an inevitable part in weakening the isolated troops, it capitulated to a superior Turkish army on 19 April 1916. The force in Mesopotamia was rebuilt and did finally capture Baghdad. After that it was decided that it should remain on the defensive whilst the main thrust of the war against the Turks was made along the eastern Mediterranean seaboard with the object of capturing Jerusalem and Damascus.

After their initial attack on Egypt, which had been repulsed with only a few allied casualties, the Turks remained on the defensive in Palestine. General Murray had attacked the Turkish positions in Palestine through Gaza in 1916 but had been unsuccessful and suffered many casualties. After much prodding and prompting by the War

Cabinet in England, he launched another attack on Gaza, regarded as the gateway to Palestine, on 17 April 1917. The Cabinet had told Murray that they were anxious that Jerusalem should be captured quickly since a success was urgently needed to boost civilian morale after a series of disasters on the Western Front.

Murray's second attack failed, suffering nearly 3,000 casualties, and the Cabinet had no hesitation about replacing him. General Allenby took over from Murray in June 1917 after being told somewhat ominously by Prime Minister Lloyd George that Jerusalem was wanted as a Christmas present for the British nation. Jerusalem fell on the 8 December after hard fighting and the imaginative use of deception and some military innovations. His success persuaded the government to give Allenby the reinforcements he needed to capture Damascus but this took rather longer than he anticipated. The Turkish army of about 33,000 men, approximately half the number of men available to Allenby, sick and starving, their communications almost non-existent and open to attack by T.E. Lawrence's Arab guerrilla raiding parties, fought with stubborn, doomed heroism. Two attacks by the British across the Jordan were thrown back and Amman remained in Turkish hands.

Allenby's plans were severely disrupted by a period of very bad weather, and the German 'last gasp' offensive in France meant that he had to go short of munitions and replacements which were diverted to the Western Front. Allenby kept his nerve and used the early part of the Summer of 1918 in defensive operations and in reorganising and retraining his troops. His final plan involved the use of deception again and whilst his real intention was to break through along the coast, by various subterfuges he convinced the Turks that he would attack in the Judaean Hills and the Jordan Valley.

Allenby's plan worked to text-book perfection. The attack opened on 18 September and in less than six weeks he had captured Damascus which he entered on the 1 October, with Lawrence and the Arab Princes in his triumphal procession. He advanced to Aleppo, 350 miles from his starting point, where the exhausted Turks asked for an armistice. The Middle East war was over.

Many soldiers and statesmen looked upon the campaigns in the Middle East as no more than sideshows and there is still a body of opinion which regards all the treasure and human lives poured out in the battles against the Turks as a waste of precious resources that would have been better expended on the Western Front in the main battle against Germany. In the narrow sense, this argument might be sustainable but only with the advantages of hindsight. At the time, there was little doubt that the effort to break the deadlock on the main battlefront seemed sensible and necessary in terms of morale.

Even more important was the need not to appear to be abandoning what the majority of the British public regarded as vital national interests in the Suez Canal, and to safeguard them against rival powers, whether Russian, German or Turkish. The growing importance of oil, by now obvious to all industrial nations, of trade through the canal and the determination of successive governments to retain a hold on India, left Britain no option but to fight in the Middle East when necessary. The necessity continued until after another world war. The strategic and political gains which accrued from British actions in the Middle East during the First World War allowed us to survive, if only by a hair's breadth, in the war which followed the long armistice which lasted from 1918 until 1939.

The Last of the Spoils

When Allenby entered Damascus, with Lawrence and the leaders of the Arab Revolt, he knew, and Lawrence probably guessed, that the Ottoman possessions in the Middle East had already been divided up between Britain and France. There was no hope for the unified Arab State that Lawrence had promised on what he believed to be good authority, and all that could be hoped for now was a parcel of Arab land for each of them, with an Arab ruling house under the tutelage of one of the victorious Allied Powers. The 'Mandatory System' devised by President Wilson aimed at advancing the inhabitants of the mandated territories towards self-government within a reasonable but unspecified period and thus towards independence. This was an idea to which only lip-service was paid by both Britain and France and by most of the other states which received 'mandates'.

In the special case of Palestine the mandate instructed the British government to 'facilitate Jewish immigration and . . . encourage Jewish settlement of the land'. The mandates were not officially issued by the

League of Nations until 1922, by which time it was clear to British administrators that the establishment of a Jewish State in Palestine, in pursuance of earlier British promises, would lead to another Arab Revolt. No one had troubled to consult, or consider the views of, the Arabs actually living in the country. An uneasy compromise, limited immigration, and angry discontent usually aimed at the Jews and occasionally breaking out into armed violence, and finally a series of bloody wars which has still not settled the fate of the Israelis or the Palestine Arabs, was the unhappy result.

Egypt and Kuwait at the head of the Persian Gulf, had meanwhile had their status regularised from that of *de facto* protectorates. At the time of the Turkish declaration in favour of Germany in 1914, Egypt, which had nominally been within the power of the Porte, was officially declared a Protectorate of Great Britain. In fact, the practical difference between a Mandate and a Protectorate was very slight. A new ruler of Egypt was chosen from Albania's Egyptian ruling family and his ministers were even more under the control of their British advisers than they had been before. Despite some local protests, Egypt found that it was now part of the British Empire and coloured unmistakably red on British maps. Kuwait had come under British protection in 1904 and no real change in status was involved in 1922.

Hussein, Sharif of Mecca, was Britain's ally in the war to drive out the Turks. His reward was confirmation as Sharif of Mecca, the Arabs' most holy city, absolute rule over a desert kingdom and the assumption that he spoke for all Arabs. The Sharif's son, the Emir Feisal, was given the most important of the old Turkish provinces, Syria, with the understanding that he would have a government fully independent of the allied powers. Unfortunately Britain had agreed that France should have the last word in Syria as well as in The Lebanon. Feisal lasted for less than two years before the French threw him out. The British, obviously feeling guilty about the course of events, renamed Mesopotamia 'Iraq' and gave it to Feisal as a consolation prize. The Royal Air Force set up a large base at Habbiniya and effectively policed the country from the air. Another of Sharif Hussein's sons was given the artificially created Kingdom of Transjordan, later to become Jordan, where His Majesty King Hussein rules today. Iraq overthrew the Hashemite monarchy in 1958.

Britain's holdings in and around the Mediterranean were now at

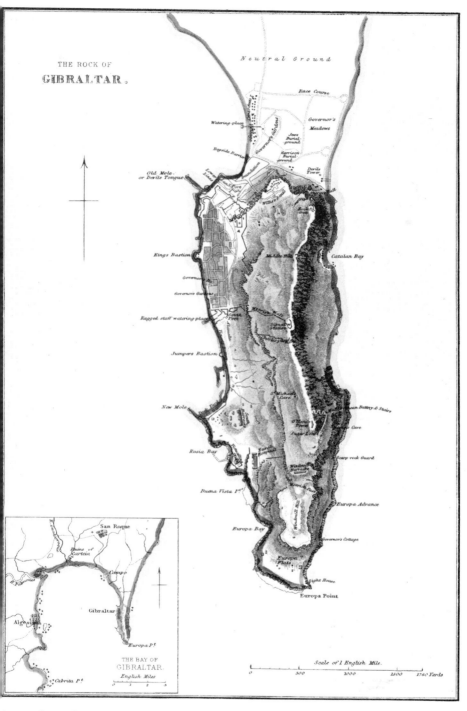

An early 19th century map of Gibraltar.

The Monument in the Alameda Gardens, Gibraltar, to General Elliot Governo of Gibraltar during the Great Siege of 1778–1783.

*...semates, with 19th century garrison. The plaque reads 'Muy Noble, Muy Real
...Heroica Ciudad de Tarifa.'*

Tarifa, the main gate.

The newly restored walls of Tarifa.

rrivals in Nicosia, 19th century.

Walls of Nicosia, early 19th century.

The Trafalgar Cemetery, Gibraltar

The Somerset dry dock at Malta, opened in 1871.

General Sikorski with General Lord Gort in Gibraltar before the fatal crash.
(courtesy of the Imperial War Museum)

28 Bomb Disposal Squad, Royal Engineers, who defused and removed
the bomb from Mosta Cathedral.

The Mosta bomb as it is today.

Gibraltar Dockyard, now almost completely in civilian hands.

Civilian activity in the Old Naval Dockyard, Malta.

Valletta, part of Grand Harbour and the Hydrofoil link to Sicily and Libya.

Moorish Castle, Gibraltar, now a great tourist attraction.

A cannon from the Great Siege now in place on the Line Wall.

18th century guardroom in Gibraltar Town.

Curium near Limassol, now restored.

Colossi Castle and sugar factory, built and garrisoned by the Knights Templar.

Early 18th century fortifications at the entrance to Port Mahon Harbour, Menorca.

All that remains of the 18th century gates to Port Mahon.

The simple burial place of Robert Graves in Deia, Majorca.

Gibraltar today, the new marina.

their most extensive. Although there were social problems and nation-alist-inspired unrest in Malta and Cyprus, they always appeared to be kept well in hand. Even when the trouble in the dockyard during the war led to a token strike in Malta, this seemed no worse than similar troubles in Britain at the same time. There had in fact been more seri-ous unrest in 1919, when troops were called out to put down riots during which four Maltese were shot dead. This had involved some incitement to violence which fell on fertile ground in the immediate post-war economic recession, but the new Governor, Lord Plummer, with the agreement of the British government, handled the situation with a mixture of firmness and conciliation. A large bread subsidy was introduced, a programme of public works was inaugurated and there were promises of more self-government. By the early 1920s an upswing in trade had removed the most immediate causes of distress and polit-ical unrest.

Cyprus, whilst remaining firmly within the British fold, presented a more serious problem because of the constant undercurrent of agitation and propaganda in favour of 'enosis' with Greece. The Cypriots had been encouraged in the belief that Britain would hand over the island to Greece after the 1914–18 war. After the collapse in 1914 of the 'leasing' agreement that had been entered into with Turkey in 1879, it was assumed in certain circles in Britain as well as in Cyprus that 'enosis' was only a matter of time. The principle of self-determination, strong-ly advocated by the League of Nations, strengthened the Cypriot demand, although Greece was not prepared to antagonise Britain by pressing the matter. In fact Greece was not in a very strong position having, it will be remembered, been offered Cyprus in 1915 in return for coming into the war on the Allied side. It had looked to Greece at that time that Germany might win the war and it was necessary to hedge bets even at the expense of Cyprus.

After the war, although popular feeling sided with a union of Cyprus with Greece, and King George V had strongly supported the offer to Greece in 1915, a wave of old-style imperialism swept through the British government, triggered by revolts against British rule and actions in Egypt, Iraq and Persia. British politicians of all parties could not resist the attractions of the spoils available from the collapse of the Ottoman Empire. So events in the Mediterranean moved from open riot to underground agitation, swinging from sullen compliance to overt action as the home government introduced local reforms and the level of local prosperity provided or denied a following for more drastic action. By the time of King George V's Mediterranean cruise in 1925, arranged as far as the sight-seeing was concerned by Thomas Cook's, all seemed to be quiet in the Mediterranean empire.

The Rock and the Spanish Civil War

Until quite late in the present century, Gibraltar lacked the facilities of accommodation and amusement essential for the middle-class traveller. For visitors, the Rock was merely a stop on the way to the more exciting pleasures of southern Europe and the Middle East. When the British Mediterranean and Home fleets combined at Gibraltar after their annual exercise, there would be hordes of visitors on the streets who would certainly have shocked the more genteel sight-seers. The usual visitors, apart from sailors 'at liberty', were friends and relatives of the officers and men of the garrison and of civilian officials employed in the colony. They were usually accommodated by their friends, and official visitors and especially privileged travellers were still sometimes put up in messes and even by the Governor at the Convent. But none of this amounted to tourism on the scale of the parties visiting the antiquities in Greece, or cruising on the Nile, or of those making pilgrimages to Omdurman, Gallipoli or Mesopotamia. No real attempt to develop tourism on the Rock was made until the late 1960s and 1970s when the closure of the Naval Dockyard forced the Gibraltar government to look for alternative employment for the native Gibraltarians, and new ways of adding to the revenue.

The real problem of Gibraltar and its viability as a separate entity is one of size. The Rock occupies less than three square miles, most of it mountain, and usually houses about 30,000 people plus the garrison, now reduced almost to nil. The colony is today no more than a very small garrison town without a garrison. Compared with Cyprus and even Malta, Gibraltar has remained a quiet, loyal and prosperous military station. The only rioting the colony has ever known, apart from the occasional drunken excesses of the soldiery and sailors and the rioting between factions during the Spanish Civil War, was in recent years when a riot developed aimed at a few, well-meaning but misguided Gibraltarians, known on the Rock as 'The Doves' who had suggested that it was worth thinking about a closer relationship with newly-democratised Spain. In 1967 a referendum was held in which all the adult people of Gibraltar were asked whether they wished to continue the link with Britain or whether they would prefer an association with Spain. Of an eligible electorate of 12,762, 12,182 valid votes were cast, only 44 votes in favour of a link with Spain.

But what the colony lacked in subversion or political ambition was made up for in the eccentricity of some of its governors and by a rather sad, standoffishness of some of the garrison's officers and soldiers and their families towards the Gibraltarians. The eccentricities were not all of the robust, worldly, O'Hara type with his mistresses rotated once a week, but of a more sporting, tub-thumping Christian variety, which could be guaranteed to cause more trouble. There was a brief respite with the arrival of General Smith-Dorrien as Governor in 1918. He came having had experience of a garrison town, with all its problems, as the GOC Aldershot District where he had introduced friendly and enlightened principles into the army's association with the town at all levels. His aim was to introduce the same system to the Rock. He was able to form an elected City Council which was responsible, for the first time, for the administration of local affairs and he set up an Executive Council to advise the Governor on all matters of a non-military nature regarding the Rock.

Smith-Dorrien, being a great sportsman, was able to persuade the military and the Navy, who had always guarded their precious sports-grounds on the few flat areas of the Rock, to allow the local people to make use of some of their sports facilities. To his surprise, he found that the Gibraltarians took readily to all ball games and were soon serious sporting rivals to the Service teams even when they were at full strength on the Rock. Smith-Dorrien's keenness on sport was a legend in the Army. His friend J. W. Fortescue, the great military historian, author of the monumental *History of the British Army* and Librarian of Windsor Castle, after a visit to the Rock said: 'I never saw a house with fewer books than Government House. Anyone would have thought that he gave no thought to anything but games and racing'.

Gerald Pawle, in an article entitled 'The General's Last Campaign', published in *Blackwood's Magazine* in 1949, describes the antics of two, rather less sympathetic 20th Century governors. Sir Archibald

Hunter lashed himself into an absolute frenzy of reforming zeal just before the First World War and held public meetings at which he harangued the unfortunate populace. He would condemn their poor command of the English language, their indolence and their insanitary habits. He objected to almost everything on the Rock including the uncouth behaviour of the dockyard workers, the siting of the Jews' Market, the Gibraltarian habit, he claimed, of reading obscene literature and the design of the donkey shelters. In the end his extraordinary behaviour was brought to the attention of Whitehall and he was removed.

General Sir Alexander Godley, the new Governor, was a mixture of good and bad news for the colony. He was not particularly interested in the Gibraltarian population of the Rock but he was passionately interested in the Calpe Hunt, apparently founded, as we saw in an earlier Chapter, from the hounds left in Spain by the Duke of Wellington after the Peninsular War. The pack was kennelled in Spain and hunted the Spanish countryside from Gibraltar. The hunt was a joint venture with the local aristocracy and occasioned much jollity and mutual hospitality which could only have been a good thing in the circumstances. However, it had joint Spanish and English Masters which General Godley found unacceptable and he at once set about having the Spanish Master removed. Godley never really recovered from the controversy this caused on the Rock. The British members of the hunt were equally divided between those who approved his action and those who were bitterly opposed. The Governor carried on an unfortunate vendetta against those who opposed him, and they were made to feel outcasts even at the Garrison Church. A wag on the Governor's staff described the warring factions as the 'Godleys and the Ungodley'. But, as has been said, apart from the foxes and anything else they hunted in the Campomento of Gibraltar, General Godley did some useful work for the colony. He interested himself in the setting up of a regular air service between the Rock and Tangier. The race course was used as a makeshift runway and amphibious aircraft were also used.

The history of aviation on the Rock before the Second World War is surprisingly sparse, no doubt because there was no regular Royal Air Force presence there until the outbreak of war. In 1903, a Royal Engineers Balloon Section was stationed on the Rock for trials which do not appear to have been very successful since the Section left in

1905 and never returned. During the First World War, BEs (Bleriot Experimentals) were flown from the race course until one crashed just over the Spanish border, putting an end to flying on the Rock for a time. The notorious 'Levanter' wind, blowing from the east, made take-off and landing a very unpredictable business and can even cause problems for today's much more powerful aeroplanes.

In the 1920s the Governor of Gibraltar and his opposite number, the Spanish Governor of the adjacent Spanish Province, who had his head-quarters in Algeciras, worked out a plan for a joint Anglo-Spanish airfield on the Spanish side of the border. Needless to say, the object of the mutual co-operation was to avoid interference with the race course, which was an amenity much prized on both sides of the border. Unfortunately, the plan was not approved in London or Madrid, where it was considered by both countries that the diplomatic problems caused by a jointly operated venture, implying a degree of joint sover-eignty, were not worth the presence of an airfield in a comparatively peaceful period of Western Mediterranean history.

In 1931, the War Office requested General Godley to prepare plans for an airfield which could be made operational at short notice. This was treated as less than urgent and the race course was preserved for a little longer. Eventually it was the brash claim of Mussolini to Italian ownership of the whole Mediterranean, which he called after the Romans *Mare Nostrum* which overcame the inertia and ensured that there was a permanent runway at North Front just in time for the out-break of the Second World War.

Italy was not the only threat to peace in the Mediterranean in the 1930s. In 1936 the nationalist uprising and the army mutiny against the Spanish government began with the landing of troops from North Africa at Algeciras. From then on Gibraltar provided a grandstand view of the Spanish Civil War, a haven for refugees and a base for newspaper reporters and other visitors to the war. Gibraltar was soon crowded with refugees – there were never less than 2,000 on the Rock, and sometimes as many as 10,000. The air war waged against the Spanish government forces by proxy by the Italian and German air forces was usually at some distance from Gibraltar over the larger Spanish cites, which were bombed unmercifully. On the odd occasion when the action was nearer everybody turned out to get a good view. A *Daily Express* reporter noted on 4 August 1936: 'Rooftops overlooking

Gibraltar Bay were used as grandstand seats at half-a-crown each'. The battle on this occasion was between a government seaplane and the rebel forces it was trying to bomb in Algeciras. The plane was damaged and had to land at Gibraltar where the mechanic quickly disappeared whilst the pilot and other crew members were interned.

The sea war on the other hand was often visible close by in the Strait of Gibraltar, the passage of which was important to both sides. An international patrol was set up ostensibly to secure non-intervention in the war, but since the patrol often included Italian and German warships, countries which were already fighting on the Franco-Falangist side, it was obvious that the Spanish government would regard the patrol as hostile. The German battleship *Deutschland* came into harbour after being damaged and the British destroyer *Hunter* struck a mine and was towed into Gibraltar in a sinking condition. In 1938 there was a naval action to the east of the Rock between a Spanish government destroyer and a nationalist cruiser. The destroyer had been trying to force a passage into the Mediterranean but was badly damaged and had to seek asylum in Gibraltar where she was interned until after the war. At least these events emphasised the importance of Gibraltar as a base and ensured that the airfield at North Front would be operational by 1939.

Although some scenes and evidence of battle, obvious although sometimes ignored by the people of Gibraltar, were insignificant compared with the ordeal of Malta and the bombing of Britain in the war which would begin in a few years time, it provided an insight into the confusion of views and ambiguity of purpose that characterised Britain in the decade before the war. Despite the battles and the bombardments, the refugees and the many innocent victims of the Spanish Nationalist uprising, Britain and France were tortuously neutral in their stance. As late as 1939 the Franco Agency, which functioned unimpeded in Gibraltar, gave a reception to celebrate the fall of Barcelona. Guests, it was reported, sang insurgent songs, cried, 'Heil Hitler, viva Mussolini' and cheered General Franco. A crowd estimated at 3,000 gathered outside the Agency to protest, and an officer in the uniform of the Spanish *Guardia Civil*, and armed with a revolver came out and threatened the crowd, which by now had become enraged, and had to be dispersed by a baton charge of the Gibraltar police. All this on British territory. It was true that some well-to-do Gibraltarians favoured Franco and the Falange Party and liaison and social contacts continued between British army officers and their mutinous counterparts in the Nationalist forces. But this only reflected the situation in Britain until Winston Churchill was able to instil an unambiguous sense of national purpose and an awareness of the overriding threat from Fascism and dictatorship in whichever part of Europe it manifested itself.

French and British apprehensions about the growing strength of the combined power of Germany, Italy and Spain in the western Mediterranean in the event of a now inevitable Nationalist victory in the Spanish civil war were reflected in a French plan to seize Spanish Morocco and the Balearics. The French were convinced that their communications with North Africa could be compromised. In February 1939 there was a reported agreement between Britain and France to recognise Franco as ruler of Spain if he agreed to an occupation of the Balearics by Britain and France. Franco did not agree and any such deal was forgotten when the British cruiser *Devonshire* took a Franco negotiator to Minorca to arrange a bloodless takeover by the Nationalists. However, Italy did protest at the British role in the surrender negotiations which were said to have prevented an Italian takeover of Minorca. In fact, Italy did occupy Minorca for a while after the Nationalist victory, without further action from Britain or France.

The *Daily Express* had consistently advanced the theory that Spain would not join the Axis powers after a Nationalist victory, recalling a precedent in an earlier war when Russia had helped Austria to crush the Hungarian revolt of 1848. When asked what price the Austrians would have to pay for Russian help, Schwartzenberg, the Austrian Prime Minister, had said: 'We shall astonish Europe by our ingratitude'. So it was with Spain who was similarly 'ungrateful' towards Italy and Germany. By a series of procrastinations and the imposition of increasingly impossible conditions, Franco managed to keep Spain out of the war, and there was no attack on Gibraltar.

Italy's involvement in the Spanish civil war was not the only cause of complaint about her behaviour in the 1930s. The brutal and unprovoked invasion of Abyssinia in 1935 was embarked upon because of the need to divert attention from economic distress and unrest in Italy. Mussolini claimed that he had the tacit approval of France and Britain for his actions, and this may have been partly true, but his aggression broke the ties between Italy and Britain and turned the British public from indulgent, if rather patronising, friendship to bitter hatred and contempt.

At the same time, there was some well-informed apprehension about the current strength of the Italian navy and its apparent superiority over the British Mediterranean Fleet. In 1937–8 Italy had two battleships, 26 cruisers, 42 destroyers and 83 submarines. She also had a strong, shore-based air force stationed within striking distance of Malta. In addition, Italy had a naval building programme which would add four more battleships to her fleet by 1940. Britain's Mediterranean fleet consisted of an aircraft carrier, four old battleships, 12 cruisers, 15 destroyers and a flotilla of submarines. The four battleships were a considerable proportion of the British battle fleet, and replacements would take a long time to come into service. There was no adequate fighter protection over the fleet and the air defence of Malta was non-existent. The decision was taken to move the battle fleet away from Malta to Alexandria where it would be out of range of Mussolini's bombers. Again the wrong signals were being sent and were read as appeasement in Italy and Germany, and probably also by Britain's Mediterranean ally, France.

Between the wars the Italian Fascists made several attempts to infiltrate Maltese society. The democratic processes introduced by the British often foundered because of opposition from the Roman Catholic Hierarchy, and on at least one occasion because of direct intervention by the Pope. The Italian language had been taught in Maltese schools and it was the language of the professions and of commerce. But because of Fascist propaganda, bribes and subsidies the British dropped the teaching of Italian and raised the Maltese language to its proper place as the cultural and judicial language of the islands. The church in Malta, eager to emphasise its independence from Rome, recognised the importance of the local language by translating the Bible and catechism into Maltese. A new constitution was introduced in 1939 but it failed to incorporate all the changes demanded by the Maltese and once war broke out future discussion was postponed for the duration.

Cyprus, as we have said, did not play an important part in the First World War, belying the expectations of the imperialists who had advocated its acquisition in 1878. Similarly, it did not fulfil the vital rôle that might have been expected because of its strategic position in 1939–45. Even after 1941, when it was poised off the exposed southern flank of the Nazi drive into the Soviet Union, its potential remained largely unused. Turkey's neutrality in the Second World War removed some of the pressure in the eastern Mediterranean but Cyprus was still important enough to hold on to, if only to prevent some other power from taking over in an area where the growing range of military aircraft brought Britain's territories in the old Turkish dominions within striking distance.

The Turks in Cyprus remained loyal or at least quiescent in both world wars, but since they were outnumbered four to one by the Greek Cypriots, a more inveterate enemy than the British, they needed British protection. After the First World War, progress towards democracy and full economic viability was rapid but irksome for the Greek Cypriots who continually called for 'enosis' with Greece. A Council to govern local affairs was set up but in 1931 a series of riots was set off by the world economic recession. During the riots, Government House was burned down by a mob incited by the Bishop of Kyrenia, who was promptly exiled for sedition. The Council was dissolved and Cyprus reverted to Crown Colony status. The bishops were very much in favour of 'enosis' because they hoped that once union with Greece was a fact, they would regain their old powers as secular heads of Cyprus.

Despite the troubles, many new roads were built, the perennial problem of peasant debt was tackled with some success, and free elementary education was provided for anyone who wanted it. Unfortunately, the petty repressions always associated with absolute rule only increased the rising tide of Greek nationalism. But Italy's invasion of Abyssinia brought a little more realism into Greek Cypriot affairs. The Italians still held the Dodecanese Islands, which they had gained from Turkey in 1919 and which to some extent cut Cyprus off from Greece. This Italian bastion across their communications with Greece, and the Italian expansionist policy in the Mediterranean seemed to threaten Greece and Greeks everywhere. The Cypriot Greeks entered the Second World War, as they had the first, hoping for better things to emerge with the peace.

So, war came to the Mediterranean in September 1939 and, as with the earlier war, it brought some immediate relief from pressing problems, but only in the short run. The underlying problem of holding a subject population against its will, remained. Gibraltar did not want to be independent of Britain but did want self-government, and some assistance in the diversification of the economy against an eventual British withdrawal from the all-important naval dockyard. The predominantly Greek population of Cyprus continued to dream of 'enosis'. Malta was sufficiently large to envisage an independent future but a British withdrawal would leave the economy under severe strain, possibly leading to a search for some bedfellows who could turn out to be undesirable. In Egypt, the native population and the cosmopolitan aristocracy did not wish to be left to the capricious and corrupt rule of an effete family, nor to the re-emerging threat of Muslim fundamentalism, without a stern nanny supervising the household. To them, no solution other than British over-lordship was immediately apparent. For them all, the Second World War would change everything and nothing.

CHAPTER VI

The Second World War in the Mediterranean

British strategists have held the opinion, at least since the late 17th Century that 'he who holds the Mediterranean holds the world'. A gloss on that comment might be: 'He who holds Malta, holds the Mediterranean and, ergo, holds the world'. This would certainly seem to be true of the Second World War. But there were those at home who thought otherwise. Whilst France was in effective alliance with Britain the inland sea could be held without too much trouble, as had been amply demonstrated in 1914–18. In both wars the assumption was that France would have a preponderant rôle in the Mediterranean and would be particularly responsible for the central and western basins of the sea. Britain would guard the eastern basin and the waters close to her own possessions. Italy was a bonus to the allies in the Mediterranean in the first of the two wars and, with a much more powerful fleet, was neutral for a short while in the second. The Anglo-Egyptian Treaty of 1936 authorised Britain to maintain a peacetime garrison of 10,000 men and 400 planes in Egypt and these, together with the naval base at Alexandria, made up a strong force in the Eastern Mediterranean. Egypt did not declare war on Germany until February 1945 but at least the country remained inert, even when Rommel advanced close to Alexandria and the canal.

There was considerable apprehension about the capabilities of the Italian navy and perhaps some over-estimation of its fighting spirit. Italy had developed a navy particularly suited to Mediterranean conditions with fast new battleships well-armed but not designed for long cruises. The crews normally lived in barracks ashore, their quarters at sea being very cramped, and they did not favour fighting at night. The Italians were pioneers in the development of towed and piloted torpedoes (MAS), and of miniature submarines which they operated with great courage and imagination. The sea areas between Sicily and North Africa were the scene of unremitting naval operations and air battles until the Mediterranean was finally cleared late in 1944. The Italians guarded the Sicilian Straits, about 90 miles wide, by the strongly-fortified island of Pantelleria. Between Sicily and Pantelleria the water is shallow and easily mined but south of the island the 32 mile stretch to the North African coast is much deeper and could be patrolled by submarines and the light craft which Italy had developed especially for inshore waters.

Gibraltar conceived herself to be at considerable risk at the beginning of the war, and more especially when the collapse of France brought the German army to the Pyrenees. But the British naval presence was strong, the Rock was well garrisoned and, providing that the Germans did not come through Spain, all was well. Cyprus still appeared to maintain its rôle as a potential asset whose future, whilst Turkey remained neutral, was uncertain. But Malta was the key.

At the beginning of the war, the situation in the Mediterranean did not appear to be very different from that in 1914, but with the advantage to the British that Turkey, against us in the earlier war, was now neutral and the chances were that she would remain outside the conflict. All this changed with brutal suddenness with the defeat and total collapse of France at a terrifying speed in June 1940. Compared with the other immediate calamities the loss of the French fleet with its rôle in the western Mediterranean and its possible takeover by the Germans may have seemed trivial but it was important enough to warrant a reluctant attack on the French fleet at Mers-el-Kebir near Oran where two French battleships and a battle cruiser were immobilised by the British. One battle cruiser and five French destroyers escaped to Toulon where, with the remainder of the French fleet, they stayed, out of action until nearly the end of the war. A sizeable French fleet at Alexandria allowed itself to be demilitarised. Even before France had capitulated, but not before the outcome of the German invasion of France was clear, Italy had come into the war on the side of the Axis powers. Hesitation in the First World War and hesitation in the Second did not guarantee that the right choice would be made. After a few months of self-congratulation, the war at sea, even before their massive defeats on land, showed the Italians that the wrong decision had been made once again.

With the defeat of France and Italy's opportunist decision to join the Axis powers, the position of Britain in the Central Mediterranean looked bleak in the extreme. Voices were raised in Britain, but not in the Churchill government nor amongst the Service chiefs, suggesting that Britain should for the time being at least, withdraw from the central Mediterranean. Malta should be abandoned and our naval and military resources concentrated on Gibraltar and Alexandria. To have adopted such a policy would have been to admit that the war was irretrievably lost. To give up Malta would have closed all communication through the Mediterranean. The reinforcement of Alexandria and the supply of our forces in Egypt, the Canal Base, Palestine and Cyprus by the Cape route would have added to our difficulties by a factor of at least three. The nearest of the Middle East bases, Alexandria would then have been 11,608 miles from the United Kingdom, as against 3,097 miles through the Mediterranean.

The defeatist assumption was that nothing would be able to get through to Malta or the Eastern Basin of the inland sea. That convoys could get through, though sometimes at horrific cost in ships, lives and vital cargoes, was subsequently demonstrated on many occasions. The so-called 'Cape School' arose at the time of Italy's Abyssinia adventure when it was felt by some critics that the Canal could not be kept open in wartime in the face of attacks by modern bomber aircraft and the vital route to India and the Far East could only be maintained via the Cape. This 'Cape School' was really a product of the pre-war philosophy that 'the bomber will always get through', which had bedevilled and diverted much of our rearmament planning in the pre-war decade and at the same time contributed to the prevalent defeatism. That defeatism was soon discarded when strong leadership emerged and the armed forces were able to demonstrate that they were capable of hitting back at a seemingly invincible foe. De Belot in his *Struggle For the Mediterranean* says:

> By tradition they [the British] attributed the most fundamental importance to the Mediterranean. Realising from the beginning that it would

be one of the major theatres of operations of the war, they made the decision to hold Malta and without hesitation accepted the risks of sending their fleet, at times with the weakest of air support, close to the Italian coasts.

The Opening of the Battle for Malta

Until August 1940, the air defence of Malta rested on the brave but obsolescent shoulders of three Gloucester Gladiator aircraft nicknamed, Faith, Hope and Charity. They didn't survive long in aerial combat but, in that month, Hurricanes from the carrier *Argus* had been flown in to reinforce the island. At the end of August a convoy arrived with troops and materials from Gibraltar. The inspiring British attack on the Italian naval base at Taranto had to wait until Glen Martin reconnaissance planes were based at Malta and could ascertain that the Italian fleet really was at Taranto. The attack was made by aircraft from the Eastern Fleet on 11 November 1940 and, at the cost of two aircraft lost, three Italian battleships, one cruiser and one destroyer were put out of action. As a result of the victory, Admiral Cunningham was able to release the battleships *Ramillies* and *Malaya* to the Atlantic. This was the first British naval victory of the war and provided a much-needed boost to morale. By June 1940, the British ships in the Mediterranean had been divided into 'Force K', the submarines, destroyers and light cruisers based on Malta, and 'Force H' based on Gibraltar. In addition, there was the strong fleet based on Alexandria which had launched the carrier-based attack on Taranto.

On 6 January 1941 a convoy of four merchant ships, escorted by Force H, reached Malta. Here escort duties were taken over by the Eastern Fleet as the convoy proceeded on to Alexandria. On this convoy, the aircraft carrier *Illustrious* was damaged and had to be towed into Malta. It was not possible to repair the carrier in Malta since the great floating dock had been sunk by Italian bombing. However, despite air attacks whilst she was in Grand Harbour, *Illustrious* was patched up and reached Alexandria safely, but eventually had to go to the United States for the repairs to be completed. For several months, the Alexandria fleet was without a carrier and could not help Malta which was bombed incessantly through the winter of 1940–41.

By then the great land battles in North Africa had begun and the importance of Malta was emphasised by the need to get supplies through to Wavell in Egypt and to Admiral Cunningham with his fleet at Alexandria. It was also imperative to disrupt Axis supplies and reinforcements being shipped from Italy to Tripoli. The Italian army under Marshal Graziani, invaded Egypt with 200,000 men in September 1940. Wavell's army of less than 30,000 withdraw to Mersa Matruh but as their supply line lengthened and reinforcements and air cover were diverted to Mussolini's ill-timed attack on Greece, the Italian army in North Africa came to a halt. Mussolini had hoped that a successful campaign in Greece would keep the Germans out of the Mediterranean. The failure of his campaign had the opposite effect and brought about the German invasion of Greece. In the meantime, the Italian advance into Egypt was stemmed. Another effect of the Italian attempt to invade Greece was that the British occupied Crete, giving them another sea and air base from which to threaten the enemy supply routes to North Africa. Mussolini's plan for an exclusively Italian capture of the Suez Canal came to nothing.

Hitler had his own plans for the Mediterranean and tried to persuade General Franco to allow German troops to pass through Spain to attack Gibraltar so that he could close the Strait. A more grandiose plan involved the crossing of the Strait from Gibraltar and an advance from Spanish Morocco along the whole of the North African coast to Egypt and Suez. The closure of the Strait and the advance to Suez would make the retention of Malta impossible and Britain would be barred from the Mediterranean. All Hitler's plans for the Mediterranean foundered on Franco's unwillingness to allow German troops to cross the Pyrenees. The German plan to invade England had also run into difficulties and by the end of October 1940 both Operation 'Sea Lion', the invasion of England, and Operation 'Felix' against Gibraltar, had been abandoned and other projects were being examined at Hitler's headquarters.

By December, Wavell had built up a force with which General O'Connor confidently attacked the Italians on the borders of Egypt. By 9 February 1941 he had captured 130,000 prisoners and had reached El Agheila, 600 miles from his start point in Egypt. At the same time Italian East Africa was cleared, removing the threat to Aden and the Sudan. These victories gave the British a breathing space during which

Malta could be resupplied and 18 more Hurricane aircraft were flown in, bringing the total on the island to 33. But Britain's success in North Africa increased Hitler's concern with the Italian failure there and in Greece. With characteristic speed and strength of purpose, he reacted in three ways. The Luftwaffe was established in Sicily in January 1941 and, as we have seen, took up the challenge with its attack on the convoy which had reached Malta on 6 January, putting the carrier *Illustrious* out of action and sinking the cruiser *Southampton*.

Hitler's second directive brought about the German invasion of Greece. He was understandably furious that the Italians had created a situation in which the British could establish air bases in Greece from which they could bomb the Rumanian oil fields and even Italy itself. The third reaction to British pressure and Italian ineffectiveness in North Africa was to send the *Afrika Korps* under General Rommel to Cyrenaica from where they attacked Wavell's forces on 31 March.

Wavell's army had been depleted by the need to send troops to Greece to bolster our one ally now remaining on the mainland of Europe. During Wavell's and Rommel's offensives, Malta was bombed mercilessly. British fighter strength on the island was by now too weak to give much protection to the convoys still trying desperately to bring succour. The position was made worse by the Germans dropping magnetic mines in the Suez Canal. The *Afrika Korps* was now back on the Egyptian frontier from where the Italians had been driven by Wavell. Hostile air-fields established again in the Cyrenaica bulge threatened Malta and the British fleet. Cunningham took his whole fleet to sea in an act of defiance in which the battleships and planes from the carrier *Formidable* bombarded Tripoli and under this cover, a supply ship was run successfully into Malta. Five days earlier, British destroyers had annihilated an Italian convoy of five ships off the Italian coast.

No British surface ships were able to remain in Malta but the Hurricanes were replaced from time to time whenever they could be flown in and British submarines continued to use the island as a base for their attacks on Rommel's supply lines. Although the German High Command tried to encourage the Italian fleet to take offensive action, sometimes by deliberately under-estimating British strength in the Eastern Mediterranean, on the few occasions when they were in contact with the British fleet they were invariably worsted. On the night of 28-29 March 1941 the Italians lost the heavy cruisers *Fiume*, *Zara* and

Pola as well as two destroyers at the battle of Matapan. Air reconnaissance and the use of radar contributed much to the outcome of the battle but it was their determination to close with the enemy which made the victory possible for the British.

Defeat in Greece and Crete

The German lightning attack on Greece began on 6 April 1941. Such was its strength and ferocity, supported by 1,000 aircraft, that an evacuation of the British force of 58,000 men, which was woefully short of air support, soon proved to be inevitable. Fifty-one thousand men were taken off, some of them to Crete from where, in the face of an overwhelming paratroop and airborne landing by General Student's crack division, the survivors were again evacuated. Student's troops fought with great bravery and determination against an equally gallant defence, mainly by New Zealand forces. The parachute troops were so mauled in their attack that they could never be used again in any strength and the battle for Crete was finally won by seaborne reinforcements. However, there is still some argument about the final and crucial German reinforcements. General Rielkhoff, who commanded the Fourth German Airfleet, insists that the reinforcements, 5th German Alpine Division, were landed from the sea. As an airman he is unlikely to have given the credit wrongly to a seaborne landing. The losses sustained by the Royal Navy in Greek and Cretan waters were exceptionally heavy, mainly because of the intervention of German dive bombers from nearby bases on the Greek mainland. The supremacy at sea was still held by the British but in the air the Luftwaffe commanded the skies.

Whilst the battle for Greece was raging, a vital convoy, code-named 'Tiger', managed to fight its way eastwards from Gibraltar to Alexandria; 238 tanks and 43 Hurricane fighter aircraft were safely landed in Egypt. The aircraft were urgently needed in the land battle and could not be spared to influence the sea and land battles to the north. On 21 May, Malta was re-fuelled and restocked with food; 48 Hurricanes were flown off *Ark Royal* and *Furious* to land safely on the island. *Formidable*, the only carrier with Admiral Cunningham's Alexandria-based fleet, lost most of its aircraft in supporting the convoy as it moved east from Malta, many in aerial combat but, sadly also, many through flying in bad weather conditions. The carrier had to remain in Alexandria during the crucial battle for Crete and on its next sortie, still with only 12 aircraft embarked, it was struck by two bombs as it retired from an attack on the Luftwaffe airfield at Scarpanto. Cunningham was again without a carrier. The Navy, under heavy attack from the air, evacuated from Crete the 18,600 men who were able to fight their way to the beaches.

Naval losses, many of which could not be replaced until the Americans were effectively in the war, were so serious that the whole of naval strategy in the Mediterranean was once again questioned. By the end of the Crete evacuation, RAF long-distance fighters were able to play a part but they had been sorely missed earlier in the campaign. After their victories in Greece and Crete, and Rommel's successful attack in Cyrenaica, the Axis airforces were able to concentrate their attacks on Malta and on the British forces who now had their backs to the Egyptian frontier. The Royal Navy was still licking its wounds and was not ready to re-enter the battle immediately. In the Greek campaign two cruisers, *Gloucester* and *Fiji* and six destroyers had been lost and the carrier *Formidable*, the battleships *Warspite* and *Barham*, two cruisers and two destroyers put out of action for many months.

In the post-mortem following the campaign, it was suggested that there should have been an immediate follow-up to the Taranto attack, and that the seven months that had elapsed between our occupation and evacuation of Crete could have been well spent in constructing more airfields and in improving the anti-aircraft defences. Much of the criticism benefited from hindsight but the lack of an accurate intelligence assessment and imaginative forward planning must have added much to the disaster. The loss of Crete meant that the route from Malta to the east was flanked on both sides by the enemy but at last a new event in the north swung the balance of advantage decisively towards the Allies. On 22 June 1941 the Germans began 'Operation Barbarossa', their gigantic attack on the Soviet Union. This gave the British in the Mediterranean a new breathing space. A frequently unreckoned gain from the British intervention in Greece was that it had thrown Hitler's timetable for Barbarossa out of gear. It is possible that the time lost over Greece and Crete, and the virtual loss of the paratroop arm, delayed the attack long enough to prevent a decisive battle from being fought in front of Moscow before the first winter of the campaign set in. Many commentators have suggested that this early failure was the cause of the ultimate defeat of Germany in Russia.

Gibraltar and the Western Mediterranean

General Franco seized the chance to take over Tangier in 1940 when France was defeated and Britain desperately engaged further east in the Mediterranean, but he made no attempt against Gibraltar or Allied interests in the Strait. The French battle cruiser *Dunkerque* was bombed for a second time in the Mers-el-Kebir base towards the end of 1940 and a few French planes bombed Gibraltar in a rather desultory fashion by way of retaliation. It is said that the French would have mounted further bombing attacks on the Rock but they desisted when Winston Churchill threatened to bomb Paris, despite its having been declared an open city after the fall of France. Italian aircraft also attacked the Rock on several occasions without causing significant damage. After the evacuation from Dunkirk it had been decided to withdraw most of the civil population on the Rock who were not in essential jobs. About 4,000 Gibraltarians remained behind whilst the remainder were dispersed in Britain and Northern Ireland and as far away as Jamaica and Canada. Ironically those who went to the British Isles were probably exposed to more danger than those remaining on the Rock.

A far more potent threat to Gibraltar and the shipping using the port than French or Italian bombs lay in the midget submarine and manned torpedo attacks which were launched from Algeciras across the bay. The Italians had established a base for their underwater swimmers and torpedo weapons, with the connivance of the Spanish authorities, in a hulk which looked directly across the bay towards their target, the Allied shipping in Gibraltar harbour and at anchor in the roads just outside. The Italian attacks were pressed home with great bravery. Although the early ones all failed, with a high loss of life among the one- and two-man crews, later attacks on shipping in the roads caused some sinkings and damage. The attacks were finally abandoned after a midget submarine attack in which all the craft were lost and five of the six crew men were drowned. The underwater raiders did, however, achieve conspicuous successes in other parts of the Mediterranean.

The British, and later the Americans, maintained constant patrols in the Bay of Gibraltar and also in the Strait where the enemy was not of the miniature variety but ocean-going submarines from their bases on the coast of Brittany, trying as in the previous war to slip through into the Mediterranean. It was relatively easy to get into the Mediterranean because of the depth of water and the strong current flowing through the Strait from the Atlantic end. Submarines were now more powerful and were able to remain submerged for longer than was possible in the First World War. In some cases they could outrun their pursuers. Five submarines were destroyed in the Strait before the end of 1941 but many did get through. As in the earlier war, submarines were brought overland from Germany to the Mediterranean and assembled in Marseilles and other ports.

In Hitler's 'Plan Felix', for the capture of Gibraltar through Spain, Portuguese neutrality was not to be respected and the Portuguese islands of Cape Verde, Madeira and the Azores were to be seized at the outset. At the beginning of 1941 Hitler wrote to Mussolini, 'all our preparations for entering Spain on 10 January and attacking Gibraltar at the beginning of February are complete'. But he still complained of lack of co-operation from Franco. Although the attack on Gibraltar was never put into operation, it was never finally abandoned, merely postponed and kept available for the right moment, until almost the end of the war. Even after the Allied landings in North Africa Mussolini was still urging Hitler to attack the Rock. Kesselring, in command of the German airforce in the Mediterranean, urged that only the bombing of Gibraltar and the North African embarkation ports could prevent the invasion of southern Europe. Hitler replied that he could not spare the shock troops, and he was afraid Spanish guerrillas would attack the Germans if they entered Spain without invitation. He thought that Spaniards were 'the only Latin fighting people'. Admiral Doenitz suggested the use of radio-guided bombs and that more submarines should be sent down the river Rhône. But there was no time left and nothing was accomplished by the time of the Allied invasion of Sicily in July 1943.

Gibraltar became the headquarters and main base for the invasion of North Africa. Many of the attacking troops sailed directly from the

United States or Britain but were controlled and supported from the Rock. The airstrip at its northern end finally came into its own. After the invasion, it was used by the Americans as a staging post from Britain, first to North Africa and later to Sicily and the Italian mainland. Flying from the Rock was always difficult but there have been surprisingly few accidents to aircraft flying in and out. Unfortunately, one of the few serious accidents involved General Sikorski, commander of the free Polish Forces whose Liberator aircraft crashed into the sea on take-off. The death of Sikorski came at a time of political tension between him and the Soviet Union and this, together with a series of minor mishaps in Gibraltar, which might have been caused by sabotage, lent an air of mystery to the event which even now has not been entirely dispelled.

As late as August 1943, only a month before the armistice with Italy, another attempt was made by the Axis on shipping anchored in Gibraltar Bay. The *Olterra*, an Italian ship which had taken refuge in Algeciras when Italy declared war on the Allies, was used again. Piloted torpedoes sank three more ships in the roads. Italy lost 116 conventional submarines in the Mediterranean but there were no great sea battles like those in the Pacific. Some 20 convoys sailed from Gibraltar to Malta and Alexandria but the Italian main battle fleet never got close to them. The battleship *Barham* and the carriers *Eagle* and *Ark Royal* were sunk by submarines but there was no great fleet action. This was not for lack of courage on the part of the Italian seamen but a lack of leadership at the top. There was also a policy of keeping the Italian fleet intact and near the mainland for fear of attack and this inhibited aggressive tactics. Even so, as we have seen, there were many small boat and underwater attacks on British ships and bases.

Malta Under Siege

At the other end of the Mediterranean, Italian underwater swimmers managed to get into Alexandria harbour on 19 December 1941, attaching explosives to the hulls of the battleships *Queen Elizabeth* and *Valiant*. Although the swimmers were captured and brought on-board the battleships, they refused to reveal the whereabouts of the explosive charges which, when they subsequently blew up, put both capital ships out of action for the rest of the war. The balance of naval power in the Mediterranean was dramatically changed in favour of the Axis. By now the Russian counter-offensive in front of Moscow had halted the German drive to the east but Japan was now in the war.

Britain still held Gibraltar, Alexandria and gallant, battling Malta but the Axis, for the moment, had air and sea supremacy in the central Mediterranean. General Auchinleck launched a land offensive in December 1941. Successful at first, his army was counter-attacked by Rommel and forced back. Tobruk, which had been under siege for so long, fell to the Germans in June 1942. Britain's fortunes in the Mediterranean were now at their lowest ebb. The seriousness of the situation in Malta was evident in Britain as well as in the islands. Malta's loss would have meant the end of any immediate hope for another counter-offensive against Rommel's forces. Spitfire fighters were flown off carriers to the island but on at least one occasion they were destroyed on the ground before they could be refuelled and sent into action.

The civil population of Malta, unlike that of Gibraltar, could not be evacuated from the islands even if they were prepared to go, which the majority were not. There were many good rock shelters available on the Maltese islands and these saved many lives in the continuous bombardment that went on through 1941 and most of 1942. But as the raids went on and rations and fuel were reduced to the minimum necessary to sustain the fight, new measures to boost and maintain morale were instituted. The Maltese people were strengthened by their deep religious beliefs. On one occasion an enormous bomb penetrated the dome of the church at Mosta where a large congregation was praying. Mercifully, the bomb did not explode and this was attributed to Divine intervention. The church at Mosta has the fourth largest free-standing dome in Europe and is now, with the marks of the bomb's penetration still visible, a great attraction to visitors. The bomb, weighing 2,000 kilos, was defused on 10 April 1942 by 128 Bomb Disposal Section, Royal Engineers, and is now displayed, polished and icon-like but still with an air of menace, in the vestry of the church.

Another morale-raising event at this dangerous and exhausting time was the award of the George Cross to the island on 15 April 1942. This made a deep impression on the people of Malta and the Cross was at once incorporated in the arms of Malta. It remains there today and provides a proud reminder of an heroic time, despite the break with Britain and the flirtation with Libya. In its intensity, the danger shared by all and the triumphal outcome the siege of 1941–43 stand alongside the Great Siege of 1565 as a record of the devotion and bravery of the Maltese people.

The morale of the people of Malta and the servicemen on the islands was further raised with the arrival of Lord Gort VC as Governor on 7 May. He took over from Sir William Dobbie who, though his personal courage and patriotism were not in doubt, seemed to have difficulty in communicating his resolve and intentions to the people. Lord Gort, from the time of his arrival, made it his business to speak to and, more important, to listen to the Maltese.

He arrived with the turning of the tide in Malta. A vital merchantman, *Welshman*, (and they were all vital by now) got in with munitions on 10 May and was unloaded under cover of a smoke screen which completely blotted out the harbour area from attacking bombers. By now Spitfires had arrived in some strength and were beginning to take a serious toll of the attackers. They also took some weight off the antiaircraft batteries, which were manned partly by the Royal Malta Regiment and partly by British gunners, and which had been fighting back fiercely for months against what seemed to be overwhelming odds. The air battles over Malta in May were the most hard-fought of the war but at last the British had air superiority over the islands. Towards the end of the battle, 63 Axis aircraft were destroyed in one day and during the last few days before the assault was called off, 112 planes were brought down for a loss of only three Spitfires. In the last five weeks of the assault, the Axis air forces flew 11,500 sorties against Malta, and although Kesselring reported that the British naval and air bases had been eliminated, in reality he was trying to justify the removal of the Luftwaffe squadrons to the Russian front.

Malta had taken a frightful pounding from the bombers but she had survived, and the island was still very much in business with raids on Messina, Palermo, Augusta and Catania by a new force of Wellington aircraft now Malta-based. The islands hung on desperately during the summer of 1942. Kesselring had planned to invade Malta on 10 July but adverse reports on the possibility of a successful attack and the need to divert part of his air forces to support Rommel in his second attack at El Alamein forced yet another postponement of the attack on Malta.

The plan was never renewed and the Luftwaffe was withdrawn.

On 23 October, having held Rommel's attack at El Alamein, the 8th Army under Montgomery attacked in their turn, broke through the enemy lines and started the great pursuit which ended only when the whole of North Africa had been cleared of Axis forces. On 8 November Allied forces landed at Casablanca, Oran and Algiers and so, by the end of the battles in Tunisia, what remained of the Axis troops had been caught in a gigantic scissors movement and over 200,000 prisoners had been taken. By May 1943 the Allies were in complete command of North Africa and only two months later, on 10 July, British and American troops stormed ashore to capture Sicily.

The war did not stop for Malta once North Africa had been cleared of Axis forces any more than when pressure on the islands had been removed when the bombing eased. It was still necessary to fight hard to get convoys through from the west and the story of the Santa Maria convoy is a classic of its kind. The Santa Maria convoy, so named because it arrived at Malta on 15 August 1942, Feast Day of Santa Maria, left Britain and passed Gibraltar on 10 August. The Italians already knew of its existence and its departure date. The convoy was one of the largest to leave Britain and when it picked up its new escort at Gibraltar, the stage was set for one of the biggest battles in the Mediterranean. As it was leaving the Strait of Gibraltar, the convoy was seen by a Spanish passenger plane flying to North Africa, which promptly reported its sighting to Italian representatives in Spain. The next morning, the convoy received its first attack by Junkers 88's. Thirty-eight Spitfires were flown-off for Malta when the convoy was just south of the Balearics and all but one landed safely. But during the flying-off the carrier *Eagle* was sunk by submarine attack.

From then on the air attacks were continuous and pushed with great determination. The Axis air forces were well aware of the coming battle at El Alamein and were prepared to go to almost any lengths to prevent the succour of Malta and the building-up of Montgomery's army. By 12 August the convoy was in great disarray with many ships sunk. The surviving ships dispersed and two badly damaged vessels lagged a long way behind the other ships making their individual way towards Malta. To the joy and relief of Malta, four ships straggled in late on 12 August but the most precious cargo for the defenders of the islands had not arrived; The tanker *Ohio*, carrying aviation spirit, was limping along far behind the four surviving ships. The *Ohio* had been hit twice by bombs and a blazing Stuka dive bomber was deliberately crashed on to the tanker by her Italian crew. The *Dorset*, the other badly damaged ship was sunk and the *Ohio*, with decks awash, was held suspended on cables between two destroyers which finally managed to drag her into Grand Harbour. Again, many devout Maltese were prepared to put the saving of the *Ohio* down to Divine intervention but others, including the intrepid submarine commander Alastair Mars himself, put it down to a willingness to disobey orders in the best tradition of the Royal Navy and also an instinct for being in the right place at the right time.

What had happened was that the five submarines which had returned to be based on Malta when the bombing had eased, had been sent out to provide a screen to prevent Italian warships from attacking the convoy as it approached. Lieutenant Commander Mars in the submarine *Unbroken*, rather like Wellington's cavalry officers in the Peninsula, who regarded every order as a basis for discussion, did not agree with the station he had been given, and after arriving there and being attacked by depth charges which drove him 15 miles off his allotted station, he decided to go to the Lipari Islands. A powerful Italian squadron was waiting there for orders to attack the convoy. When the Italians received the order to finish off the stragglers from the convoy Mars was able to attack them, torpedoing two cruisers; whereupon the remaining cruisers and destroyers spent valuable time depth-charging around *Unbroken's* position, and finally giving up the hunt completely. So *Ohio* got in to port, perhaps with Divine intervention but if so, surely Alastair Mars was its chosen instrument.

Malta, like Gibraltar and Alexandria, had its share, of unconventional attacks and raids. Its proximity to Sicily and the southern Italian ports made the island the obvious target for the enemy's E-boats, human torpedoes and torpedo launchers. The first of these attacks took place on 26 July 1941 and was targeted on a newly-arrived convoy. The attack, comprising all types of small assault craft, was a complete failure, apart from the destruction of one span of the viaduct leading to the harbour defence boom. This only succeeded in more effectively blocking the entrance to the harbour and no damage was done to installations or shipping. Of the attacking force, only the Italian tender *Diana*, which had been kept well away from the coast, was able to get back to its base in Sicily. All the rest, including 14 boats and two human torpedoes, were destroyed. Fifteen Italians were killed and 18 taken prisoner.

There were several more raids on Grand Harbour and other installations round the coastline, none of them particularly successful although they demonstrated the great bravery and determination of the crews who could have had very little hope of returning from their raids. An interesting sidelight on the raids and on the loyalty of the Maltese people is given by a remark of Commander Moccagatta who was in command of the Italian raids. He said that the Italians had to rely on reconnaissance by swimmers and small-boat parties because they did not have a single spy in Malta. Moccagatta was later killed in a raid on Grand Harbour.

The battle at sea and in the air went on until almost the end of 1942. Small raids continued but the battles of October were Kesselring's last fling. The last week of blitz in October 1942 saw 1,400 enemy sorties during which the enemy lost 114 planes and at least 200 almost irreplaceable aircrew. In the same week the British lost 25 Spitfires, 14 of whose pilots were saved. Montgomery's offensive opened on 23 October and brought what seemed to be peace after the previous two years of holocaust.

For the Allied attack on Sicily, 8th Army headquarters was moved forward from Cairo to Malta and much of the heavy allied bombing of Italy and support of the landings was conducted from there. In September 1943, following the Italian armistice, 65 Italian warships sailed into Maltese waters to surrender; they could not bring back the thousands of civilians and military, Maltese and British, who had died defending the islands, but there could be no doubt left about the completeness of the victory. The German invasion of Russia in June 1941 had removed so many strategic options from the military plans of the Axis powers that it is almost true to say that the battle for the Mediterranean was won in Russia. The slackening of pressure on Malta when the island was at its last gasp was only one of the fortuitous bonuses that it was necessary to accept. There were many others. Cyprus could have been occupied, probably at little cost to the enemy, and a force pushed into Syria and beyond, bypassing Turkey and securing the southern flank. Even Gibraltar, at the western end of the inland sea, was spared invasion because Franco insisted on good news from

Russia before he would open Spain to German troops. Furthermore, as Hitler said, he could not spare the shock troops from the Russian front.

Cyprus had a comparatively quiet war. After the German attack on Greece, Cypriots joined the British and some local forces served and were taken prisoner on Crete. When the situation looked serious for Cyprus, an Indian division was stationed on the island but it was not needed. Egypt, apart from some brief moments of panic when Rommel and his army were poised to push into the Nile Delta and seize the Canal, kept remarkably cool. Cairo and Alexandria presented an extra-ordinary picture even at the height of the Desert War. Helen Long, in her book, *Change Into Uniform*, published in 1978, gives a picture of the 'flesh-pots' that anyone who was lucky enough to escape to them will recognise:

> Alexandria was attractively cosmopolitan, sophisticated and full of restaurants, bars and night clubs. Allied uniforms were to be seen every-where, it was the thing to be tanned, bleached, sandy and randy! In Cairo we sat on the balcony at Shepheard's sipping cocktails, gin slings and freshly crushed lime drinks and swatting flies. At night the sky was ablaze with stars and the lights of Cairo.

General Alexander soon put a stop to all that. Like Allenby before him, when he arrived he moved his headquarters to a site in the desert. His comment on the 'high jinks' in Cairo was:

> There were too many opportunities for the 8th Army to surrender to the curiously seductive charms of Lili Marlene. It was all too much divorced from the battlefield.

What the austere General Montgomery made of it all is not recorded. But what is known is that when the opportunities presented them-selves, the desk-bound staff officers, those at least that survived Montgomery's 'new broom', did what was asked of them with exper-tise and efficiency. The girls sitting on the balcony at Shepheard's changed out of their 'little white dresses' and into more workmanlike uniform to cope with the many thousands of casualties from the battle of El Alamein. Compared to what was happening to the garrison and civilians of Malta at the height of their blitz, or to the daily life of the front-line soldier in the desert, the goings on in Cairo must have seemed unbelievable, but there can be no doubt that many of the 'base wallahs' in the rear areas would have given much to be able to say 'I fought at Alamein'.

Italy Changes Sides – the Partisan War in Greece and Yugoslavia

It took the Allies less than six months to clear the Axis forces out of North Africa but it took them almost another two years to clear the northern shores of the Mediterranean. American and British armies invaded Sicily in July 1943 and after consolidating their hold on the island they moved quickly across the Straits of Messina into mainland Italy. By September, assault landings at Salerno, fiercely resisted by crack German units like the Hermann Goering Division, secured the whole of southern Italy and brought about the collapse of all the Italian forces and an armistice with Italy. It was still only September and the Italian surrender raised false hopes of an early end to the war in Europe. Winter now intervened and, despite another leapfrog landing further up the coast towards Rome at Anzio in January 1944, Rome was not liberated until June. There was still almost a year to go before the war would be over.

Meanwhile, across the Adriatic in the Balkan countries, the Russians had begun to advance around the right flank of the retreating German armies. Already, with the defeat of Italy and a partial change of sides by the Italian armed forces, there had been a battle in September 1943 on the Greek island of Corfu between the German army, which wanted to secure the island because of its strategic position, and the Italians who, although defeated, may have had ambitions to retain the island for Italy after the war. The Germans took over the island but only after heavy fighting during which Corfu town was badly damaged.

But elsewhere in the Balkans the German army fell back and evacuated Greece in August 1944, apart from some of the islands where a bitter war continued between the Germans and local partisans supported by British commandos. In both Greece and Yugoslavia partisans had been fighting a particularly brutal war of terrorist attacks, hostage-taking and bloody reprisals for over three years. Towards the end of the war, Britain had maintained contact with the partisans in both countries and was able to provide food and other much-needed stores. Through these contacts Britain was able to provide some slight counterweight to the Soviets, whose clear ambition was to make the Balkans into a Communist satellite of the Soviet Union.

Yugoslavia, which during the war was overrun by the German forces in their move south into Greece, produced two partisan groups. One group under Mihailovitch harried the Germans but seemed to be half-hearted in its actions and was intimidated by German reprisals. The second group emerged after the German attack on Russia and was led by a Croat Communist, Josif Broz, who adopted the *nom de guerre* Tito. The effectiveness of both groups was reduced by quarrelling and their frequent clashes. Eventually Britain, led forcefully by Winston Churchill, swung all her support behind Tito. At the end of the war, despite the strong Communist sympathies of his government, and perhaps because he knew he could rely on his British friends, Tito did not follow the other Balkan states into the Soviet fold. He managed to maintain a precarious independence, austere and undoubtedly Communist but neutral in the Cold War which was now developing.

In Greece there was a different situation. In October 1944, when the Germans withdrew from the Greek islands, the British occupied Patras, Corfu and the Piraeus. With overwhelming Allied air power over Italy and complete dominance at sea, only the extrem inland ends of the Adriatic and Aegean seas could be used by the Germans. Even in these restricted areas, they were subjected to the raids and supporting missions of the Allied forces. It had been agreed with the Soviets that Greece should be left to the supervision of the occupying British. With these forces in place, Greece did not follow the Balkan states into the Soviet orbit, despite the existence of a large pro-Soviet Communist party. It is possible that if the Communists had waited for even a short while, they would have come to power by the quasi-legitimate means employed elsewhere. In Poland and Czechoslovakia, governments previously in exile and supported by the Allies, were rejected after populist style pro-Russian pseudo-elections.

In Greece, the Communist party mounted their coup but without sufficient popular support and in the vital absence of an intimidating

Russian presence. The British Army fought a short war against the Communists in Greece whilst the Greek army was being reorganised and trained so that it could take on its own defence. The ensuing civil war, with both sides being supported by a major Allied power, dragged on for several years. The Communists were well armed and fought in the northern Greek mountains where it was always possible for defeated elements to slip over the border into Albania or Yugoslavia where they could rest and re-equip.

The war might have continued indefinitely if Russia and Yugoslavia had remained friends. But when the quarrel between Stalin and Tito, now President of Yugoslavia, deepened into the threat of a Russian attack, Tito looked round for support. The price of Western support against Russia was the abandonment of the Communist insurgent army in Greece. The cutting-off of Yugoslav aid and the loss of the refuge across the northern frontier spelled the end for the Greek Communists, some of whom made their peace with the regime in Athens whilst the majority went into exile behind what was already known as the Iron Curtain. Because of the bitter civil war and the prominent part played in it by an extremely conservative officer corps, Greek politics has since been subject to right-wing pressures and the threat of military take-over. This legacy has had a baleful influence on Greek relations with their neighbours, not least in Cyprus.

The war in Europe ended in May 1945 and peace of a kind descended for a while on an exhausted and war-weary Mediterranean. The British still held firmly to their prewar possessions, in some cases, because of the strong moral position they had maintained during the war (with one or two regrettable exceptions), with an enhanced position. This encouraged some subject peoples to expect more than the British were prepared to give. In Gibraltar, Britain appeared to be once again in an unassailable position, but in the middle and eastern Mediterranean the situation was much less happy. The quest for Maltese self-government had developed into a demand for complete independence and it could only be a matter of time before this was achieved.

Egypt, which had been more or less independent since 1922, could at last look forward to the reality of an Egypt without an overseeing power. New elements in the Egyptian equation were the rise of the Arab League, a growing Russian interest in the Near and Middle East and the growth of Arab nationalism fanned by the beginnings of Muslim fundamentalism, with its undercover terrorist organisation, the Muslim Brotherhood. Problems were also re-emerging in Iran where a pro-German political group had had to be removed during the war, but had returned with a heightened dislike of the British and their control of Iranian oil. The Mandate in Iraq had been given up in 1932, although two large British air bases were maintained there. During the war it had been necessary to counteract German penetration in Iran and Iraq as well as to safeguard the overland supply route to the Soviet Union from the Arabian Gulf. Even with the enhanced British presence in the Middle East, Iraq was the only Arab country to join the pro-Western Baghdad Pact and even she did not remain a member for long.

The Cold War affected the Mediterranean countries and the Near East as much as central and eastern Europe. In some ways, perhaps because of the absence of the Iron Curtain, the intrigue and conflict between Soviet and Western interests in the countries at the eastern end of the Mediterranean were more overt, and presented a higher profile than the infinitely more dangerous game of nuclear confrontation going on in central Europe. To the new super-weapons now available to the major powers was added the more pragmatic and more easily-concealed weapon of terrorism. Terrorism had become the super-weapon of the people and quickly transformed the politics of most Arab countries.

Transjordan became the Kingdom of Jordan in March 1946, retaining its Hashemite ruling family and its army, the Arab Legion, still with a British commander. The old mandated territory of Palestine survived the war under British control but its problems were steadily growing. Even if the Hashemite rulers of the Arab states had been prepared to accept an influx of Jews into Palestine, many of their subjects and the Arabs in Palestine itself were ready to take up arms to prevent the emergence of a Jewish state. From 1921 onwards, there had been anti-Jewish riots and occasionally, as in 1929, there were bloody massacres, providing a portent of the horrors to come in Germany and Eastern Europe. From 1936 to 1939, there was a full-scale Arab revolt against Jewish immigration and against the idea of a Jewish state carved out of Arab lands. The Arabs' resistance led to confusion and vacillation in the British government which left them with enemies in both camps and a basic mistrust of Britain amongst both Arabs and Jews. British policy, even where it was understood in Palestine, was not acceptable to either party and the stage was already set for the abrupt relinquishment of the mandate, the partition of Palestine and the series of bitter wars that followed.

CHAPTER VII

The Birth of the State of Israel and the Suez Invasion of 1956

In terms of international boundaries, there was a remarkable reversion to the *status quo ante* around the Mediterranean after the Second World War. Whereas in the areas of eastern Europe conquered briefly by Nazi Germany there was a frantic redrawing of the map between the Soviet Union with its satellites, and the Western Powers, particularly with regard to the boundaries of Poland; the swallowing up of the Baltic Republics by the Soviets was formalised and accepted by the West. There were minor changes in the frontiers of some of the Balkan states and there were problems over the future of Trieste. But by and large, if only temporarily, the boundaries of all the states bordering the Mediterranean remained as they had been in 1939. The North African territories of France and Spain remained unchanged at their prewar frontiers. The British and French Mandates and Protectorates remained as they had been when first taken up after the First World War. Turkey and Greece, whilst continuing to snarl at each other across their frontiers, were not prepared to go to extremes to change them.

Immediately after the war in most European countries there was a thankfulness to have survived, a need to draw breath before the new situation could be weighed up and a new course of action embarked upon. What was clear was that the establishment of the United Nations, with its strong mandate to work for the removal of colonialism, its propagation of the principle of self-determination for subject peoples, and nationalism as a guiding and self-justifying reason for revolution, would lead to a diminution of control by the Western powers. This applied to the democracies but hardly seemed to affect the countries to the east of the Iron Curtain who were now under a different and more ruthless yoke. Above all, the subject peoples in the old colonies and mandates could see in the establishment of the Iron Curtain and the political manoeuvring by both sides in the Cold War the possibility of playing off the new non-colonial superpower against their old European guardians and protectors. The new powers may have been non-colonial in the old sense but their concern with subject peoples was just as self-interested and exploitative as that of the old colonial powers. The Cold War between the Communist states and the Free World presented an opportunity for Third World Countries to accept favours from both sides and often to set up an auction in which the winner would be allowed to provide aid of various kinds without any obligation by the recipient to repay, except by way of lip-service to the donor's political ideology.

Despite the Cold War and the sealing off of whole sections of the globe to travellers and tourism, the demand from affluent and pleasure-loving members of Western society quickly brought about the return of holidaying abroad. During the Second World War, as in the First, tourism had completely ceased over the whole of Europe and the Mediterranean. But by the middle of the 20th Century leisure travel had again become an important industry in Europe and the Mediterranean where accommodation and travel facilities were increasing and improving rapidly. While there was limited suitable accommodation available for tourists in the run-down hotels and *pensions* of postwar Europe, camping in tents was an acceptable and cheap alternative for hundreds of thousands of ex-servicemen, their girl-friends and families, all released at last from the fears, restrictions and discipline of wartime. Tourism was too profitable not to be revived at the first opportunity. Ostend and the French Channel ports and then Paris and Brussels were soon crowded holiday resorts again and the Mediterranean area followed quickly. The experienced prewar holidaymaker could return to his favourite resort on the Riviera, and a new class of traveller took to voyaging abroad with a determination and appetite which the austerity years had rendered more desperate. It remained only for the package holiday trade to provide a combination of cheap air transport, accommodation and food, tailored to the as yet unsophisticated tastes of the mass British holidaymaker, for the steady flow to turn to an unstoppable and rather frightening flood. In Gibraltar, at the time, there was an apocryphal saying that General Franco could recover the Rock overnight merely by threatening to ban all British holidays in Spain unless it was returned.

The Spanish coast and the Balearic Islands were probably first discovered as a cheap holiday destination by the British, and for them they may still be the most popular areas in the Mediterranean. From the period immediately after the Second World War, army officers and colonial servants from Gibraltar, who looked forward to a cheap retirement in a warm climate and, in the days of Franco, reassuringly near a safe haven across the nearby frontier, bought houses and villas in Spain. Their numbers were modest and their houses were discreet and hidden away in the hills and cork woods between Algeciras and Tarifa. Soon all this changed. The 'Moorish Style Village' developments, ubiquitous along the Spanish coast and most other beach areas throughout the Mediterranean, have taken over. The coastal road, almost from Gibraltar to Valencia runs through a concrete jungle of apartments, clubs, pubs, souvenir and junk shops and fast food outlets which could be found in any popular holiday resort on the British coast. Even this unattractive vista may well represent the top end of the popular holiday market abroad, and the genie has only recently escaped from the bottle!

The problems arising from popular tourism were confined in the early days after the war to the western half of the Mediterranean. In the eastern half, the trivial concerns of the holiday-making Briton, if they surfaced at all, were quickly lost sight of in a series of upheavals, disturbances and minor wars which occupied the British and their much reduced forces during the two decades after the end of the war with Germany. These disturbances and wars were overlaid throughout the whole period by the Cold War with Russia and its client states and also by the emergence of terrorism and hostage-taking by dissident groups, usually but not always Arabs, as a means of enforcing the will of a minority upon a more powerfully armed group.

Terrorism was not a new phenomenon and hostage-taking had been indulged in by Britain and France in their colonial adventures, and by Germany in Europe in the Second World War in its attempt to crush resistance to the occupying Nazi forces. The emergence of the Cold

War meant that it was impossible for countries losing hostages to underground groups, or sustaining terrorist acts, to take strong action against the sheltering and protecting states for fear of starting a large-scale conflagration. In addition, in the Middle East especially, it was never a single cause like the West's need for oil or the re-emergence of Muslim fundamentalism or anti-colonialism or anti-zionism that brought about the frictions but a 'stew' of all these elements which frequently boiled over into violence and atrocity.

The End of the Palestine Mandate and the Founding of Israel

It is a habit of politicians trying to redraw the world's political boundaries to promise more than they can really deliver. The promises can be contradictory, or the same 'prize' can be awarded to two different contestants without either being told that there had been an appeal and a revision of the placings. This is what happened in much of the old Ottoman Empire and to the Jewish and Arab interests in Palestine. The Balfour Declaration of 1917 purported to further the establishment of a Jewish National Home within the bounds of Palestine, but promises had been made to the Sharif of Mecca in 1915 about the disposal of the Turkish Empire which were not compatible with the 1917 declaration. In 1920 there were approximately 83,000 Jews living in Palestine compared with about 700,000 Arabs. But the Jewish immigration continued between the wars, encouraged by the Balfour 'promise' and supported and organised by Zionist agencies around the world, particularly in the United States. By the outbreak of the Second World War there were probably at least 450,000 Jews in Palestine plus many illegal immigrants who had evaded the quota restrictions. By 1936, the Jews were talking about a Jewish state and this, with the increasing number of Jews continuing to arrive in the Mandate, brought about the Arab Revolt.

Typically, a British government in difficulties appoints a Royal Commission. In 1937 the Peel Commission produced a report which recommended the partition of Palestine into an independent Jewish state in the north and an Arab state in the south of the country with a buffer state between them which would include Jerusalem, Jaffa and Tel Aviv, presumably still to be controlled by the British. The Zionists would not accept the plan, especially since it meant giving up their claim to Jerusalem. The British government abandoned the Peel plan, and with war against Germany now seeming inevitable, returned to the classic policy of muddling through.

The end of the war brought added problems for Britain. The Holocaust had caused an immense wave of sympathy for the survivors and now a larger, better organised and well-armed Jewish element in the Mandate made no bones about its determination to have an independent state. Terrorism had become endemic in Palestine and both Arabs and Jews directed their frustrations against the occupying British. After a particularly horrifying series of outrages against the British army and no sign of compromise from either side, Britain had had enough. To the hurt surprise of the United Nations in February 1947, Britain declared that she was surrendering the Palestine mandate in May of the next year. The United Nations appointed a Commission under the leadership of Count Folke Bernadotte. The United Nations plan was again for partition but this time, so much had circumstances and sympathies changed, offering the Jews almost two-thirds of Palestine as against the one third offered by the earlier Peel Commission. The Jews reluctantly accepted the partition proposals on the assumption that any state was better than no state. The Arabs did not accept the proposals and both sides prepared for all-out war. The Jews had the advantage of being able to switch their defensive effort from one threat to another as the situation developed. They also had the gruesome advantage of believing that they would be subject to a second holocaust if they were defeated, and they were strengthened in that belief by lurid Arab propaganda.

Another advantage for the Jews was that a large number of them had fought in the British forces against Nazi Germany, and had used modern equipment and understood modern training and logistical methods. The opponents of the Jews were not just the Arabs of Palestine but effectively the forces of all the Arab States. But despite their effectiveness on paper the only thing they had in common was a hatred of the Jews and a determination to crush any Jewish state in Palestine. At the moment of the laying down of the mandate by Britain, the Jews proclaimed the new state of Israel. At dawn on the next day, regular troops from Egypt, Transjordan, Iraq and Syria began to move into Palestine.

The Arab League could not bring together an efficient fighting alliance. Rivalries between members of the League and intrigue and jealousy made a concentrated effort difficult and a co-ordinated strategy impossible. The Arab Legion of Transjordan fought valiantly; well-armed and officered in part by seconded Britons, it occupied and managed to hang on in Jerusalem, but with a total strength of only 10,000 men it could not change the overall situation. After their initial advances, the invading Arab armies were thrown out of Israeli territory by the Israeli citizens' army which fought with a courage and determination which surprised the world. The Israelis made some strategic gains in the course of the short war and, when an armistice was arranged, they had occupied more territory than the United Nations plan called for and were determined not to give it up.

In the series of wars that have followed, the Israelis have fought with equal courage and dedication and the frustrated Arabs and Egyptians have not been able to reverse the situation. Few Arab States have ever accepted the existence of the state of Israel and its continued survival has provided a cause or at least an excuse, for the bitterness and intransigence occasionally escalating into outright war that has plagued the area for more than 40 years. The state of belligerence between Israel and her neighbours has poisoned relations between Britain and its former Arab friends and has led to the replacement of war by terrorism as the 'other means' by which politics are conducted in the Middle East.

For Britain, one of the most important casualties of the Arab/Israeli war was its relations with Egypt. Although Britain found it difficult to treat Egypt as anything but a subject state and British soldiers and colonial servants were often contemptuous and openly rude to its nationals, as indeed some of them had been in India, both nations found it advantageous to work together if only on the commercial level. The alleged betrayal of the Arabs over the establishment of the Jewish state ended this uneasy arrangement and from 1947 onwards relations became increasingly strained. The importance of the Suez Canal had not diminished since the end of the Second World War and Britain believed she had an immense stake in guarding it and preserving her defensive bases in Egypt. For her part, Egypt regarded the control of the Canal as her prerogative, and with the continued existence of Israel, wished to see the removal of all British influence from the area.

The Rise of Nasser and the Flight From Egypt

In 1936, Farouk, following his father Fuad, became King of Egypt and Anthony Eden, the then British Foreign Secretary negotiated a new Anglo-Egyptian Treaty with Mustafa Nahas Pasha, the Egyptian Prime Minister, who had been continually in and out of power from 1927 onwards. As leader of the nationalist Wafd party, which always gained a majority at the elections, he had some claim to be Prime Minister in perpetuity but he was an uncomfortable man to have in power. Whenever King Fuad, and later Farouk, felt strong enough Nahas was dismissed, only to be recalled at some moment of crisis. Being a nationalist, Nahas was not popular with the British but he was accepted as the legitimate leader of the Egyptian people and he was the only Egyptian politician who was in a position to negotiate the Treaty in 1936.

As far as Britain was concerned, the treaty was for public consumption but not for expert analysis. It started, as one would expect, with the statement: 'The military occupation of Egypt by the forces of His Majesty the King and Emperor is terminated'. But it then went on to say that considering the importance of the Suez Canal, and despite its being an integral part of Egypt, the British army would guard it from bases on Egyptian soil until such a time as the Egyptian army was sufficiently strong and well-organised to take over the defence of the Canal on its own. The British would presumably be the judges of when the Egyptians were ready to take over. The position of Egypt, should Britian be involved in a war or in an 'emergency', was also covered by articles of the treaty. In these circumstances Egypt could remain neutral but she was to make all her facilities and territories available to Britain and be prepared to enforce a long list of emergency measures including martial law and press censorship under British direction.

In the Second World War, Egypt did remain neutral as far as she was allowed to, but, like Turkey, she declared war on Germany in February 1945 so as to qualify as a founder member of the United Nations. During the war the realities of power were made clear to the Egyptians. First, in 1940, Farouk was forced to dismiss his Prime Minister, Ali Maher Pasha, who was regarded, probably wrongly, as pro-Italian. Later, in 1942, Farouk was forced to accept Nahas Pasha as Prime Minister under threat of enforced abdication. By bowing to British pressure Farouk alienated the young nationalist officers like Nasser and Sadat who were instrumental in 1952 in bringing about his removal from Egypt. Nahas Pasha repaid the British for his reinstatement as Prime Minister by keeping his country solidly on the side of the Allies until he was dismissed once again by Farouk at the end of 1944, but not before he had brought about the formation of the Arab League. At the time of its formation the League included Egypt, Saudi Arabia, Yemen, Transjordan, Iraq, Syria and the Lebanon. It claimed to be a federation of Arab countries but it was neither entirely, nor in terms of population even predominantly, Arab. It certainly was not a federation since the only point of agreement and unity was a common opposition to the Jews. In its petty squabbles and jealousies it probably, as we have said, made the first intervention in Palestine in 1948 even less effective than it might have been.

The weakness of Farouk, demonstrated in his abject subservience to the British during the war against Germany, influenced two forces in Egyptian society which had existed for some time but which were now brought into a sharper focus. The Muslim Brotherhood, an extremist organisation allegedly based on the teachings of the Koran, was the forerunner of what we now know as Muslim fundamentalism and preached a form of primitive morality and a social organisation which has been responsible for a fanatical attack on Western influence in the Arab, or more properly, the Muslim world. The second force was that of the growing technical and professional élite, especially in the armed forces, who banded together to bring about a modernisation of Egyptian society and to enlarge the technological base of the country.

The new forces were obviously opposed to each other but the modernising element had certain affinities with the aims and organisation of the Young Turks under Ataturk after the First World War. In the Egyptian Army the forces of reform came together in an organisation called the Free Officers and it was from this cadre that Gamil Abdel Nasser emerged as leader. Farouk's impotence and ineptness in his dealings with the British was an early cause of shame and discontent amongst young Egyptian officers and the professional classes but it was the poor showing of the army in its first war against Israel that stirred them to active revolt. In December 1948, the Muslim Brotherhood was declared illegal in Egypt. This had the effect, usual in such cases, of driving the organisation underground from where it turned with relish to a campaign of political assassination and terrorism which remains today a threat to any secular political party or politician in Egypt, as it was to the British whilst they remained in that country.

Whilst a condition of ' No war, No peace' continued between Israel and the member states of the Arab League, Britain had already withdrawn its widespread Egyptian garrisons into its bases along the Suez Canal. The Muslim Brotherhood then transferred its activities to the Canal base where they were aided by the Egyptian police in the zone. A British order to surrender the police barracks along the canal only ended after hours of bitter fighting in which 46 police were killed. This led, not surprisingly, to a mass reaction from the notorious Cairo mob. Anarchy and the frenzied behaviour of crowds on the Cairo streets gave Farouk an excuse to sack the nationalist Prime Minister Nahas, who was once more in high office.

In July 1952, the army seized power. General Mohamed Neguib, known to be an anti-royalist, was named as leader of the coup, but it was well known that the Free Officers, chief amongst whom were Nasser and Anwar Sadat, were the real leaders behind the conspiracy. There were three days of confusion during which the British did nothing to help Farouk, and he then abdicated, departing on his yacht on 26 July. For a few months the monarchy was preserved by a regency but in March 1953 Neguib became President and the monarchy ended.

The British reaction was mixed. A group of British elder statesmen led by Churchill advocated a tough line involving the retention of the Sudan or, if the worst happened, separating it completely from Egypt, and there was much support for this course of action in the Sudan. The group also advocated a strong British presence in the Canal Zone. Another group, reported to be under the influence of Anthony Eden, the Foreign Secretary, favoured a more conciliatory approach and suggested a softening of Britain's attitude towards Egypt. In the event, Britain's deteriorating financial position persuaded both Churchill and Eden that she could no longer afford to keep the 80,000 troops in the Canal Zone, the minimum number considered necessary to defend both themselves and the Canal. Britain decided in principle on the evacuation of the canal base and in future to rely on the Americans and their Sixth Fleet, now a permanent feature in the Mediterranean, to defend the international integrity of the Canal. British interests in the

Eastern Mediterranean did not coincide precisely with those of America but the British bases in Malta and Cyprus were important to the Western alliance. It was hoped that the carriers and assault ships of the US fleet permanently on patrol in the Mediterranean would safeguard British interests in Egypt by preserving freedom of movement through the Canal, under British influence if not actually under British control.

It quickly became apparent that Nasser was the man to deal with in Cairo and after a brief power struggle between Neguib and Nasser in which, according to Keith Kyle, in his exhaustive study of the Suez invasion, Nasser and the Free Officers' movement was backed by the CIA, Nasser assumed the office of Prime Minister in April 1954.

No doubt after much prompting by the CIA, Britain began to see Egypt as a possible ally. Both Nasser and Eden paid lip-service to the idea of co-operation. Talks about a complete withdrawl from the Canal base began. Britain's treaty with Iraq, which gave her use of the air bases at Habbiniya and Shaiba, as well as the right to provide the instructors and advisers for the Iraqi armed forces, was due to expire in 1957. Social unrest, amounting at times almost to open rebellion, had brought on a frantic hunt to patch together a treaty which would give better terms to the Iraqis, before the expected revolution rendered all co-operation with the West impossible.

Under the circumstances, the British preferred instrument was the Baghdad Pact, which initially united Turkey and a reluctant Iraq. It was meant to provide a shield along the northern borders of the Middle East against Soviet expansion towards the south. It immediately proved to be an extreme irritant to Egypt and Nasser, who saw the Pact as a direct challenge to the Arab League which was, after all, an Egyptian invention.

More important, the Baghdad Pact as an instrument of British policy was not compatible with another scheme which had, without much examination, recommended itself to Eden and some other Western diplomats. In April 1955, Eden succeeded the 80-year-old Winston Churchill as Prime Minister. It is said that he had had to wait too long in the wings and that he was a sick man who had lost much of his decisiveness and clear vision. Kyle says, rather unkindly but with evident truth in the context of Eden's sickness and hypochondria: 'Eden replaced Winston Churchill in the Prime Minister's bed at Number

Ten'. Nevertheless Eden pursued the scheme which was to be negated by the temporary success of the Baghdad Pact. 'Project Alpha' was the name given to a secret plan, known only to Eden, Foster Dulles and a few close colleagues, aimed at making Nasser the chief negotiator and peacemaker between Israel and the Arab States.

Once Nasser knew that Iraq had agreed to join the Baghdad Pact and had signed a treaty of mutual defence with Turkey, all hope of his acting as an intermediary between Israel and the Arabs was gone. Nasser feared that, with Arab League members joining other alliances and making bilateral defence agreements, Egypt would become isolated and lose the leadership of an anti-Israel coalition. A meeting between Nasser and Eden had been arranged for February 1955 but it was doomed by the imminent signing of the Baghdad Pact, which had been rushed through by Menderes, the Turkish Prime Minister before Eden was fully prepared for it. The Pact was signed on 24 February, only four days after the Eden-Nasser meeting in Cairo.

Under the shadow of the Baghdad Pact Eden decided not to raise the Alpha proposals. Despite the cloud over their meeting, Nasser was not entirely negative over Israel and suggested that he was the only person able to bring about peace but that it was a matter of timing. For his part Eden agreed that something should be done about the Palestine refugee problem and declared that Britain was willing to help. Both leaders said that relations between Britain and Egypt had been improved by the meeting.

The reduction of British forces in the Canal Zone was by now well under way but was being delayed by a dispute over the technicians who were to be left behind to run the base. Britain wanted them to wear uniform but Egypt was strongly opposed to this reminder of the British forces on Egyptian soil.

After Eden took over from Churchill, there was some relaxation in relations between Egypt and Britain and another attempt was made to launch the Alpha scheme. Egypt was desperate for modern arms and it was hoped that in this context Nasser could be persuaded by the Americans to sponsor an accommodation with Israel. Nasser demanded as his price for intervention in the Israel dispute the whole of the Negev, which had been awarded to Israel under the United Nations partition plan. Israel refused point blank to give up the Negev and enunciated the principle 'Israel will not give up land for peace'.

Ben Gurion saw the future of Israel as being away from the Mediterranean and, like many Israelis, looked towards the Negev and the port of Eilat at the head of the Gulf of Aquaba as the direction in which expansion and development should take place. Egypt, to counter Israeli development in the Negev through Eilat, which was being rapidly expanded to compensate for Israeli exclusion from the Suez Canal, fortified the Sharm al-Sheik at the entrance to the Gulf of Aquaba and declared the Gulf closed to Israeli shipping. Despite these aggressive actions, Nasser had not entirely closed the door on an accommodation with Israel. But his hand was finally forced, by the scale and intensity of the Israeli retaliation against Arab incursions across the armistice lines in the Gaza Strip and elsewhere. Violent Arab and Egyptian denunciations removed any chance of an agreement.

A particularly bloody Arab-Israeli clash resulting from determination to inflict exemplary punishment on intruders who crossed into Israeli territory on 1 March 1955, showed Nasser that Egypt was not strong enough at that time to protect the Palestinians and turned him to urgent war preparations. His immediate reaction was the formation of fedayeen commando units from amongst the Palestinians and the issue of instructions to the Egyptian units in the Gaza Strip to pursue a more active rôle in the defence of the Palestinians. But his aim above all else was to build up the Egyptian army.

Britain and America dragged their feet over the supply of arms to Egypt and so Nasser, in exasperation and perhaps reluctantly, turned to the Soviet Union. At the same time, as though to emphasise his political independence, he suppressed the three Egyptian Communist parties, imprisoning their leaders, including two who were Egyptian Jews. The Pentagon, at last seeing the danger, offered arms but at an impossible price which, according to Kyle, would have taken all that remained of Egypt's fast-dwindling dollar reserves. The Russians were quick to make a counter offer that was too good to be refused. They offered 100 Migs, 200 tanks and other arms, but even more important they were prepared to accept payment in surplus Egyptian cotton. To clinch the deal the Russians offered to build the multi-purpose high dam at Aswan, a project that had long been a favourite ambition of the Free Officers. Again the payment was to be in raw cotton, and so the Egyptian people would not have to choose between 'guns or butter'. There was no way in which the Egyptians could refuse such 'generosity'. The arms deal was contracted out to Czechoslovakia by the Soviet Union. Meanwhile, the French, quick to seize an opportunity in the seeming absence of British or American interest, supplied arms to Israel to balance the weapons coming to Egypt from behind the Iron Curtain. The Israelis, aware of the Egyptian build-up, prepared plans for a pre-emptive strike at the Egyptian positions at Sharm al-Sheik and elsewhere in the Sinai Peninsula.

A consortium of German, French and British firms had been pre-pared to build the dam at Aswan but there was continual delay and evasion on both sides over an agreement. Some of the arguments about the viability of the project are a little reminiscent of the objections put forward to the building of the Suez Canal. In particular, once the World Bank was involved, the cost of the dam, put in the original estimate for the Egyptian government at £E 241 million, shot up to £E 470m ($1.3 bn), meaning that Egypt would have a deficit of $400 million before work could start. The World Bank was willing to advance $200 million, leaving Egypt to find the remaining $200 million. Although the British and the Americans were quite keen to sponsor the dam, the terms demanded were driving Nasser into the hands of the Russians.

Meanwhile, the Turks, who were the most impatient if not the prime movers amongst the Baghdad Pact members, were anxious to get Jordan to join them. Britain sent General Sir Gerald Templer, chief of the British General Staff, to Amman to try to persuade King Hussein to join the Pact and thus loosen his links with Egypt. The mission was a complete failure. The King wanted to join but his ministers wanted to side with Egypt. The scheme was almost certainly doomed from the beginning because the Pact was concerned with the Russian threat and not with the fate of Palestine and its refugees which was, and remains, the immediately critical problem for Jordan. Hussein's ministers were only being realistic in bowing to the wildly pro-Egyptian and pro-Nasser sentiment in Jordan.

The failure of the Templer mission led directly to the dismissal of General Glubb, the British commander of the Arab Legion, Jordan's army, since 1939. Templer had been authorised to promise Jordan more arms and an expansion of the Legion to include its own air force if she joined the Baghdad Pact. Nasser agreed to make good these losses but his price was the dismissal of Glubb. Glubb had already warned the British government of his isolation and of Egypt's eagerness for his dismissal. But the myth of Glubb, beloved of the Arabs, and a crass refusal by the Foreign Office, despite all the evidence, to believe that the British were not universally liked and admired, particularly in the Middle East, allowed him to be thrown out of Jordan to the incredulous disbelief of Britain. Eden could not understand what had happened. It was clear by now however that Egypt and her friends saw British and American support for the dam as purely anti-Russian and not as evidence of a pro-Egyptian stance.

The dismissal of Glubb hardened British attitudes towards Egypt and constituted a severe blow to Eden's self-esteem. He had to accept that Alpha had failed and he turned to more direct methods of influencing Nasser. Negotiations over the dam were allowed to languish, arms sales to Egypt were stopped and commercial aid, including humanitarian aid, was abandoned. Britain, despite her rebuff by Jordan, continued with her side of the bilateral agreement with that country in the now vain hope of keeping Jordan out of the Egyptian camp. Finally, France and Canada were encouraged to supply more arms to Israel. Canada demurred at what she saw as a surrogate rôle, but ever-ready France was more than willing and filled the Canadian portion of the order for arms as well as her own. Eden was clearly showing signs of strain and he made some indiscreet statements about Nasser. The Americans, and especially the CIA, which seemed to be operating in the Middle East were now beginning to get cold feet over some of Britain's more ambitious plans, which included armed co-operation with the Israelis. The signs of the rift were evident and although Britain did not expect the United States to intervene unless Nasser closed the Canal, an American estimate that three or four divisions would be necessary to effect a successful landing on the Mediterranean coast of Egypt, and the sudden awareness that Britain was very short of landing-craft of all types, served to dampen the aggressive spirits in the government.

The Assault on Port Said

By June 1956, it was clear that the United States would not take part in any adventure in Egypt which might be construed as pulling British chestnuts out of the fire for them. The American attitude had hardened partly because of British intransigence over the Buraimi Oasis, a collection of villages on the borders of Saudi Arabia, Abu Dhabi and Muscat, all of which claimed the oasis. The British supported Muscat and Abu Dhabi, having a special relationship with both of them including responsibility for their foreign policy. If oil was found in the oasis area, the concession would go to the British-controlled Iraq Petroleum Company. The Americans supported the King of Saudi Arabia partly because if oil were found in a Saudi area it would fall to the Americans to exploit it but also because Nasser, who sided with the Saudis, accused Britain of playing the old, discredited, colonial game and this revived misgivings in America. The Saudis continued to press their claim to the oasis and something like open war developed. All this encouraged Eden to look still further for ways to harm Egypt. The result of what was becoming an obsession with Eden was a war alliance with France and an undisclosed, and subsequently denied agreement with Israel.

Kyle refers to France as the *tertium quid* in this situation – the third factor in the equation without whose participation the Suez situation could not have come to a head. France had her own reasons for getting involved in the Suez crisis. Britain and Israel were directly concerned with Egypt but France, although she had financial interests to protect and could claim de Lesseps as a son of France, had a more pressing reason for her involvement, centred at the other end of the Mediterranean. Morocco and Tunisia had obtained their independence from a France that was reluctant to see them go. They were entirely free of their previous colonial status by March 1956. Algeria was another matter. The three northern *Départements* of Algeria, Algiers, Oran and Constantine were by law an integral part of Metropolitan France. France was shocked and surprised when the Berber and Arab population turned to open rebellion in November 1954. By 1956, the war in Algeria had escalated into a horrifying cycle of atrocities and reprisals and had become a matter of extreme political embarrassment to the French government. The revolt was led by the *Front de Libération Nationale*, (FLN) and despite the one-and-a-half million Frenchmen who had made their home in Algeria the insurrection seemed impossible to crush. Egypt supplied arms and trained the insurgents in Cairo. Nasser was a steady supporter of the FLN and his broadcasts on Radio Cairo were effective propaganda on their behalf to the chagrin of the French.

Under these circumstances France formed links with Israel, and supplied the Israelis with their first jet fighters. Many of the French
ex-Resistance leaders, through their experience of the German war,
were pro-Israel and anti-Nasser, who was reputed to be employing
German ex-army, and in some cases ex-Nazi, officers. At a conference
at Chantilly in April 1956, France agreed to supply Israel with 72
Mystère fighter planes, 120 AMX tanks, 40 Super Sherman tanks, 18
105mm mobile guns and ammunition and radar equipment. The agreement was signed by French intelligence chiefs so as to avoid French
parliamentary scrutiny. Lacoste, the French Resident Minister in
Algeria complained that Nasser was the main enemy. The Egyptians, he
said, were not only supplying arms but also providing the military
direction of the FLN rebellion. General Jacques Massu, the legendary
commander of the 10th (Foreign Legion) Parachute Division, said the
same thing but in more forthright terms.

Nasser became the President of Egypt on 23 June 1956. At the same
time the Russians made their offer of aid in the construction of the
Aswan High Dam unconditional. The Egyptians chose this time to
recognise Communist China, to the great indignation of America.
The official reason for the refusal of American finance for the dam was
because of Egypt's alleged inability to handle so large a project and
this Nasser found particularly insulting. He waited only for the last
British troops to evacuate the Suez Canal bases before using the
opportunity of a broadcast speech to a crowd in Manshiya Square in
Cairo to announce the codeword 'Ferdinand de Lesseps'. This was the
pre-arranged signal which set in train the immediate take-over of the
Canal.

Anthony Eden realised rather late in the day that there could be no
immediate response to the nationalisation of the Canal. The British
Mediterranean fleet was concentrated at Malta and could have picked
up the Royal Marine Commando Brigade which was 'peace-keeping' in
Cyprus, and landed them at Port Said but they could not have been supported in less than six to seven weeks. The French offered an infantry
division and a parachute brigade which would have been available within 30 days but the British were wary of what Kyle calls the 'halitosis
effect'. The British were still convinced that they were loved by the
Arabs in a general way whilst the French, they thought, were unpopular because of their earlier actions in Syria and the Lebanon and

increasingly in Algeria, and more than anything because of their open support for Israel.

However, because of their general unpreparedness and shortage of specialised troops and modern equipment, the British overcame their misgivings and accepted the French as allies. This was very important since the French were able to provide 2,000 battle-hardened paratroops with better equipment and better air transport than was available to the British Parachute Brigade. In almost every respect, the British were unprepared for a serious engagement. The Parachute Brigade had to be brought back to England for training before being returned to Cyprus from where it would be launched against Egypt. The reserve formations in Britain were in a poor state. They were dispersed, under strength, under-trained and in many cases on leave. The infantry could not use their new anti-tank gun because there was no ammunition available and so the obsolescent and withdrawn 17 Pdrs, despite their known ineffectiveness against the Soviet tanks they could expect to meet in Egypt, were re-issued. The confusion over weapons and formations was only matched by the chaos resulting from the constant change of plans for the landing and, indeed, its objectives.

On 16 August a so-called Maritime Conference was held in London under the chairmanship of Robert Menzies, the Australian Premier. The object was to set up a small committee which would explain to Nasser a plan originating with John Foster Dulles, which would effectively hand over the Canal to a Canal Users' Association (CUA). The Users' Association would handle all the Canal transit dues and Egypt would thus have gained nothing financially from its nationalisation of the Canal. Needless to say, Nasser would have none of this. Eden was very much relieved by Nasser's rejection of the CUA plan because he was determined to topple the Egyptian President by fair means or foul.

Britain and France had already agreed that they would attack early in September if their grievances had not been met in full by then. Mountbatten, and possibly other Service chiefs and many ministers were opposed to military intervention, and there was much talk of resignations though little came of it. Admiral Mountbatten, then First Sea Lord, actually wrote a letter of resignation to Eden, but he didn't send it although it remained usefully on the file. The most outspoken opponent of intervention was the Defence Minister, Walter Monckton who, incredibly, Eden would not allow to resign until the end of October, and even then he was kept on in the government as Paymaster General. The effect of Monckton's, or any other Minister's, resignation on the fate of the government was very much in Eden's thoughts.

By the end of August General Keightley was appointed overall Commander-in-Chief, with the French military intellectual General Beaufre as his deputy. The original plan for the invasion of Egypt, code named 'Musketeer', called for a bombardment and then a landing at Alexandria. But as time went on, fear of high civilian casualties, and an increasingly vociferous public outcry at home and around the world, persuaded Eden and his War Cabinet, known to Parliament as the 'Egypt Committee', to switch the landing to Port Said and the entrance to the Canal itself. This plan, known as 'Musketeer Revise', was agreed and adhered to.

Opinion in America and the United Nations had hardened against Britain and France and it became more and more essential to find an unassailable moral case for the invasion. Keightley, who became extremely uneasy as the attack was delayed, emphasised the necessity for an unimpeachable reason for the attack. To what extent he was echoing service opinion is not known although Mountbatten had made clear his opposition. Lord Hailsham was brought into the Admiralty to stiffen its backbone when Lord Cilcennin, who was violently opposed to the bombardment of Alexandria, departed. It was Hailsham who persuaded Mountbatten that he could not resign 'in wartime'.

Yet another new plan was mooted, involving 10 days of psychological warfare to be followed by the neutralisation of the Egyptian air force by RAF bombing, and then, it was optimistically hoped, an unopposed landing from the sea. This new plan was accepted although it was clear to many in the know that it would not work. The over-reliance on 'Psywar' and indeed a stubborn reliance on the efficacy of bombing from the air, flew in the face of all the evidence collected by combat analysis teams during and after the Second World War. The psychological warfare effort was based upon a British radio station in Cyprus. Bombing planes could not be used to drop leaflets since they were not equipped to fly at the low altitudes necessary for the successful targeting of populated areas. The propaganda war from Cyprus was run by the former Chindit commander, Brigadier Bernard Fergusson, and was characterised as ill-directed, uninformed and ineffectual. Unfortunately, many of the broadcasts seemed to have an anti-semitic twist, Nasser, for example, being portrayed as a sinister agent of Zionism.

Finally the British and French came up with a plan which they were sure a gullible world would swallow and which, whilst its genesis was kept secret, would justify and almost sanctify their intervention. On 23 October, with the sands of time really running out, a conference was held at Sèvres, outside Paris, in, appropriately enough, a one-time French Resistance 'safe house'. France, Britain and, for the first time Israel, met to concert a plot to bring about the downfall of Abdel Nasser. Selwyn Lloyd, the Foreign Secretary, represented Britain with Eden's full consent and approval. Israel had already told her French friends that she was contemplating an attack to capture Sharm al-Sheik and open the Gulf of Aquaba so that shipping could reach the Israeli port of Eilat. It only remained to persuade the Israelis to extend their attack right up to the Suez Canal. This would provide an excuse for France and Britain to intervene, with the apparently laudable intention of separating the two sides and safeguarding the Canal. Israel and Egypt would be told to disengage and withdraw an equal distance from the Canal and the two allies would then interpose a peace-keeping force between them along the whole length of the waterway.

Eden replaced Monckton as Minister for Defence on 18 October with Antony Head, who had been Minister for War throughout the crisis and now became responsible for all three Services. As an ex-brigadier, and because of his familiarity with the plans for the invasion, which presumably he approved of, he was considered to be 'hawkish'. He was, however, soon to tell Eden that the troops could not be held in a state of readiness, many of them actually embarked, for much longer. By the time Head took over, 1,000 officers and 26,000 soldier reservists had been recalled and 6,000 regular soldiers due for discharge had been retained. Many of the reservists were resentful of their position and were suffering financially. Their families were experiencing real hardship since in many cases the reservists received in pay and National Assistance only about half of what they had been earning in their civilian jobs. There were instances of disaffection and incipient mutiny including a demonstration by guardsmen in Malta.

The disturbances evaporated as the prospect of action approached, which is usually the way with British soldiers, but they were sufficiently serious to worry the Service leaders and to prompt a paper from them calling for a speeding up of the invasion plans. Everyone with access to the plans was afraid that if action was too long delayed and there was no more provocation on the part of the Egyptians which could be used as a *casus belli*, the long gap between the nationalisation of the Canal and the landings would give many opportunities for further outcry against the allies. Even the civilian members of the crews of the requisitioned ships, standing by to take the British contingent to Egyptian waters, were complaining (and involving their unions) about their inability to earn overtime whilst their ships were tied up waiting for orders to sail.

The Sèvres agreement, which Eden wished to keep verbal only, was brought home as a document much to his horror, but it probably came just in time to prevent the complete abandonment of the Anglo-French plans. It was agreed that the Israelis would be allowed to capture Sharm al-Sheik before the ultimatum to the Israelis and Egyptians expired. After that the Israelis had only one more qualm and that was over the supposed vulnerability of their towns from bombing by Egypt's newly-supplied Russian bombers. The French solved that problem by secretly stationing two squadrons of fighter aircraft on Israeli airfields. It was also agreed that the British would 'take out' the whole Egyptian air force before the planned truce came into effect.

The Suez Débâcle and the Aftermath

At 5 pm on 29 October, an Israeli parachute battalion dropped on the Mitla Pass on the southern route across the Sinai Peninsula from Israel to Suez. They were near enough to Suez to convince the Egyptians that a full-scale attack across the Canal was in prospect. The Egyptians were taken completely by surprise and many of their units had been withdrawn from the frontier to be re-equipped and trained with the new weapons arriving from Czechoslovakia. The allied bombing of Egypt began on 31 October. The prepared ultimatum, which treated Israel the invader and Egypt the invaded with what the British government called even handedness, was ignored with disdain by all the parties involved. The Egyptian air force was eliminated, largely because it very sensibly retired most of its planes out of harm's way to Upper Egypt and Syrian and Saudi airfields. (Iraq played much the same game in the Gulf War 35 years later.) But, despite the large number of bombs dropped, the Egyptian airfields were not put completely out of action. Radio Cairo and the main Egyptian air base at Cairo West were not attacked for fear of inflicting heavy civilian casualties. When the main bombing effort from the Canberras and Valiants was over, the battle was taken up by ground attack aircraft which destroyed the remaining 200 aircraft in two days.

The landings were originally planned to follow eight days after the beginning of the bombing campaign but the hullabaloo around the world and in the British Parliament was such that this was reduced to six days, the minimum time necessary to sail from Malta to Port Said. On 5 November one British parachute battalion and two French parachute battalions dropped to secure vital points around Port Said and the following day the seaborne landings of the Commando Brigade and 6 Royal Tank Regiment were successfully completed.

Although the landings were a success, General Keightley was worried by the number of civilians killed and wounded and Eden, on being told that it would take six more days to reach Suez, lost his nerve and agreed to a cease-fire to take effect from 2 am local time on 7 November. General Stockwell, who was in command of land operations pushed a squadron of 6 RTR supported by 2 Para down the Canal to try to secure as much of it as possible before the cease-fire came into effect. Although they overran the start of the truce by a few minutes, they were still four miles from Al Quantara and many more from Suez when they were ordered to halt. General Massu, who was the French commander on the ground and under General Stockwell's orders, had always wanted to drop his paratroops right down the Canal to Suez and, despite the risk involved, this was probably the only way in which the Canal could have been captured within the time frame and in a comparatively intact state.

The United Nations proceeded to organise an Emergency Force under the command of General Burns of the Canadian Army. The atmosphere at the United Nations was painful and embarrassing. Sir Brian Urquhart, a senior British representative, in his book, *A Life in Peace and War*, says: 'Virtually everyone I knew was violently opposed to the Suez expedition, which we regarded as a doomed, dishonest and contemptible aberration by the British and French governments.'

The immediate effect of the Suez fiasco was the abrupt severing of the 'special relationship' with the United States which Britain had so assiduously cultivated since the time of President Franklin Roosevelt and before. Britain and France were excluded from the close councils of their former allies and it was made clear that they would not be welcomed amongst the comity of decent nations until both had purged their transgressions by the removal of all their troops from Egypt. The 'comity of nations' at that time, it should be noted, included the Soviet Union which had just brutally crushed the movement for freedom and democracy in Hungary and which had made threats about the use of nuclear weapons against British and French aggressors.

In the longer term, France decided to 'go nuclear' and to leave the command structure of NATO. From that time Britain and France were seen throughout the world as essentially second-rate powers without the ability to defend themselves adequately. The rebellions in Cyprus, Algeria and elsewhere in the world were strengthened and the rebels comforted. At the same time the confidence of the Western democracies was undermined and a period of self-doubt and self-questioning set in. Eden, who had a history of illnesses, not all of them minor and not all of them the manifestation of hypochondria, succumbed at last to the strain of running the Suez affair as a one-man show, and went off on doctor's orders, to Jamaica, for a complete rest.

When he arrived back in England he was faced in the House of Commons with questions hinting strongly at collusion with the Israelis. He replied that he had been aware of the risk of an Israeli attack but that he had not known the date fixed, its objective, or the form it would take. This was clearly a lie. Question Time in the House on 20 December was the last time Eden spoke in Parliament, which went into the Christmas recess immediately after his statement. On his doctor's advice he resigned on 8 January 1957.

Whilst Eden was away, the government had been led by 'Rab' Butler as Deputy Prime Minister and he was left to clear up the immediate mess. Petrol rationing had been brought in on 23 November and there was much anxiety over the run on sterling. The drain on Britain's dollar reserves and the increasing difficulty over obtaining oil persuaded the Cabinet that Britain should withdraw from Egypt. Macmillan, who supported the withdrawal and who, as Chancellor of the Exchequer, had been concerned almost to the point of hysteria, over the run on the pound and the shortage of oil, was now elected under the strange Tory selection system then in force, as Prime Minister, emerging with an overwhelming majority over Butler on 9 January 1957.

The withdrawal of the British and French troops from Egyptian soil was completed by Christmas 1956 followed by the demolition and removal, by the Egyptians, of the statue of Ferdinand de Lesseps which had stood proudly at the Mediterranean entrance to the Canal. The Egyptians had gained a token revenge for the invasion. But immediately following the withdrawal, oil and financial credits started to flow again and already there was some renewal of friendly relations with America. However, as Kyle points out, Britain was undoubtedly beaten over Suez by economic sanctions and ironically Britain has played down the importance and efficacy of sanctions ever since. What was obvious after Suez was that there would be no more 'going it alone', or indeed at all without the active support of a 'real' world power.

In Britain another lesson, demonstrably not learned even by 1994, concerns the left and right hands knowing what the other is doing. It is well known that plans were being formulated in the Ministry of Defence for the contingency of an invasion of Egypt, whilst at the same time, in another part of the Ministry, cuts in all the armed forces were being actively pursued. This was happening again at the time of the Falklands campaign, the Gulf War and most recently of the Bosnian horrors.

As in the two World Wars, Cyprus was found to be of very little value in 1956, chiefly because it had been scandalously neglected. Even when it was realised that it was important as the only British air base from which the eastern Mediterranean could be covered, nothing was done until the last moment to enlarge or modernise the base. It has been left to the tourists and the package trade to bring about the construction of alternative airfields. Some of the inertia in Cyprus can be put down to the provisions of the Sovereign Base agreement, but all Cypriots north and south of the demarcation line, have a great deal to gain by closer co-operation with the British.

As a result of the Suez experience Britain took no action against Ian Smith, the Premier of Southern Rhodesia, when he unilaterally declared independence. Again, in 1974, no British forces intervened against the Turkish invasion of Northern Cyprus, although the British did help by opening the Sovereign Base areas to the flood of refugees. The Falklands were an exception which proves the rule. The British victory took place in the most favourable of circumstances. Despite their being so far away, the Falklands were unmistakably a British colony whilst Argentina was a military dictatorship. Britain had good support in the United Nations and above all, since Argentina was seen clearly to be the aggressor, from the United States.

Writing in *The Observer* of 13 February 1965, A.J.P.Taylor, at the time Britain's most highly respected historian, now sadly dead said:

> The moral for British governments is clear. Like most respectable people, they will make poor criminals and had better stick to respectability. They will not be much good at anything else.

A fitting epitaph for a sorry episode.

CHAPTER VIII

The Mediterranean Since Suez

The retreat from Suez can be seen as the watershed in Britain's relations with its former colonies and bases, not only in the Middle Sea but throughout the world. From another perspective it appears as an inevitable stage in the decline of British power, stemming from financial and physical exhaustion caused by Britain's extended and desperate struggle to survive the Second World War. The decline was first manifest in the giving of independence to India, followed by the abandonment of British territories and colonies in Africa and elsewhere. After Suez it was clear that a new era had arrived in the Mediterranean and all that was left was to make the best possible arrangements for the hand-over of power in what remained of the British possessions.

Whilst Britain accepted her changed position in the Mediterranean and in the world, it can hardly be said to have been done with good grace. The limited amount of goodwill generated by Britain's comparatively unacrimonious handing-over of power in India was quickly dissipated in the Mediterranean, in Malta where aspirations for independence were soured by an ungenerous financial and economic settlement, and in Cyprus where an admittedly difficult racial situation was made worse by a determination not to upset either of the two ethnically interested parent nations. Only in Gibraltar, with a small native population, chronically suspicious and fearful of a Spanish takeover, did the British presence remain unequivocally welcome. The fact that Spain was a fascist dictatorship until the death of General Franco in 1975, gave Britain a useful card to play in the United Nations where overt fascism in smaller nations was frowned upon, although the absence of democracy in the Soviet Union and its satellites was ignored. Gibraltar was, and still remains, a problem for Britain in the Mediterranean.

By the early 1950s, Gibraltar had settled down to a period of peaceful if uneasy co-existence with Spain. The frontier was open, workers continued to cross into Gibraltar to work in the Naval Dockyard and for those who could afford it, and that meant the majority of Gibraltarians, there was an unlimited supply of domestic labour. The native population numbered about 25,000, with the last of the wartime evacuees, almost incredibly, not returning to the Rock until 1950. The garrison, with its British civilian employees, amounted to another 5,000, and it was comparatively easy to feed everyone, even if the food was rather dull. Some foods were still rationed in Britain, of course. It was possible to get exciting meals in Spain but they were more to the Gibraltarian than to the British taste. Meals and accommodation were exceptionally cheap in Spain and for a while, and even for the British serviceman who has made an art out of complaining about his living conditions throughout the world, except when action is imminent, the Rock was a very desirable posting.

The Queen visited the Rock in 1954 and was greeted with such a patriotic, pro-British furore that the Spanish took fright, seeing their chances of annexing Gibraltar with United Nations approval slipping away. The Spanish Consul was withdrawn and restrictions were placed on the frontier crossing at La Linea. The frontier was completely closed soon afterwards and entry by sea from Gibraltar through Algeciras was forbidden. In 1964, the United Nations Commission on Decolonisation took a hand in the dispute and, despite the appearance before it of a delegation from Gibraltar asking for the status quo to be confirmed, resolved that Britain and Spain must come to a negotiated settlement of the dispute. Britain refused to negotiate under duress and proceeded to remove the remaining trappings of colonialism on the Rock in order to make its constitutional position more acceptable to the United Nations. Earlier in the year the Executive Council had been abolished and replaced by a Gibraltar Council with an elected majority. Spain, of course, was still a fascist dictatorship but the irony of the situation seemed to escape the Commission on Decolonisation. The stalemate and virtual siege dragged on until 1975 when the death of General Franco and the introduction of a fledgling democracy seemed to bring about a new situation, at least for Spain.

Not only was there a revival of democracy in Spain, but a renewed interest in an outward-looking foreign and commercial policy made membership of the European Economic Community desirable if not immediately essential. Under these circumstances, a limited agreement to reopen the frontier was arrived at in 1982 but the opening was postponed at Spain's request because of the Argentine invasion of the Falkland Islands. A partial reopening took place at the beginning of 1983 which allowed long-term residents of Spain and Gibraltar to cross the frontier. By the end of 1984, British support for the entry of Spain to the EEC had become vital and so a full opening was finally agreed and put into operation on 5 February 1985. So ended the last great siege of Gibraltar.

The Gibraltarians had made the point once more that they were not going to be bullied or coerced into joining Spain. At every test of public opinion on the Rock, the wishes of the Gibraltarians have been made clear beyond doubt. In 1967 a referendum was held in which all adult, native Gibraltarians were asked whether they wished to continue the link with Britain or whether they would prefer to join Spain. Out of an eligible electorate of 12,726, 12,138 voted to maintain the link with Britain, whilst only 44 voted in favour of Spain. It is not surprising that the only pro-British riot recorded anywhere took place on the Rock following the referendum. Some well-meaning Gibraltar business men had written to the *Gibraltar Chronicle* suggesting that with the new climate in Spain it might at least be worthwhile talking to the Spaniards. A spontaneous riot, which went on through most of the day but was quickly abandoned when the Governor put the army on stand-by, was the people's answer.

Unlike other Mediterranean bases, Gibraltar has been little used for its primary function by the armed forces since the Second World War. Even the Suez invasion force bypassed, for the most part, a base almost 2,000 miles from the scene of action. But the Rock did provide for the fleet a walk ashore in a friendly environment and an opportunity to reshuffle cargoes and reorganise landing tables even if on a small scale.

But not much of this was evident to the local population, who were just as bemused as the Service garrison over the extraordinary aberration which Britain had perpetrated at Suez. Gibraltar was loyal and remained loyal despite the run-down of the garrison, the almost complete closure of the dockyard and the occasional call from self-interested voices in Britain for the handing over of Gibraltar to Spain.

The End of the Line in Malta

Malta was profoundly affected by its experiences in the Second World War. The Maltese people, who had survived the continuous assault on the islands during the war, emerged with a new self-confidence and a determination to see the resolution of the constitutional and social problems which had been postponed for the duration of the war. Previously the majority of the Maltese worked on the land and lived in small villages which, whilst they could never be far from a city, were isolated by poor communications. Immediately after the war, a series of measures was introduced to modernise the islands. Compulsory education became a reality; the provision of fresh water and electricity and a sewage system was extended out to the villages and an efficient and frequent bus service was inaugurated throughout Malta.

A study of land usage in Malta and Gozo concluded, not surprisingly, that the economy of the islands was very largely dependent upon expenditure by the British armed services. In the expected run-down after the war the need for diversification in the primarily defence-orientated industries was obvious. Britain was expected to aid the redevelopment by establishing a fund and by providing grants and loans of about £22 million. The establishment of new industries was unfortunately rather haphazard and ill-controlled and, as is quite usual now even in more developed economies, many firms seem to have been set up in Malta merely to attract the generous grants available. A typical example of bad planning was the project to assemble Nash Rambler cars under licence in Malta, despite the very small immediate market and the well-established and heavily-protected motor car industry in Italy, the nearest mass market. That scheme and others, equally carelessly researched, soon ceased to operate.

The Suez operation and the lack of any other suitable ports available to the British slowed the run-down of the dockyard but this was merely postponing the inevitable. A £30 million war damage fund, provided by the British government to finance reconstruction and development, helped to keep the economy running at a high level after the hectic activity of the war years but, in 1959, the dockyard was taken over by a South Wales shipyard as part of a plan to convert it to commercial use. This did not prove to be a success and the yard was then taken over by Swan Hunter, Britain's largest ship-builder at that time. This too was a failure and the yard was eventually taken over by the Maltese government.

By 1960, the constitutional problems of the islands had become acute. A powerful Labour Party favoured integration with Britain but, despite a large vote in favour, the Church, fearful of coming under the domination of the Protestant Church of England, and the Nationalist Party, opposed this policy. Britain also rejected integration, an attitude which was regarded as a serious snub by the Maltese people who had voted so overwhelmingly in its favour. This rejection, together with the now acute economic decline in the islands, let to an increasingly tense situation. By 1958 the Governor had already had to assume extra powers to maintain law and order and the islands were administered by the Maltese permanent civil service.

A Commission set up in July 1960 under Sir Henry Blood recommended that more powers should be given to the Maltese government and that there should be no matters reserved exclusively to the United Kingdom government. The Blood Report was accepted and Malta regained a degree of self-government. This was followed in 1962 by a general election in which the Nationalist Party, led by Dr Giorgio Borg Olivier, gained a majority over the Maltese Labour Party. In August 1962 Borg Olivier gave notice that Malta would claim the right to full independence. Despite the opposition of the minority parties, the British Colonial Secretary accepted the demand for independence and this was finalised on 21 September 1964. Ties with Britain were not severed immediately and it is unlikely that the Maltese people would have agreed to such an abrupt break.

Malta remains a member of the Commonwealth but declared herself a republic in 1974 when, in a decade dominated by the Maltese Labour Party, with drastic reductions in the British garrison in the islands and

177

a return of economic recession, solutions to Malta's problems were sought in radically new directions. Chinese technical and financial assistance was obtained in the running of the new ship-yard in the inner Grand Harbour and even the old enemy, Libya, was welcomed in to invest Arab oil money in hotel and other developments. The building of hotels went hand-in-glove with the policy of encouraging the new tourism. In the past, Malta had been a port of call for cruise ships in the Mediterranean but more recently the package-holiday industry, self-catering and time-share property-owning has taken over as a major industry in Malta, becoming a large foreign currency earner. Britain, for historical and sentimental reasons, now provides the largest proportion of tourists to the islands.

It quite soon became apparent that Chinese technical assistance and Arab money were not being offered for altruistic reasons, any more than British interest in Grand Harbour during the period of her occupation. However, by the 1980s it was clear that the price to be paid for non-Western assistance was not acceptable. The clear link between terrorism and gun-running sponsored by Libya and channelled through Malta, without the knowledge or consent of the Maltese authorities, could only have a disastrous effect on the growing tourist industry. This was especially so in the case of Britain, where Colonel Gadaffi provided arms for the IRA, seemingly transshipped in Maltese waters. The Lockerbie bombing outrage, with its suspected Maltese connections, was probably the last straw for the Maltese people. As an increasingly popular and comparatively cheap Mediterranean holiday resort, with a ready-made British market Malta felt it should now stay firmly in the Western camp.

A New Status for Cyprus

Cyprus presents a middle way in the progress of British colonies in the Mediterranean towards a settled and peaceful existence, between the clinging attachment of Gibraltar and the total independence of Malta. When Lawrence Durrell arrived in Cyprus in 1953, intending to settle quietly into a leisurely writer's life, he bought a house, the transaction amusingly described in his book *Bitter Lemons*, in the Greek village of Bellapais in what we would now call the Turkish area of occupation.

Before the anti-British rebellion which practically coincided with his arrival, Cyprus was divided into towns and villages which were predominantly Greek or Turkish. Both races were spread throughout the island and, considering that the Turkish minority were masters of the island for 400 years and that the Greek Cypriots had always dreamed of 'enosis', the mystical union with the Greek motherland, they got along reasonably well together. It had served the British purpose to encourage a certain degree of separation between the two peoples if only to provide some counterweight to the idea of a union with Greece. It will be remembered that Wolseley, the first Commissioner, had supported a plan to settle Maltese peasants in Cyprus for the same reason. Durrell, who had lived in Corfu and spoke Greek, liked and admired the Turks but, as a true Englishman, loved the Greeks.

The question of 'enosis' had arisen before the war and had been postponed until the end of hostilities. The British attempt to stem the German invasion of Greece in 1941 and the eventual defeat of the invaders had improved, if only temporarily, relations between the Greek Cypriots and the British. However, this postponement of the reckoning could not last for ever and, with ringing declarations in favour of self-determination and decolonisation coming from the United Nations, it did not, in fact, last for long. The Turkish Cypriots took a pragmatic line and wanted the British to stay on the island to protect them from the Greek majority. However difficult an accommodation between the Greeks and Turks on the island might have been, it is not unreasonable to assume that some settlement, doubtless uneasy, could have been arrived at. But the ghost of Disraeli hung over the island. With the abandonment of Egypt and the withdrawal into the Canal Zone, the island of Cyprus had still not earned its keep. It was still inadequate as a base for British forces in the Middle East. But as pressure increased on the troops stationed along the Canal and the inclination to evacuate became stronger the government was able to convince itself, and to some extent the British public, that Cyprus was a satisfactory substitute for the bases in Egypt.

One of the most important attributes of a military base is that it should not have to fritter away resources in defending itself. The internal situation, quite apart from the inter-communal rivalry, was completely discounted in the plans for the evacuation of British troops to Cyprus. Perhaps the British were indulging, as they had elsewhere, in the belief that the Greek Cypriots would prefer decent, honest British rule to the unknown horrors they might become subject to under a benighted government of their own choice. Even Durrell betrayed traces of this somewhat smug belief. In any case, by 1955 a guerrilla war had broken out in the island.

Anthony Eden, in a state of chronic indecision over Egypt and the Canal, seized the opportunity to do something decisive somewhere. To loud Tory cheers in the House of Commons, though against the advice of his Colonial Secretary, he had the Greek Cypriot leader, Archbishop Makarios, exiled to the Seychelles. The Archbishop had been an outspoken proponent of 'enosis' and had organised a plebiscite amongst the Greek Cypriots which produced a 96 per cent majority in favour of joining Greece. Makarios had also encouraged the Greek Cypriots to take up arms against the British in the terrorist Organisation of Cypriot Freedom Fighters (EOKA), led by a Greek Cypriot officer in the Greek Army, Colonel Grivas Dhigenis. Between 500 and 600 people were killed by EOKA during the 'Emergency'. Over 200 Greek Cypriots were killed by EOKA, as against 166 killed by the security services.

The Emergency brought many changes in the lifestyle of the civilian expatriates, who were living in a kind of Cypriot Lotus-Land, as was the military garrison with its families and supporting British-based services. Before the Second World War the British garrison had consisted of one company of infantry, detached from its parent battalion which was stationed at Khartoum. The company usually occupied a camp at Polemidhia, about four miles inland from Limassol, which had been built at the time of the original take-over of the island in 1878. When Government House was attacked and burned down in the riots of 1931 the troops were moved to Nicosia. With the war, although the island's rôle was a fairly quiet one, the garrison was built up and the theatre reserve divisions were stationed there from time to time, for training and defence purposes. Immediately after the war the garrison was run down again to a single battalion with a District Headquarters and supporting services.

When the decision was made to make Cyprus a main British base in the Middle East, plans for a large-scale development were agreed. These were to include the building of a new military town, with a large headquarters, messes and barrack blocks, married quarters, a hospital, schools, clubs and other amenities, located on the coast a few miles north of Larnaca. Unfortunately, the military town was not to achieve the status originally intended for it. In the first place, as so often happens with planned military expenditure, the Treasury reduced the amount of money available and so standards of accommodation and welfare and leisure facilities were reduced. The rate of building was slowed down overall. The site was chosen and agreed by 1951 but the actual building was only just beginning when the Emergency began to feature as a factor. The construction workers were Cypriot but there was a shortage of skilled men, and because of the political situation shoddy work, industrial disputes and a lack of commitment to the project on the part of the workforce were endemic. Nevertheless, the new cantonment of Dhekalia was completed although on a reduced scale but, as it turned out, not on a sufficiently reduced scale to take account of the garrison reductions which have occurred from the time of its completion right up to the present day.

After the Emergency, when Cyprus had achieved independence although not 'enosis', the setting up of the Sovereign Base Areas, one at Episkopi which included the large air base at Akrotiri, and the second at Dhekalia around the already developed new town, meant that the forces would no longer be concentrated in one area only. With two base areas, the concept of a military town was diluted and whenever the garrison was cut, as it frequently was, after Suez, after the Emergency and in the course of three further reviews of forces' strength, spare accommodation and resources have been thrown up. In parts, the cantonment has begun to resemble a ghost town. An extreme example of this phenomenon is the military hospital. For obvious reasons military hospitals are planned with spare capacity so as to provide for the extra casualties arising in war but the British Military Hospital in Dhekalia has never been used by the forces. It is used by the Cypriot medical services whilst British casualties and cases requiring hospitalisation go to the Princess Mary's Hospital at RAF Akrotiri within the Western Base Area.

In June 1955, with the Egyptian bases all but evacuated, the British government anxious to develop its bases in Cyprus since the civilian-operated facilities left behind in the Zone were considered of doubtful value, invited Greece and Turkey to a tripartite conference on the future of Cyprus, establishing for the first time that Turkey had rights in

Cyprus. Nothing came from the conference and the problem was transferred to the United Nations which in 1959 (Resolution 1013) declared the principle that Cyprus would eventually become an independent state.

Greece agreed to the principle of independence for Cyprus and this prevented a double 'enosis' and the possibility of a Greco-Turkish war and partition of the island. As it was, the resolution left the Turkish minority in Cyprus in a permanently subordinate position. The tripartite agreement gave Britain sovereign rights over her military base areas and set up Cyprus as a unitary state with a Greek Cypriot President and a Turkish Vice-President.

The republic came into being in August 1960 but from the beginning the two races could not work together. Archbishop Makarios became the first President but he was opposed to the new constitution and did his best to secure more power for the Greek majority. The Turkish government, in its self-appointed rôle of protector of the Turkish minority on the island, resented all attempts to increase Greek power. Before long the Turks were massing troops opposite the island, threatening to intervene if Makarios introduced changes in Cyprus unilaterally. The sabre-rattling by both Greece and Turkey raised tension to fever pitch within the island and communal disturbances broke out which, even in this notoriously volatile island, were so serious that the United Nations sent a peace-keeping force there in February 1964. They also sent a mediator who, in the circumstances, could achieve nothing.

Brigadier Mike Harbottle was Chief of Staff of the United Nations peace-keeping force, (UNFICYP) and controlled its operations in Cyprus from 1966 to 1968. He helped to establish procedures for peace-keeping forces which, in Cyprus included the setting up of a 'Green Line' between the warring communities. In 1970, he published what he saw as the lessons of Cyprus in his book, *The Impartial Soldier* in which he suggests that it is necessary to maintain a special advisory staff on peace-keeping at UN headquarters. Recent events in Africa and the Balkans have given new impetus to this idea and schemes put forward for a centralised UN disaster control and aid co-ordinating body appear to be more urgent than ever. Harbottle ends his observations on Cyprus by making the often overlooked point that a peace-keeper is not a peace-maker. The real achievement of UNFICYP was that it kept comparative peace on the island for 10 years, from 1964 to 1974.

In July 1974, at the height of the Cyprus tourist season, intrigue and subversion by a small group of Greek Cypriots led to an attempted coup against the established government of the island. For a short time the coup seemed to be succeeding, but then mainland Turkey, no doubt grateful at last for an excuse to intervene, invaded the island, landing troops at the north Cyprus port of Kyrenia and driving Greek Cypriots and refugee holiday-makers before them into the south of the island. When the results of the coup became obvious the Junta, which had ruled briefly since the coup, was forced out of the country but by then the damage had been done. Thousands of Greek Cypriot farmers in the northern and central areas of the island were dispossessed and fled south. The Turkish invaders set up a new boundary between Greek and Turkish areas, giving the Turks a much greater land area than prior to the coup which could not be compensated for by the seizure of Turkish land in the south.

Britain did not intervene militarily in what was an extremely delicate situation. Greece and Turkey were both valued members of NATO and any effective intervention would almost certainly have sparked off a full-scale war between at least two of its member states. The island was effectively divided between Turks and Greeks although the Greek Cypriots claimed to be the legal government of the whole island. The UK Sovereign Base Areas served a useful function in providing a haven for the 10,000 holiday-makers who fled from the north, most of whom were British and were subsequently flown home from Dhekelia. The island remains divided into two bitterly hostile camps with neither side prepared to compromise over the sovereignty of its part of the island and with Greece and Turkey glowering at each other across the Aegean. Despite the end of the Cold War, which has raised hopes for the settlement of a number of intransigent border problems around the eastern end of the Mediterranean, the portents are not auspicious and *de facto* partition may be the fate of the island for the forseeable future.

British Authors and the Mediterranean

Lawrence Durrell, although writing at the time of the earlier 'Emergency', sums up his, and most people's feelings about the tragedy of Cyprus in his poem *Bitter Lemons*. Durrell could not believe when he arrived in Cyprus in 1953, despite the evidence of the past, and some more recent events in the Mediterranean and elsewhere, that the Greek Cypriots could turn against the British. He willingly accepted the Greeks when they proffered love and the values of Greek civilisation and culture. Even after the outbreak of violence, his only fear seems to have been that some wild, brigand-like guerrillas from Crete might infiltrate the essentially peaceful Cypriots and help or persuade them to expel the British. He lost his illusions, if not his love of the Greeks, during the first Emergency and he never returned to Cyprus after 1956. As he was being driven to the heavily-guarded airport at the time of his departure, his taxi driver said to him: 'You see, the trouble with the Greeks is that we really are so pro-British'.

Durrell lived for most of his life on or near the Mediterranean and died in November 1990 at Sommières, a village in Provence where he had finally made his home. He was born in India in 1912 where he first went to school. Then, after attending St Edmund's School at Canterbury, failing to get into Cambridge and undertaking a variety of stop-gap jobs in England, he went to live with his family on the island of Corfu. From then on, he was rarely absent, physically or in his thoughts, from the Mediterranean. His life in Corfu is illustrated with affection by his younger brother Gerald, himself a writer and world famous zoologist, whose best known book is probably *My Family and Other Animals* which was made into a very popular television series. Lawrence Durrell started his literary career by writing poetry and novels, usually with a Mediterranean background, and he was working as a teacher of English in Athens when the Second World War broke out. He left Greece before the Germans arrived and worked in the government information service in Egypt from April 1941 until the end of the war and afterwards in Greece, Yugoslavia and Cyprus. He was also Director of British Council Institutes at Kalamata in Greece and Cordova in the Argentine. By now he was well known as a poet and published his first book, *Prospero's Cell*, about Corfu, in 1945. This was followed by a book on Rhodes, *Reflections on a Marine Venus* in 1953 and *Bitter Lemons*, about Cyprus, in 1957. *Justine*, the first volume of his most acclaimed work of fiction, *The Alexandria Quartet*, also appeared in 1957, followed by *Balthazar* and *Mountolive* in 1958, and the final volume, *Clea*, in 1960.

Together, the quartet of novels and his three travel books – although they are more than that – encapsulate his views and feelings about the eastern Mediterranean. Even though his vision is a little starry-eyed for today's reader, and his disillusion comes a little late, there is no better place to begin reading about the Greek islands. Even from his semi-retirement in the south of France he could not keep away from the islands and the pervasive influence of Greek civilisation in the Mediterranean. In 1977 he travelled as a member of a package tour, by motor coach around the island of Sicily, describing his journey and the antiquities which he visited in *Sicilian Carousel*, one of his most entertaining books. He showed the package tour to be both amusing and respectable, and if he gives the impression that Sicily is essentially Greek and not Italian, at least he produces evidence for his view, and one could not expect more from one of the last great philhellenes.

Another Englishman of letters, always to be associated with the Mediterranean was Robert Graves. Almost of the previous generation to that of Durrell, Graves was as Roman in his predilections as Durrell was Greek. Born in Wimbledon in 1895, he died in Majorca in 1985 and was buried in Deia, the village he had made his home for over 50 years. Although described in *The Times* obituary as 'a great romantic poet and English eccentric', he seems, as compared with Durrell, to always have had something of the 'antique Roman' about him. This view is certainly supported by his impeccable record in the First World War and by his translations of Lucan's *Pharsalia* and Seutonius's *Twelve Caesars*. Apart from an unhappy period early in 1926 as an English lecturer at Cairo University, which lasted only three months, he had no other direct experience of the British in the Mediterranean but his life in Deia, broken only by enforced absence during the Spanish Civil War and the war against Hitler, stamped him as an English Mediterranean expatriate.

Despite his eccentricity, Graves became a close friend of T.E.Lawrence who regarded him as all that a poet should be. Lawrence had used his influence to get Graves the job of writing his official biography *Lawrence and the Arabs* which was a financial success and allowed him to become a serious professional writer. After his successful autobiography *Goodbye To All That*, he was able to remove himself and his extraordinary domestic ménage, (at one time *à trois*) to Majorca. Although Graves encouraged the impression that he was writing pot-boilers to redress a new burden of debt, his 'Roman' works, *I*

Claudius and *Claudius The God*, published in 1934, were serious, highly-researched historical novels, accepted as being at the top of their genre, and obviously inspired by Seutonius's *Twelve Caesars*, his new translation of which appeared in 1957. In 1938 Graves wrote another historical novel based on the life of the Byzantine General *Count Belisarious* which was also a great success. At the same time he was writing some of his most sensitive and introspective poetry. He was able to return to Majorca in 1946 where he wrote *The White Goddess* and then the novel, *Seven Days in Crete*. In 1961 he was elected Professor of Poetry at Oxford University which set the seal on his acceptance as an outstanding poet in Britain and America. Although he travelled widely to lecture he continued to write poetry until 1975. When he died in 1985 he was buried in the tiny churchyard above the village of Deia which had been his only real home.

After Graves and Durrell, the only other English poet of this century who comes immediately to mind as a Mediterranean resident, if only for a short period, is D.H. Lawrence. It is possible that Graves and Durrell, in company with many members of the literary establishment, would have regarded Lawrence as something of an outsider but his stature as a poet and novelist is assured. Graves, with his friendship with T.E. Lawrence, a character every bit as complicated as the son of the Nottinghamshire miner, and Durrell with his early admiration for, and later friendship with the eccentric Henry Miller, might both have found DHL congenial company. He lived for the last few years of his life in Sardinia, overlapping Graves's first period in Majorca.

During the Second World War, many writers served in the Mediterranean littoral countries in the armed services or in government agencies. Olivia Manning accompanied her husband, a lecturer with the British Council , to Bucharest, just before the war. As the Germans approached they were forced to move to Athens and eventually to Egypt and Jerusalem. The fruits of her experience are represented by, *The Balkan Trilogy*, published between 1960 and 1965, and the *Levant Trilogy* which followed between 1977 and 1980. Described by Anthony Burgess as the 'finest fictional record of the war', the six volumes were serialised by BBC Television to great acclaim. The war that Manning describes takes place in the Balkans and then in Greece and moves on to Egypt and Jerusalem. By any standards Olivia Manning possessed a major talent but her entire life did not revolve around the Inland Sea any more than that of Penelope Lively whose Booker Prize winning novel, *Moon Tiger*, about life in wartime Cairo, was published in 1986.

There are a number of professional travellers who write about the Mediterranean and the Middle East, two of whom immediately come to mind. Eric Newby, who lived in Tuscany, conceived the idea of describing a tour round the whole periphery of the Mediterranean, moving in a clock-wise direction, having been persuaded by his wife Wanda that this was a more logical way to tackle the task than 'to go dashing off in all directions like a lunatic'. Although the book is a little artificial in its format, the result, *On The Shores of the Mediterranean*, published in 1984, was described by *The Guardian* as an 'Odyssey with Newby as its Ulysses'. The second traveller of note, Colin Thubron, also describes a round trip but this time a more modest circumnavigation of the island of Cyprus soon after the second 'Emergency' in 1974. His book, *Journey into Cyprus*, earned him a Fellowship of the Royal Society of Literature and makes an interesting, as well as a complementary, counterbalance to Durrell's *Bitter Lemons*.

The advent of television has produced a market for an almost unlimited flow of documentaries, plays and serials using exotic locations which provide free advertising when, as so frequently happens, the locations are developed into popular holiday resorts. This began after the war with films set in Spain, the south of France and Italy, but with the opening up of the eastern Mediterranean the television industry has been quick to seize on Greece and the Aegean islands for its settings and Turkey will follow the trend. Television and tourism feed on each other so that a television presentation may induce a mass descent upon a previously unknown and unspoiled location, whilst a popular holiday area provides television programme-makers with a ready-made audience for their work.

None of this is really new, except perhaps, in its intensity. Film-making and coastal development in Spain led to a building boom and the speed with which the coastal strip was concreted over was startling, but those were the days of the Bible epics and ancient histories. The pace has accelerated and we can now look forward to a time when the whole of the north shore of the Mediterranean, from Turkey to Gibraltar, will become one great continuous yacht marina. Anyone who doubts this has only to inspect the latest development, the shores of southern Turkey. Bodrum and Kusadasi are fast becoming the Turkish Benidorm and Magaluf and they appear to be developing at an exponential rate. At the moment, the Turkish Mediterranean coast is concerned mainly with the upper end of the tourist market with an emphasis on sailing and 'flotilla cruising' but hotels and other facilities are being rapidly developed. Turkey has the potential, as Spain had in the 1950s and 1960s, to provide very cheap holidays.

Tourism and the Terrorists

Even during the recent deep economic depression, tourism has shown no signs of a fundamental decline. The Gulf War did produce a period of uncertainty for a few months but this seems to have affected American tourists coming to the eastern Mediterranean rather than European holiday-makers and anyway is now a negligible factor in the choice of a holiday location. A partial sense of euphoria, brought about by the much publicised rapprochement between Israel and the Palestine Liberation Organisation, only partly offset by events in the old Yugoslavia, has tended to alleviate the fear of terrorism. But the Mediterranean has, in the present century, been the hunting ground of a host of fanatical groups seeking to influence their perceived enemies and oppressors by the most ruthless terrorist acts. It remains to be seen whether this scourge is now over.

The Mediterranean has lent itself to the successful practice of terrorism because of the coming together of a number of factors. The classic act of terrorism is a symbolic act of cruelty and horror perpetrated by a weak political or religious group against a country, which, in conventional terms, is so strong as to be unbeatable in any other way. Surprisingly, Israel, from its declaration of independence in 1947, has presented just such an unbeatable power to its Arab neighbours. Terrorist acts against the state of Israel, which might just conceivably be represented as legitimate acts of war, have spilled over into acts against those Western powers which appear to be sympathetic to Israel or at least in a position to influence her to Arab advantage. Sadly, most Arab countries, whilst some of them did not oppose the establishment of Israel, now support the Palestinian cause financially and in more direct ways.

There can hardly be a better place for the great symbolic act of terrorism than the Mediterranean, usually full at all times of the year with rich, Christian tourists from the Western world. When the tourists are Jewish Americans the temptation to reap the unexpected bonus must be almost irresistible. In the case of the cruise ship *Achille Lauro*, all the factors making for a successful act came together. The cruise ship left Genoa, its home port, early in October 1985. It was hijacked by four Palestinian terrorists belonging to the Palestine Liberation Front, while on its way from Egypt to Israel. There had been no security precautions on the ship, and no search of passengers and their baggage when they had re-embarked after an excursion to the Pyramids. There were counter-terrorist forces available but their employment was not authorised until it was too late.

In the course of their peregrination around the eastern Mediterranean and subsequent return to Egypt, the terrorists murdered a crippled American Jewish tourist and threw him and his wheel-chair overboard. The incident demonstrates to perfection the conditions necessary for terrorist action to be regarded as successful, at least by the fanatic perpetrators. The seizure of the cruise ship and the brutal murder of a disabled and elderly passenger ensured that the symbolic nature of the act would be recognised and broadcast by the media. The terrorists believed that the co-operation of Egypt and Italy was more or less guaranteed, although a rebuff by Syria was a slight setback. After their surrender, the imprisonment of the four terrorists by Italy, half-hearted as it was, was easily forgiven in the light of the alternative – handing them over to the Americans. In any event, most terrorists have shown that they are prepared to give their lives for their cause. America's indecision and final weakness in this case signalled to all terrorists that America's words would not always be backed up by strong action. Once more, the incident showed that a small group of well-organised and utterly ruthless men can only be defeated by the matching of force by force, and the willingness to make sacrifices, often in the face of weak and conciliatory public opinion.

The Aftermath of the Cold War

In 1985, at the time of the seizing of the *Achille Lauro*, the first faint signs of change were becoming apparent in the Soviet Union. Until the late 1980s terrorists could act under the broad umbrella of the Cold War stalemate, assuming that East and West would not co-operate to deal with any outrage, however horrifying. It was clear that the two superpowers would avoid any conflict which might lead to a nuclear confrontation. They would restrain their satellites and client states from any act that would jeopardise this seemingly fragile *pax atomica*. Smaller countries, especially the Arab and Third World countries, could turn to terrorism without fear of massive reprisals.

The conditions of the Cold War also led to intense competition between the two blocs for 'hearts and minds' in the uncommitted nations. If the hearts and minds in the Arab countries unequivocally condemned Israel and were prepared to follow the lead of demagogues who were often Muslim fundamentalists, then national interest required that they should be treated gently and that they should be wooed on their own terms. Aid and military co-operation would continue even if some of the aid is diverted to the support of terrorist groups carrying out operations against America and other Western Powers. It has proved to be more effective and less costly to strike symbolically at the West than to target the more obvious enemies.

By 1990 it was clear that the unthinkable was actually happening. The Soviet Union was slowly but surely moving towards democracy. The process has involved great suffering in the transition from the failed Marxist economy to a system that will be based on the free market economies of the West. The Commonwealth of Independent States (CIS) is no longer the powerful rival that the Soviet Union was and the cry is now for co-operation with the West and a requirement for aid which dwarfs all previous demands by the supplicant nations of the Third World. So the terrorists have dimly perceived that their world has changed. The sight of representatives of Israel and the PLO sitting down together in September 1993 is the first tangible evidence of this change following Soviet verbal support of the Americans at the time of the Gulf War. The PLO had seriously miscalculated, and would in the future have to adopt a much more conciliatory rôle. Unfortunately, what at first appeared to be an overwhelming victory for the Allies turned out to be less than satisfactory in its outcome. Saddam Hussein was not removed from power. The large number of civilian casualties in Iraq brought about a revulsion which prevented the war being carried to a satisfactory conclusion. But the mould had been broken and a new atmosphere has emerged, leading to the freeing of the hostages in Lebanon and the rejection, on paper at least, of violence and terrorism by the PLO.

There can be no doubt that the end of the Cold War and the avowed rejection of violence by the most important terrorist-sponsoring organisation will have a profound impact on the Mediterranean and its littoral countries. The ending of terrorism may be a slow and hesitant process and will require courage and persistence but at least a real start has been made. The outcome of the charges against Libya over the Lockerbie bombing will be a measure of how the peace process is moving forward and Britain in the Mediterranean can only gain from any improvements that may come about. Our continued interest in the old British bases and colonies on the inland sea, and our continuing rôle as a world trading and maritime nation, however reduced our circumstances, dictate the need for a permanent influence on events there. The end of The Cold War – and of the present economic recession – is bound to trigger a tourist boom in the eastern Mediterranean. Apart from holidays it can provide opportunities for British business to profit from contacts and experience in many Middle Eastern Mediterranean locations. The building and servicing of holiday facilities is an obvious field where British enterprise can get a firm footing in an area which, so far, seems to have been ignored.

It has been said that tourism is only colonialism under another name and even if the aphorism does have a 'Lenin on *Imperialism*' sound about it, it may still be worth examining. The hasty development of tourist facilities around the Mediterranean is reminiscent of the earlier replacement of subsistence agriculture by the planting of cash crops like cotton and sugar-cane and silk which benefited absentee landlords, and the tenants and peasants too, but only in the short run. Of course the development of tourist resorts does produce some immediate benefits in terms of employment and an enlarged local market for vegetables and fruit and craft products. However, in so far as the labour required for building hotels and other facilities is usually highly skilled, and the personnel required to service the holiday complexes are not usually the local peasants or their children, people will be brought in from outside. Often, too, the food provided will be what the tourists are used to and will be imported. Local crafts will often prove to have been mass-produced in centralised locations. But this need not be the end of the story. Developers can be required to provide training for at least a quota of local people, local materials can be specified where they are appropriate and beneficiary clauses can ensure that some of the expected profit from development is used to provide facilities for the local population as well as bolstering the local infrastructure. It is not necessary to import all the vices and bad habits of the visitors, which may well prove to be counterproductive. Tourism may well prove to be a good cash crop for the more backward areas of the Mediterranean.

CHAPTER IX

A Short Epilogue

A *Times* newspaper report appearing in the summer of 1991 is headed, 'The Last Post for the British on the Rock'. It said that the lowering of the regimental flag of The 3rd Battalion, The Royal Greenjackets put an end to a military tradition dating back to 1704 when the British captured the Rock. The Gibraltar Regiment, now converted from an artillery to an infantry rôle, has taken over the task of guarding the Governor and the NATO installations on the Rock. However, by the 28 August a corrective report in *The Times* played down the suggestion that the British were leaving. From *The Times* Diary:

Uniform Display.
'No one can accuse Rear Admiral Geoffrey Biggs, the new commander of British forces in Gibraltar, of favouritism. When the former submarine officer dresses for work each day, he pulls on RAF boots and an army uniform, but wears Royal Navy insignia. The dress is meant to show his commitment to all branches of the Rock's military operation. Biggs feared that his appointment might lead to suspicion among the army and RAF that he was a harbinger of a takeover by the senior service.

The move has gone down well with the Island's (sic) 1,100 servicemen. "All three services are reflected even if it is only

in his boots or on his belt", says Captain Leo Callow, of the
British forces headquarters . . .'.

Despite the gentle fun, Gibraltar has been going through some worry-
ing times recently. A letter to *The Times* from Sir Anthony Kershaw
said that it was now pointless to retain Gibraltar, which no longer had
any military value and could only be compared to Andorra. Kershaw's
letter provoked a host of further letters, all of them hostile, but it probably did more harm to morale and Gibraltarian faith in British
commitment than all the troop withdrawals and flag-lowering that has
gone on over the past 10 years. One letter from an ADC to a previous
Governor made the important point that the status of Gibraltar should
be compared to that of the Spanish enclaves in Morocco, Ceuta and
Melilla, not to Andorra. In times of internal crisis, commercial or political, Spain remembers Gibraltar but not her own little peccadilloes in
North Africa. The handing-over of Gibraltar to Spain regardless of
the wishes of the inhabitants, is exactly the kind of amoral behaviour,
it was strongly suggested, we should avoid in the Mediterranean and
elsewhere in future. It would seem that most people who have no immediate financial incentive to encourage closer relations with Spain, agree.

Once the frontier with Spain was opened Gibraltar became an object
of interest to the IRA. With typical miscalculation of the mood of the
inhabitants, or perhaps naively reckoning on the Catholic connection,
a bomber group was sent into Gibraltar via Spain to select a suitable
soft target, the Governor, or a military band, a favourite target with the
Irish terrorists, or even a group of tourists. Unfortunately for the terrorists an SAS team was waiting for them and, in the course of what
was reasonably believed to be the dangerous apprehension of armed
and ruthless killers, the three terrorists were killed. The people of
Gibraltar were outraged at the action of the terrorists and more than
satisfied with the outcome. If there had been a bomb in the terrorists'
car which was parked by the forming-up place of a military band but
also next to a primary school, and if it had been detonated by the terrorists, which was a most likely assumption, the people of Gibraltar
would have saved the SAS their unpleasant task. Predictably, there were
cries of anguish about the circumstances surrounding the killing of the
terrorists, but not from Gibraltar. A coroner's jury in Gibraltar found
the killings to have been justified and unavoidable in the circumstances.

Once the IRA realised there was no further favourable publicity to be gained, they admitted that the three dead terrorists had been part of an 'active service' murder team sent to the Rock.

Although the frontier at La Linea is open and the British have withdrawn the guard at the crossing point, many other petty irritations remain. Whenever the Spanish frontier officials begin to feel the summer heat, or are so directed by higher authority, their work rate slows down and huge queues of cars and trucks build up, usually traffic trying to pass from Gibraltar into Spain and not the other way. The ferry route between Gibraltar and Algeciras has not been reopened, a once convenient and pleasant way into Gibraltar for workers from Spain and for tourists in the opposite direction.

The latest cause of disturbance is over disputed claims to Gibraltar International Airport, which was built entirely by the British and is wholly within the British frontier. Spain insists that she should have a part share and part control. British officials seem prepared to discuss the issue with Spain but Gibraltar knows that even discussions could be seen as the beginning of the surrender of sovereignty and have resisted strongly. The frontier has always been a focus of friction but now that the Rock has become a highly photogenic subject for the world's media it has attracted many of Spain's internal disputes and disturbances to the gates of the Fortress. However trivial the dispute, the place to present it to the best advantage is the entrance to Gibraltar. The world television will usually be waiting to publicise, with the Rock as a backdrop, the distressing cases of, for example, the Malaga taxi drivers or the civil servants of Seville. Spain has still to earn the trust of Gibraltar.

It is 30 years since Malta gained her independence. During this period, with the run-down of British involvement in the island and the decline of the traditional defence-orientated industries, there has been a steady build up of tourism as well as visitors seeking new industries and employment possibilities. At first the provision of capital came mostly from Arab and other non-Western countries. This was partly brought about by a rather churlish attitude on the part of the British who, in a fit of pique, appeared to wash their collective hands of the troublesome islands. It took the Maltese a little time to realise that financial penetration however discreet often implies, or gives the impression of, political involvement. But recent events, particularly the Lockerbie bombing and the naming of Malta as the base from which the terrorists were thought to have operated, will have opened many eyes on the islands. There is now a clear sign of a move back towards traditional friends.

As far as tourism is concerned, by 1990 Britain eagerly provided over half of the visitors to Malta. There is also in the islands a new interest in Malta's recent history. The Maltese protested strongly at not being invited to the 1990 Gallipoli Landings Commemoration, and have pointed out that many Maltese soldiers took part in the ill-fated campaign several of them being decorated for gallantry. In developing the tourist attractions on the islands, attention is now being paid to the period of British rule. British visitors are fascinated by the siege of 1941–43 when Malta was awarded the George Cross for its steadfastness under continuous air bombardment. For many this second siege ranks with the Great Siege of 1565. The Maltese can take great pride in the outcome of both sieges, and they have many interesting reminders of these and other historical events to show to visitors. Both as tourists and potential investors in a growth industry the British will find a fund of goodwill in Malta.

Cyprus, the land of bitter lemons still has its bitter fruit. Independence from the British has not brought peace. Hostility, to the point of hatred continues between the Greek and Turkish islanders. The running sore of the closed frontier between the two communities and the continuing need for a peace-keeping force to mediate their differences has not abated. At least the end of the Cold War means that it is no longer necessary to wear kid gloves when treating with Greece and Turkey, both members of NATO, since neither country is likely to appeal to what is left of the Soviet Union for support.

Meanwhile, tourism continues to grow in Cyprus. Now too, the northern section of Cyprus is wooing visitors. Although the facilities in Turkish Cyprus cannot as yet match those of Mediterranean mainland Turkey, an effort is being made to compete with the south of the island. It remains to be seen whether it will be as tolerant of its visitors' behaviour and mode of dress as Turkey itself, where topless dress on the beaches is as common as in many other Mediterranean countries where religious attitudes are not allowed to interfere with the profitable business of tourism. In southern Cyprus the Greek Orthodox Church has recently criticised the immorality allegedly imported into the island by 'scantily dressed German and Scandinavian women'. This may reflect the government's efforts to wrest control of family law from the Church. All this could provide another field for competition between north and south and interestingly, the newspapers of Cyprus are no less eager than those in Britain to exploit the appeal of sex stories and pictures, in the circulation battle. *The Times* recently reported that inside stories in Cyprus newspapers on sex orgies in exclusive Nicosia suburbs would make *The Sun* seem modest by comparison. But while the internal wrangles go on, Cyprus is becoming less and less important as a British base.

The response to President Bush's 1991 call for a settlement in Cyprus has not been encouraging. An attempt to get both parties together under the aegis of the UN Security Council has, so far, only resulted in a renewed and intensified propaganda war between the Greek Cypriots and Ankara which, with 35,000 Turkish troops in the island, is more directly involved in Cyprus than are the mainland Greeks. It seems sadly likely that the only compromise that will bring any hope of permanent peace to the island is a partition into two completely separate sovereign states, with international guarantees and adequate compensation for the dispossessed – though recent developments between Israel and the Arab states may yet provide a precedent of co-operation and progress towards peace that seemed equally unlikely. As the British bases become no more than an embarrassment, it may be that a Security Council agency, or the headquarters of the recently proposed UN Permanent Peace-keeping Force, might take over one or both of the bases on the island to everyone's advantage. Events in the last year or two seem to confirm the confusion in which the terrorists and hostage-taking groups have found themselves. The hostages have been released and terrorism certainly seems to be on the decline. However, the growing activities of the Egyptian Fundamentalist terrorists, especially in its selection of tourism as the target, can only serve as a warning. But even here the impact of the Israeli/Arab rapprochement may turn the scale against violence. So much awaits to be seen.

Tourism is now agreed to be the fastest growing industry in the world. Five years ago the global total of tourists was reckoned to be 355 million. America was said to be providing 40 million and Britain a staggering 20 million out of the total. The numbers are said to have at least doubled between then and now. The number of tourists visiting the most popular locations is so great that the chaos and environmental damage caused is giving some countries second thoughts about the benefits of tourism. Already Venice and the Algarve are trying to enforce a limit on tourism and even Majorca, according to a recent letter to *The Times*, is looking for ways to reduce the pressure on certain parts of the island.

Again, the pressures and disturbances associated with mass tourism are so great in some areas that there is a conscious effort to go 'up-market' and welcome only the middle class tourist with others discouraged by high pricing or the provision of inappropriate facilities. The travel correspondent of *The Times* reported that whilst only two percent of British holiday-makers go to the Caribbean, as many as one third of them would, if they could afford it, take a world cruise or lounge on a Caribbean beach. The money spent by holiday-makers, despite the recession, appears to have increased by between 15–20 per cent each year. For the moment the pattern of tourist development will ensure the continuation of the division between the cheap and near 'popular' holiday and the distant and more expensive ones. In the Mediterranean, the eastern end with its classical antiquities, Nile cruises and the rather more specialised appeal of the Holy Land, caters for a different customer from the more brash and obvious delights of the central and western end of the Middle Sea. However, all the evidence seems to show that tourism, like motor-car buying, induces an upward spiral of expectations so that this year the Costa del Sol may satisfy but next year it has got to be Istanbul or the Nile and after that, the sky is almost literally the limit. Tourism, given peace and moderate prosperity, is not going to go away.

As for the 'British abroad' there seems to be a dearth of writers, artists and composers at the moment, although there is a constant stream of travel programmes on the television. Perhaps there are not so many English-teaching posts abroad providing congenial and inspirational havens. There would still seem to be a considerable number of British expatriates living in Malta and Cyprus, not to mention Spain. Ownership of apartments and time-shared villas all along the shores of the Mediterranean is still popular with the British. Indeed, the annual winter migration to more sunny parts has reached such proportions that the departers are now known, affectionately one hopes, as 'the boat-train people' to distinguish them from their less fortunate and involuntary fellow-travellers in Asia. In time, new writers and artists will emerge inspired by the evidence of past civilisations and cultures still being discovered and preserved all the way round the Mediterranean basin. A new Coleridge or Byron or Graves is urgently needed to interpret and carry on the story of the Middle Sea, and to explain again, in a new age of divisions and national rivalries, the essential unity of the Mediterranean area and its peoples, and perhaps, to write for us a new Odyssey.

ANNEXE

Remainders and Reminders.
A Short Guide for
Travellers

The object of this Annexe is to record what remains of the British presence in the British colonies and former settlements and military bases in the Mediterranean. As in the previous sections of this book we deal primarily with those areas where the British settled for a considerable time. Egypt, Italy, Spain, Greece and Turkey have, perforce, had to be ignored, apart from those few cases where a mainland site of interest can be visited conveniently from one or other of the areas dealt with.

In most of the settlements reported on, it will be the buildings, fortresses and general fortifications which come first to mind as worthy of a visit, and this is only to be expected since most of them were fought for and held at the cost of British blood. Where the British stayed for any length of time they erected their own monuments and these in most cases still exist although they are sometimes, and perhaps increasingly now, put to a different use from that originally intended. In Malta, especially, the buildings and defences of a previous age, whilst not built by the British, were cherished and in some cases rediscovered by them so that they occupy a special place in British regard, and are noted accordingly. On a more sombre note, where the British have settled for any reasonable length of time there will be British dead. In the 18th and 19th Centuries when the majority of British possessions in the Mediterranean were being acquired, and later in the two World Wars of the 20th Century, the dead accumulated. In addition to military casualties the scourges of yellow fever, cholera, malaria, enteric fever and influenza cut swathes through the overcrowded and insanitary garrison towns of the Mediterranean. Those too have left their monuments which, whilst presenting a somewhat morbid record, do give a fascinating and comprehensive picture of the British military presence and the price which had to be paid for dominion over the Inland Sea.

As we have said, in Malta there is a revival of interest in the island's heroic achievements in the Second World War, fostered by the award of the George Cross as a symbol of the co-operation between the British and the islanders in their resistance to a siege no less fierce or unrelenting than that of the Turks in the Great Siege of 1565. Whilst the monument to the Knights of Malta in Valletta, built immediately after the end of the Great Siege, takes pride of place in the tourists' itinerary, evidence of the British presence is now strongly featured in the travel brochures. Throughout the Mediterranean the availability of funds from the European Community has encouraged the traditional links of friendship, commerce and culture.

Another recent trend in Mediterranean economics has been the unprecedented movement of workers and job-seekers from North Africa into Europe, bringing a new wave of distrust and rejection fuelled by the deep recession which is affecting all European countries in the 1990s. It is evident that some Mediterranean island countries do not want to be caught on the wrong side of the immigration line and need all the friends they can find. All this has produced a new atmosphere of friendship and co-operation which bodes well for increased association between Britain and her former Mediterranean possessions, not least through tourism and cultural and educational exchanges. Gibraltar especially, has never abandoned or wished to abandon her strong links with Britain, and British tourists can always be sure of a friendly welcome based on shared ideals and what is by now a common heritage.

Tangier, Minorca and Corfu can only be dealt with briefly. In all three cases the British severed their connections long ago and very little remains, even in local folk memory, of the British, except amongst the literati of Corfu, where interest in the eccentric British has been kept alive by a flourishing colony of expatriates with whom they keep contact. But here, as elsewhere in the Mediterranean, there are monuments and memorials to the British presence and although they are not always worth a visit in their own right they are still nostalgic and even heroic reminders of former glories, often worth a short diversion from the beaches or the golf course.

Tangier (1662–1684)

Of all Britain's Mediterranean possessions, past and present, Tangier is perhaps the most unsatisfactory in that there remains almost no trace of the British presence. The reason is not hard to understand. Tangier was the first British colony in the Mediterranean and it was given up over 300 years ago after a brief occupation of only 22 years. Even so, one could hope to have found some evidence of those turbulent years, but the absorbent quality of Islam and the raffish reputation gained by the town in the 19th Century which persisted until recent times have been sufficient to put Tangier beyond the pale for British historians and antiquarians and have had a negative affect on the unearthing or preservation of anything to do with the British connection.

It is possible to trace the line of the old walls and the probable location of the Great Mole, completed just in time to be comprehensively demolished by the English garrison when they left in 1684. There are several early engravings and helpful paintings done during the occupation, in some cases by the engineers and surveyors employed on the Mole and the defences. Many of these are held in HM The Queen's collection, at the Queen's Gallery, Buckingham Palace, but they are rarely on view, and never in Tangier. The old town within the walls coincided roughly with the modern Medina district and it contains amongst other things the site and ruins of York House, the English headquarters. The house now presents a machicolated if improved appearance and is owned by the French perfume and fashion business Givenchy. The house is situated on the seaward side of the road curving up and to the left round the kasbah.

Tangier has its English Church with a graveyard though no early graves are preserved. The only other building of interest, apart from the residences of the notorious expatriate colony of European and American writers, drug addicts and wastrels, is Malcolm Forbes House, which contains the Forbes Museum of Military Miniatures. The collection depicts military life and includes war posters, photographs and huge models of battles, many of them relating to Moroccan history. There are various roads and avenues with familiar names including a Rue S.Pepys, presumably in recognition of the famous diarist's part in removing the English garrison. But that is about all!

Both, *Morocco – Insight Guide (1989)* and *Morocco* (Cadogan Guides 1989) have useful Chapters on Tangier and are recommended. Many of the early prints of Tangier from HM The Queen's Collection are reproduced in Routh's book on Tangier. (See bibliography.)

Gibraltar – Captured in 1704

Gibraltar, in sharp distinction, is a living museum of the British presence extending from 1704 until the present time. Like most other resorts on the Mediterranean, Gibraltar has now succumbed to the urgent requirement to attract tourists. The sad side of this is that in the restricted areas available for development on the Rock the new hotels stick out like sore thumbs. The positive side is that more money has now been invested in amenities like the aerial cable car to the summit ridge of the Rock. From the top station the visitor is provided with an absolutely stunning vista of Spain, the Mediterranean and North Africa. Incidentally, it also shows why Gibraltar, properly defended, was impervious to attack from the landward side for almost 200 years. Money has also been found to refurbish the Gibraltar Museum, an outstanding model of its kind, and to bring to life the galleries and batteries hewn out of the living rock, by placing authentically dressed models of soldiers, sappers and gunners in the chambers where they worked and fought to defend the Rock.

Most of the early barracks and the Naval Hospital mentioned in such ingratiating terms by Francis Carter in 1777 are still in place although many have enjoyed a change of use; St. Jago's Barracks for example, has been converted into a school. The convent, which has been the Governor's residence almost from the start of the British occupation, with its splendid garden so much admired by Carter and Disraeli, still serves its original and symbolic purpose, and whilst most of the military offices and installations have been moved to a new military estate at the south end of the Rock, the Governor remains in his town house, close to the people of the colony.

The Spanish walls of the town, named after Charles V, are still intact for much of their length and are pierced at the northern and southern ends by medieval gates which now, unfortunately, have had to be widened to accommodate the vast increase in motor traffic. There are also Moorish walls and a Moorish castle in a well-preserved state but dating back to only a few years before the Moors were driven out of Spain in 1462. The Gibraltar Museum is situated in the restored old Moorish baths in the centre of the town. The seaward side of the town was defended by the Line Wall which included in its fortifications the King's Bastion which played a prominent part in defeating the last Spanish attack on the Rock towards the end of the Great Siege. The Line and the Bastion are still very much in evidence, now overlooking the Services' sports grounds and a large area reclaimed from the sea when the lagoons and inundations were finally filled in along the west side of the town.

Gibraltar also has its share of graveyards and historical monuments to the illustrious dead. The most visited of them is the Trafalgar Cemetery situated just outside the Southport Gate. A garrison burial ground is located at North Front, immediately underneath the galleries and batteries of the great northern rock face. But the most evocative of Gibraltar's memorials are to be found in the King's Chapel, at one time the chapel of the Convent and now the Garrison Church. There are plaques commemorating Governors who have died on the Rock including General O'Hara and there are memorials to the more important residents who died from the many endemic diseases; most poignant of all, are the engraved slabs erected by their comrades to officers who fell in the Peninsular War.

With all the wealth of historical monuments and the many surviving buildings dating mainly from the 18th Century, the true memorial to the many humble soldiers and sailors who served and died at Gibraltar lies within the Rock itself, in the tunnels and galleries, roadways, reservoirs and storage chambers dug continuously over the nearly three centuries when the British have been 'in garrison'. Apart from the human endeavour, nature herself has been at work within the Rock. St.Michael's Caves, high on the west face of the Rock, have been known to exist at least since the 18th Century. Although the caves were ignored for some time, apart from exploration by local and Service cavers, they have now become a tourist attraction almost rivalling the Rock's famous Barbary apes. Both attractions are now easily accessible via the cable car. The caves, complete with stalactites and stalagmites, make an interesting venue for concerts, pop as well as classical, and for the dramatic performances which are mounted from time to time in the flood-lit caverns.

One of the most attractive older buildings in Gibraltar is the Garrison Library, established for officers and their families in 1793. The typically Georgian building is set on a terrace overlooking Library Square, now dominated by the Gibraltar Holiday Inn. Until recently there was a well-maintained garden behind the Library and drinks were served to the accompanying hoots of a family of Scop's Owls. But alas no more! With the run-down of the Services, the Library seems to be lacking a rôle and is becoming semi-derelict. Urgent action is needed to save it from the hands of the developers. Another feature of Gibraltar which was beginning to slide into decay is the Alameda Gardens, with its collection of Mediterranean and semitropical plants, a delight to visitors and residents alike. For a while the gardens became the target for local vandalism but at the end of 1991 a determined effort was made to rehabilitate and restore the garden to its former glory. Four full-time gardeners have been employed and a roster of volunteer gardeners has been enrolled.

Now that the frontier with Spain has been reopened, Gibraltar is well placed for visiting that 'Most Loyal and Gallant Town of Tarifa'. It is situated about 20 miles to the west, along a most picturesque road that runs through the Cork Woods above the Bay of Gibraltar on the way to Cadiz. The town was held by a combined force of Spainish and British troops from Gibraltar. Tarifa is quite interesting and worth a short diversion off the main Cadiz road which bypasses the town. Further along the road towards the west, just above the sea, is the Peninsular War battlefield of Barossa, the only one, apart from Tarifa, within easy reach of Gibraltar.

Gibraltar – The Island Series, is a useful general guide. *The Rock of the Gibraltarians* by William Jackson, (1990) provides a good account of the history of Gibraltar, written by an ex-Governor. Dorothy Ellicott has written many short books on Gibraltar, which are useful and detailed but only seem to be available in Gibraltar.

Minorca (1708–1802, with interruptions)

Like Gibraltar, Minorca was occupied by the British in the name of Charles III, contender to the Spanish throne, who was put forward and supported by the British. However, when the island was secured all the Spanish soldiers were removed and only the British were allowed to garrison the forts from then on. Charles III was coerced into handing over Minorca as mortgage for the expenses the British incurred in the War of the Spanish Succession, and in 1713, like Gibraltar, it passed legally to Britain under the Treaty of Utrecht.

Colonel Richard Kane, who had been at the Battle of Blenheim with Marlborough, became Governor of the island in 1713 and immediately set to work to improve living conditions for the islanders. He built a road from Mahon to Ciudella when he transferred the capital of the island to the port. He also drained the land at the head of the Port Mahon inlet to make a very valuable market garden area.

Kane brought with him a large clock from England which was erected in the tower of Fort St.Philip. The Fort has now gone but the clock may still be seen in the Gothic Tower, all that now remains of the old city walls. The Coat of Arms of the Fort was also removed and is now in the City Hall. The city walls, which were still intact in 1740, can now only be traced at the Gothic Tower and at the bridge of San Roque, a prominent feature of the Playa Bastion. The Playa was known to British garrisons as the Grand Parade. The town of Mahon is situated on the highest part of the cliffs overlooking the harbour and the sea. The architecture of the town is mainly neoclassical Georgian, not found elsewhere in Spain. Many of the houses have sash windows which are also not found in mainland Spain. The main shopping street is still called Hannover Street. A monument was raised to Sir Richard Kane in 1926 and replaced by another in 1972, at the head of Port Mahon.

Although traces of the British occupation are scanty there are sites worth visiting. There are many megalithic sites on the island and the largest of these, Trepuco, is on the outskirts of Mahon. The settlement is still partly encircled by an 18th Century gun emplacement from which the Duc de Crillon once tried to terrorise the inhabitants of the town. There are over 1,000 megalithic sites on Minorca. There are also excellent beaches and pleasant walks on the island and the blight which has settled on parts of Majorca has, thankfully, not arrived in Minorca to any extent.

Minorca – *The Island Series*, is an adequate guide. Dudley Pope's, *At 12 Mr Byng Was Shot* (1962) provides details of Minorca's most celebrated incident regarding the British. There is also a useful *Blue Guide*.

The Maltese Islands (1799–1964)

The whole of urban Malta is a memorial to Malta's military past. The two most stirring events in Maltese history, the defeat of the Turkish Siege in 1565 and the resistance to the Italian and German attempts to bomb Malta into a state of helplessness in 1940–43, rank equally in the heroic story of the islands. The town of Valletta, built by the Knights of St John after the siege of 1565, contains most of the important buildings and monuments of the period including the Grand Master's Palace, now the House of Representatives. The Palace Armoury, where Thackeray's 'truculent little scimitar' is housed, the principal Auberges, the museums of the Cathedral, of Archaeology and of War, the Manoel Theatre and the Malta Library, are all within easy walking distance of central Valletta. The Library, situated in Queen's Square, houses the original deed of donation of the Maltese Islands and Tripoli to the Order of St John by Emperor Charles V, in 1530 and photocopies are on sale at the Library. Although most of the buildings in the town were completed well after the siege, they convey an impression, situated as they are within the massive fortifications designed to dissuade the Turks from another attack, of a city and a people continually at war or at risk of war.

The Manoel Theatre, in Old Theatre Street, helps to dispel this atmosphere of living under a threat. It was built by Antonio Manoel de Vilhena in 1731 when he was Grand Master of the Order and illustrates the beginning of that decline, noted by Gibbon, into a more worldly and sophisticated way of life in the 18th Century. As Gibbon said, 'The Knights were more prepared to die for their God than to live for him'. The theatre has maintained its position as the artistic centre of Malta and enjoys the reputation of being the third oldest theatre in Europe. A Royal Opera House was built in the mid-19th Century but was destroyed by fire in 1873, allowing the Manoel to come into its own again. The Opera House was rebuilt but it was destroyed in the Second World War. Before the war the Manoel had served intermittently as a dance hall and a cinema, and was no doubt well patronised by the fleet. It was restored and reopened in 1960 and has remained without a rival since then. The British were very much concerned with the theatre in the 19th Century, influencing the choice of programmes, which then as now, were mainly in English, and following the long tradition of British garrisons abroad, putting on amateur productions themselves. Interestingly, the Knights produced and acted in some of the earliest performances in the theatre.

The best view of the peninsulas of Senglea and Vittoriosa (Birgu), giving an 'attacker's eye view' of the towns defended by the Knights and their Maltese soldiers, is from the Victoria Gate of Valletta, or further to the west from Magazine Bastion. Fort St Elmo, the scene of the self-sacrificing battle to the death of its garrison, and Fort St Angelo, across Grand Harbour, which was vital in the defence of Vittoriosa against the last desperate attacks of the Turks, are both still standing and can be visited. St Elmo houses the Malta War Museum. But the best way of all to view Valletta and the fortified peninsulas is by boat. There are guided tours of Marsamexett and Grand Harbours daily in winter and more frequently in summer, leaving from The Strand below Sliema. The boat trip round Valletta and into the creeks of Grand Harbour provides an excellent introduction to the architecture and layout of the towns and harbours surrounding the central urban area of Malta. If, in addition, your guide is an ex-member of the Royal Navy you will receive an informative and amusing bonus.

The fortifications on the landward side of Valletta and another complete system of bastions, batteries and dry moats on the landward side of the suburb of Floriana were completed in the late 17th and 18th Centuries according to the principles of Marshal Sebastien le Prêtre de Vauban, one of Louis XIV's military advisers and the greatest military engineer of his age. Between the two lines of fortifications on the landward side of Valletta can be found, near the City Gate, the famous Triton statue, almost completely obscured by Malta's central bus terminus. From the Triton it is possible to get buses to almost every village, however small, across the whole of the main island. Further out, but still within the fortifications is the Royal Air Force Memorial which bears the names of all the air-crew members who failed to return from missions whilst based on the island during the Second World War. It provides a poignant reminder of the intensity of the air battles over the island and shows in its sombre details when the crisis of the air battle came in 1942. One can see too, that the air battle, with all its attendant casualties, went on into 1945, well after the Mediterranean Sea was cleared of its Axis enemies, and that the island was defended by squadrons from the Commonwealth and from many of the Allied nations.

Most British visitors, certainly those with Service connections, will find the War Museum of interest. Details of the convoy battles and of the air war are on show together with a reconstructed 'operations room'. There is an exhibition of weapons and uniforms mainly from the Second World War, and a special section devoted to the achievements of the Royal Malta Artillery, and the decorations awarded to Maltese Servicemen and civilians. Pride of place goes to the George Cross awarded to Malta in 1942 and the illuminated scroll presented by President Roosevelt when he visited the islands in 1943. Sadly, it is pointed out in the Souvenir Handbook of the Museum, in words which bring to mind the circumstances of the British withdrawal from Corfu in the 19th Century and from Tangier two centuries earlier, that although there are German and Italian mementoes in the museum, the guns which shot down so many enemy planes, many of them manned by men of the Malta Regiment, are not represented; all were broken up and sold for scrap when the British left.

Outside the urban areas surrounding Grand Harbour there are still many reminders of the British connection. West of Sliema is the main site of what was the British military cantonment, and many of the barrack buildings, family quarters, hospitals and schools are still very much in evidence although they are being demolished or adapted for new purposes, in one case being transformed into a holiday complex. The ubiquitous British military cemetery is also situated in the area within the lines of the old St Andrew's Barracks. Throughout the islands there are towers, bastions and battery sites, some of them dating from medieval times, but most of them reminders of the bitter battles with enemy aircraft in the Second World War. There are also satellite airfields and old RAF stations now abandoned; one of them, at Ta' Qali has been made into a flourishing 'Crafts Village', its Service origin still recognisable in its hutted accommodation and even more in its café, which was obviously an Officers' Mess at one time; one can almost hear the old songs being sung round the piano. Near Ta' Qali is Mosta with its church where the miraculous failure of a bomb to explode saved a large number of people sheltering in the church during a raid. Above Mosta is the ridge called Victoria Lines, stretching right across the main island of Malta, on which was built a massive defensive system in the 1870s, designed to bring most of the island within the fortified works. Below the lines and easily visible from the ramparts of Medina, the ancient and exceptionally visit-worthy capital of old Malta, is the Mtarfa Clock Tower. A very large military hospital was built on this site after the First World War, and it was here that Sir David Bruce isolated the cause of Malta Fever, Brucellosis Melitensis. The hospital is now used as an old people's home.

In medieval times, before the coming of the Knights of St John, Malta, as an appendage of Sicily, produced little of artistic or architectural note, and the constant threat of Turkish raids discouraged much enterprise in the islands. But with the arrival of the Knights, and especially after the defeat of the Turkish attack and siege of 1565, the Maltese 'Golden Age' commenced. The city of Valletta, built by the Knights in what Coleridge described as a 'Southern Baroque' style, in its adornment and in its town planning by the outstanding architects and artists of the day, emerged as a monument which could rival Venice in its aesthetic appeal.

There is a very wide selection of books available on Malta. New histories and guide books appear regularly. For a brief introduction to the islands the following are recommended:

The Blue Guide to Malta. Stuart Rossiter.
The Story of Malta. Brian Blouet (1987).
The Great Siege of Malta. Ernle Bradford (1961).
The Battle of Malta. Joseph Attard (1980).

There are many short specialist guides printed in Malta, and an excellent map, *Hildebrand's Travel Map of Malta*, which includes a useful bus route guide for the main island, published by Progress Press of Valletta.

Corfu and the Ionian Islands (1814–1864)

As we have said, Britain's impact on Corfu is not very evident from the surviving monuments on the island and there is even less evidence on the other islands which made up the British Protectorate of the United States of the Ionian Islands. The Venetians, who colonised the islands for over 400 years, have naturally influenced the domestic architecture and the style of the early public buildings. They also erected a strong system of defences around Corfu town which successfully kept out the Turks through the whole period of their rule. Even the French, in their two short periods of control over the island, 1797–99 and 1807–14, made more impact than Britain in her 50 years on Corfu.

De Lesseps the elder, father of the Suez Canal entrepreneur, designed and built the elegant arcaded block on the inland side of the Spianada, in the same style as his colonnaded row on the Rue du Rivoli in Paris. Tourists, having their own interests which are not always concerned with self-improvement, sit having their drinks in the shaded cafés of the Liston, often paying small attention to the buildings and monuments in front of them around the main open space and public gardens of the town. From the Liston Colonnade it is possible to see the huge neoclassical palace built as the official residence of the British High Commissioners. The palace was built in 1819 and housed the Ionian Senate and the headquarters of the Order of St Michael and St George, after whom the palace is named. In the Spianada, and around it, are found monuments to note-worthy High Commissioners. Maitland's Peristyle, now frequently defaced with graffiti, a bronze statue of Sir Frederick Adam, who constructed the town aqueduct, and a statue of Lord Guildford, a prominent philhellene and educationalist are sited on the Spianada, as is the Club House of the Corfu Literary Society founded in 1836. The Club House contains an excellent library and a collection of icons and paintings. The Palace of St Michael and St George was used as a summer residence of the Greek Royal Family until 1913 and is now a museum and the headquarters of the Archaeological Service. Apart from a certain amount of road building, most of it in the environs of Corfu town, the only work of any importance carried out by the British was the partial rebuilding of the New Fort. Most of the building disappeared in the demolition carried out when the British left.

The destruction was sanctioned as part of the agreement on the future neutrality of Corfu but it left an understandable legacy of bitterness.

Holiday Which? Guide to Greece and the Greek Islands (1989) is recommended.

Also *Corfu – History – Monuments – Museums* (1979) by A.B. Tataki, published in Athens. An English version is available.

Prospero's Cell, Lawrence Durrell (1945) still makes an agreeable companion on a visit to the island, if only to show what we have missed. Maps are available on the island.

Cyprus – Occupied in 1878

When the British took over the island of Cyprus by arrangement with the Sublime Porte, they found almost every building, fortress and town to be in a state of intense dilapidation. Famagusta, the only port of any importance in the island, was still in much the same condition as when it was left after the Turkish siege and capture of the town in 1571. The harbour was silted-up and none of the 200 guns mounted on the walls and in the Citadel appeared to be in working order. Paphos, an important port in Roman times, was in a similar condition and both harbours had to be dredged and refurbished by the British early in the 20th Century.

During the first years of the British occupation the troops lived in temporary camps near Limassol with small detachments at Nicosia, Famagusta and Paphos. The main camp near Limassol was at Kato Polemidhia but little remains now except for the inevitable military graveyard. The graveyard itself contains some interesting reminders of the past including the graves of some White Russian officers, including two Generals. The cemetery, which was in use from 1882 until 1965, provides an outline of the British occupation, indicating the various regiments 'in garrison' and the many family members as well as Servicemen who died there, often of 'fever'. In Cyprus the fever was known as enteric but variants were common and stoically born in all overseas garrisons. The summer camp in the Troodos Mountains can still be seen and is used as a base by skiing parties. The High

Commissioner's summer residence was established near the camp and a plaque in memory of Arthur Rimbaud, 'who contributed with his own hands, despite his fame as a French poet and genius, to the construction of this house', was affixed to it in the 1940s.

The history of the development of the new military town of Dhekelia was told in an earlier Chapter and the base has very little of interest to tourists. The Western Base Area, on the other hand, contains the site of the ancient settlement of Curium, with its Greek Temples and Roman villas and the splendid Greco-Roman theatre, recently restored and now used for dramatic presentations and concerts.

Larnaca, just outside the perimeter of the British Eastern Sovereign Base, has had a British community for several hundred years. It was a main overseas base of the Levant Trading Company, set up by Royal Charter in 1581. An English Consul is reported as being based in Larnaca in 1626, and by the 18th Century the British Consul's house was said to be the best on the whole island. By 1841, Larnaca was slightly larger than Nicosia and it housed the largest 'European' (i.e. non-Greek or Turkish) population on the island. As the century progressed Larnaca declined in importance compared with Nicosia, Limassol and Famagusta, and was noted only as a town on the site of ancient Kition where, as in Salamis, just north of Famagusta, antiquities, carvings and statues could be purloined, especially by a rapacious breed of Consuls of all nations, under the benevolent and adequately compensated eyes of the Turkish authorities. In the churchyard of the Ayios Lazaros is an English cemetery which contains graves dating from 1685 to 1850, mainly of members of the Levant Company and of Consuls and their families. There is also an English Church in Larnaca, St Helena's, dating from the early 20th Century, the choice of patron saint confirming its original connection with the Army and its families.

Between Larnaca and Limassol is the site of the Phoenician, later Greek and still later Roman, town of Amathus. Much of the old town is now beneath the waves, and several generations of British Servicemen first learned sub-aqua swimming and the elements of marine archaeology in the area. In Limassol there are some small public buildings of the typical, one-storey type with verandas, some now used as police stations, which betray their British military origins. But the principal antiquity of Limassol town is the castle where Richard Coeur de Lion and Berengaria were married in 1191. The castle was later walled and became a crusader base. It was destroyed on several occasions by earthquake and fire but always painstakingly rebuilt. It was garrisoned by the Knights Templar and, after their disgrace and the dissolution of their order, by the Knights of St John. The castle has been recently adapted to house a museum and a collection of tombstones, plaques, sculptures and ceramics of the Lusignan and Venetian periods.

On the eastern outskirts of Paphos another international airport is being rapidly developed to cope with the burgeoning holiday traffic using the large new hotels springing up along the coast in New Paphos. Paphos itself, whilst it was important in antiquity when the Roman Governor had his residence and headquarters there, was, like most other places on the island, neglected by the Turks, although it was one of their District Headquarters and used by Wolseley as such. Sir Sidney Smith established an agent there during the Napoleonic Wars to attend to the provisioning of British ships. Smith also followed the established pattern by making off with some marble carvings.

There is a semi-ruined fort built on the harbour wall which appears to have consisted of two keeps joined by a curtain wall but there is no trace now of the second keep. A much larger Frankish Crusader Castle was situated above the beach. Excavation of the site was started in 1957 but much of the masonry and many granite columns are still scattered around the site. Near the site of the Crusader castle, which was completely destroyed by an earthquake in 1222 soon after its completion, is the recently discovered site of several Roman villas with excellently preserved and displayed mosaics, a Roman theatre, and remains of sections of the old town walls. The mosaics are quite outstanding and the best of them are to be found in the villa of Theseus, the house of Dionysus and the House of Orpheus. A thousand yards north of this site is the area known as the Tombs of the Kings, which were cut down into the rock and date from the third century BC. A feature of this site is the profusion of mandrake plants growing around the tombs. It is an obvious place to test the ancient legend about the uprooted mandrake's scream. You should be warned, however, that apart from the ancient curse there is a modern prohibition on digging up plants.

Cyprus is a beautiful island and everyone finds his or her favourite spot. In the past it was possible to make an almost instant comparison between the north and the south of the island, and each had its enthusiasts. Now of course, it is difficult – though not impossible – to cross the arbitrary frontier. In Nicosia, a pass to cross into the Turkish-occupied area of the island can be obtained from the United Nations office. Passes are valid for one day only and not overnight. Despite some obstruction, brave hearts can cross and pick up a taxi just over the border which will take them to any part of Northern Cyprus.

Outside Nicosia the main attractions in the north are the three great Crusader castles of Buffavento, St Hilarion and Kantara. All three are situated in the Kyrenia range, with Buffavento the highest at 3,000 feet. All the castles are accessible with only a minimum of climbing on foot. Kyrenia, with its attractive harbour and its own large and easily explored castle is now popular as a tourist resort reached through mainland Turkey. Only a few kilometers from Kyrenia is the Abbey of Bellapais, a magnet for all visitors who have read Durrell's *Bitter Lemons*. All these places are within easy reach of a one-day trip from Nicosia, as is Famagusta and ancient Salamis just to its north.

There was bitter fighting for Famagusta in 1974 during which the Turks retained what was largely the old Turkish, medieval town and drove out the much larger Greek Cypriot population from the modern suburb of Varosha, renamed Maras by the Turks. In 1960 Famagusta had a total population of 34,750, making it the third largest town in Cyprus after Nicosia and Limassol. The old town is still completely walled and the defences are very much as the Venetians left them in 1571, faced in many places with the massive stone blocks quarried from the ruins of old Salamis. Artefacts found at Salamis date back to the 11th Century BC. The town was, in its turn, Phoenician, Hellenic, Persian and then Hellenic again. Eventually allowed to decay by the Venetians, it was lost to the Turks with Famagusta in 1571.

The modern Greek suburb of Varosha (Maras) is now quite deserted and overgrown. It lies right up against the border between Greeks and Turks and is a constant reproach to the Turks and an incitement to the Greeks. What has happened in Famagusta is a microcosm of what has happened throughout the island. To the casual visitor the division seems unnecessary and many tourists cannot distinguish between Greeks and Turks; but to the inhabitants the tragedy of Cyprus is real and is rooted in history – as much in the history of the two protecting (perhaps one should say *provoking*), mainland powers as in the long and turbulent history of the islanders themselves.

The Blue Guide to Cyprus, by Ian Robertson is highly recommended.
Journey Into Cyprus, by Colin Thubron (1974), is very readable.
The Bartholomew Leisure Map is useful and shows the ancient sites.
Bitter Lemons by Lawrence Durrell (1957) is still essential reading, not
   so much as a guide book, although the advice to potential house-
   buyers may be useful, but as an insight into the atmosphere and
   attitudes of the Greek and Turkish Cypriots, not to mention the
   British, during the rebellion of the 1950s.

Bibliography

Alexander, Field Marshal The Earl of Tunis *Memoirs*. Ed. John North, Cassell, London, (1962).

Baker, Sir Sam White. *Cyprus as I Saw it in 1879*. Macmillan, London, (1879).

Barnett, Correlli. *Engage the Enemy More Closely*. Hodder & Stoughton, London, (1991).

Bekker, Cajus. *Luftwaffe War Diaries*. Macdonald & Co., London, (1968).

Blake, Robert. *Disraeli's Grand Tour*. Weidenfeld & Nicolson, London, (1982).

Blouet, Brian. *The Story of Malta*. Progress Press Co. Ltd., Malta, (1987).

Borghese, Valerio, J. *Sea Devils*. Translated Jane Cleugh, Melrose, (1952).

Borrow, George. *The Bible in Spain*. Ward, Lock & Co. 2nd Ed, London, (1889).

Bradford, Ernle. I. *The Great Siege of Malta*. Hart-Davies, London, (1961). II. *Gibraltar, The History of a Fortress*. Hart-Davies, London, (1971).

Braudel, F. *The Mediterranean and the Mediterranean World in the Age of Philip II*. 2 Vols. Collins, London, (1973).

Brendon, Piers. *Thomas Cook. 150 Years of Popular Tourism*. Secker & Warburg, London, (1991).

Brett-James, Anthony. *General Graham 1748–1844*. Macmillan, London, (1959).

Carter, Francis. *A Journey From Gibraltar to Malaga*. London, (1777).

Chapman, Olive. *Across Cyprus*. Bodley Head, London, (1937).

Childs, Virginia. *Lady Hester Stanhope*. Weidenfeld & Nicolson, London, (1990).

Chitty, Susan. *That Singular Person Called Lear*. Hodder & Stoughton, London, (1991).

de Belot, Raymond. *The Struggle for the Mediterranean*. 1939–1945. Oxford University Press, (1951).

Drinkwater, John. *The Great Siege of Gibraltar*. London, (1785). Reprinted (1905).

Durrell, Lawrence. I. *Prospero's Cell*. Faber & Faber, London, (1945).
  II. *Bitter Lemons*. Faber & Faber, London, (1957).
  III. *The Alexandria Quartet*. Faber & Faber, London, (1957–1960).
  IV. *Sicilian Carousel*. Faber & Faber, London, (1977).

Ellicott, Dorothy. *Gibraltar's Royal Governor*. Gibraltar Museum Committee, (1981).

Elliot, Peter. *The Cross and the Ensign*. Cambridge University Press, (1980).

Fortescue, Sir John. *A History of the British Army*. 13 Vols. Macmillan, London, (1899–1912).

Foss, A. *Ibiza & Minorca*. Faber & Faber, London, (1975).

Fyers, Sarah. *Journal*. The Royal Engineers Journal.

Galea, Michael. *Historical Sketches* and *More Historical Sketches*. Malta Library, (Several appear in the *Malta Times*.)

Graves, Robert. I. *Lawrence and the Arabs* Cape, London, (1927).
  II. *Goodbye To All That*. Cassell, London, (1929).
  III. *I Claudius*. Penguin Books, London, (1934).
  IV. *Claudius The God*. Penguin Books, London, (1934).
  V. *Count Belisarius*. Cassell, London, (1938).

Green, Miriam. *Journal*. The Royal Engineers Journal.

Hakluyt, Richard. *The Principal Navigations, Voyages, Traffiques & Discoveries of the English Nation*. 8 Vols. J.M. Dent, London, (1927).

Hallam, Elizabeth.*Chronicles Of The Crusades* (Ed). Guild Publishing, (1989).

Hogben, Major Arthur. *Designed To Kill*. Patrick Stephens, (1987).

Hoskins, J.L. *British Routes to India*. Frank Cass, London, (1966).

Howes, H.H. *The Gibraltarian*. Medsun, Gibraltar, (3rd Edition.) (1991).

Jackson, General Sir William. *The Rock Of The Gibraltarians*. Gibraltar Books, (1990).

Joyce, James. *Ulysses*. Bodley Head/Penguin, (1986).

Kesselring, Field Marshal. *Memoirs*. William Kimber & Co., London, (1953).

Kitchener, Field Marshal H.H. Anonymous Articles in *Blackwood's*, January & June 1897. Vol 125.

Kyle, Keith. *Suez*. Weidenfeld & Nicolson, London, (1991).

Lane-Poole, S. *The Story of The Barbary Corsairs*. Putnams, New York, (1890).

Lewis, Mrs. E.A.M. *A Lady's Impressions of Cyprus*. Remington, London, (1984).

Lively, Penelope. *Moon Tiger*. Penguin Books, London, (1986).

Long, Helen. *Change Into Uniform*. Dalton, London, (1978).

Luke, Sir Harry. *Cyprus Under the Turks*. London, (1921).

Bibliography

Magnus, Philip. *Kitchener, Portrait of an Imperialist*. Penguin Books, London, (1958).

Mahan, A.T. *The Influence of Sea Power Upon History*. Sampson Lowe, London, (1889).

Manning, Olivia. *Fortunes of War*. Penguin Books, (1960–1980).

Maurice, Major General F. & Arthur, Sir G. *The Life Of Lord Wolseley*. Doubleday, New York, (1924).

Newby, Eric. *On The Shores of The Mediterranean*. Picador, London, (1984).

Noakes, Vivien. *Edward Lear*. Ariel Books, BBC, Collins, London, (1968).

Nutting, Sir Anthony. I. *No End Of a Lesson*. Constable, London, (1967).
II. *Nasser*. Constable, London, (1972).

Pack, S.W.C. *Sea Power in the Mediterranean*. Arthur Barker, London, (1971).

Pawle, Gerald. The General's Last Campaign. *Blackwood's*. (1949).

Pepys, Samuel. I. *The Diaries and Companion Volume*. Revised Edition (1983). Ed. Lantham & Matthews, Bell and Hyman, London, (1970).
II. *The Tangier Papers*.

Pocock, Tom. I. *Horatio Nelson*. Bodley Head, London, (1987).
II. *Remember Nelson*. Collins, London, (1977).

Routh, E.M.G. *Tangier, England's Last Atlantic Outpost*. John Murray, London, (1912).

Selwyn-Lloyd, Lord. *Suez 1956. A Personal Account*. Jonathan Cape, London, (1978).

Sheppard, Edgar. *HRH George, Duke of Cambridge*. 2 Vols. Murray, London, (1906).

Smith-Dorrien, General Sir H. *Memories Of Forty-eight Years Service*. Murray, London, (1925).

Sultana, Donald. I. *Samuel Taylor Coleridge In Malta And Italy*. Barnes & Noble, New York, (1969).
II. *Disraeli In The Mediterranean. 1830–1832*. Tamesis, London, (1976).

Tataki, A.B. *Corfu, History, Monuments & Museums*. Athens, (1979).

Thackeray, William Makepeace. *Sketchbooks, Notes Of A Journey From Cornhill To Cairo*. John Murray, London, (1846).

Thomas, Hugh. *The Suez Affair*. Weidenfeld & Nicolson, Revised Ed. (1986).

Thompson, Nathaniel. *A Choice Selection Of One Hundred & Eighty Loyal Songs*, London, (1685).

Thubron, Colin. *Journey Into Cyprus*. Penguin Books, 1975.

Williams, St John N. *Judy O'Grady And The Colonel's Lady*. Brassey's, London, (1988).

Woodhouse, C.M. *The Battle of Navarino (1827)*. Hodder & Stoughton, London, (1965).

Index

Index

Index

Index

Index

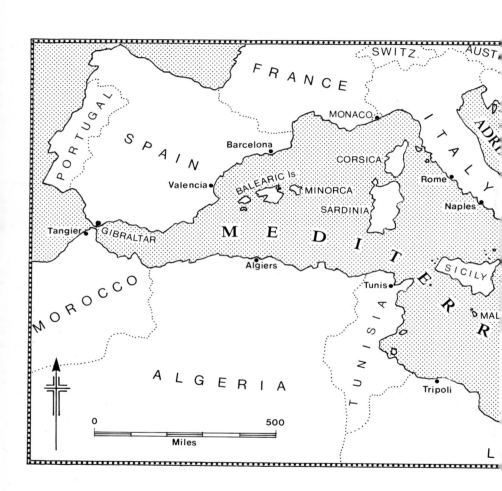